CW00959336

Inside the City

INSIDE THE CITY

A guide to London as a financial centre

WILLIAM M. CLARKE

London
GEORGE ALLEN & UNWIN
Boston   Sydney

First published in 1979
Reprinted 1980

GEORGE ALLEN & UNWIN LTD
40 Museum Street, London WC1A 1LU

©William M. Clarke 1979

British Library Cataloguing in Publication Data

Clarke, William Malpas
    Inside the City.
    1. Financial institutions – England – London
    2. Money market – England – London
    I. Title
    332. 1´09421´2   HG186.G7   79–41108

    ISBN 0–04–332070–8

Typeset in 11 on 12 Baskerville by Northampton Phototypesetters Ltd
and printed in Great Britain
by Unwin Brothers Limited, Old Woking, Surrey

To Faith

Preface

Over the past two years the City's institutions have been baring their activities to public view, at the prompting of the Wilson Committee of inquiry, in a way that neither the Macmillan Committee, in the early 1930s, nor the Radcliffe Committee in the mid-1950s, fully succeeded in doing. In this new book, therefore, I have tried to keep abreast of the thousands of words of evidence which the Wilson Committee, to its credit, has published as it went about its probing task.

Post-war developments in the City have been dramatic and continuous. The City of ten or even five years ago was not what it is today. Its operations have changed; its environment has changed; the external pressures on it have changed. In two previous books about the City, one in 1957, one in 1965, I barely mentioned the Eurodollar market. Each City market, each City industry also has its own new developments to be explored. In a book of this length I could hardly hope to analyse in any great detail the score or so markets and industries that make up what is loosely termed 'the City'. I have, therefore, used a broader approach, combining a brief up-to-date sketch of each part of the City, sector by sector, drawing on personal experiences to highlight some of the main changes, along with an assessment of how one part of the City affects another, how it still manages to have a coherence of its own and how commentators, friendly and otherwise, regard its role today. I have also been tempted to draw some independent conclusions. It is not, therefore, a textbook, rather a bird's-eye view of the City as one observer, helped by Sir Harold Wilson, sees it on the threshold of the 1980s.

I have several acknowledgements to make, not only to City institutions but to a number of their critics, all of whom have helped me in preparing the book. Two particular individuals have borne the brunt and helped the most: George Pulay, an old friend and former Fleet Street colleague, was in the venture from the outset as an original co-author, though pressure of City work eventually forced his withdrawal to the sidelines. His influence, his encouragement and even some of his words, have remained. To Peter Leek of George Allen & Unwin go my thanks for any coherence the book possesses. The blemishes are mine.

I must also thank Gaye Murdoch and Caroline de Beaufort-Suchlick for the cheerful way in which they grappled with the preparation of the innumerable drafts, Vanessa Harding for invaluable help on the historical references, and Pamela Clarke for holding my hand (in a filial way) in the preparation of the glossary of City jargon.

Contents

	Preface	*page* ix
1	What is the City?	1
2	The Banks: A Vast Supermarket?	7
3	The Banks: Enough Help for Industry?	32
4	Insurance: World's Biggest Risks?	50
5	The Stock Exchange: Still Necessary?	71
6	Private Investors: A Vanishing Race?	92
7	Investing Institutions: Too Much Power?	107
8	Money Markets: A Billion a Day?	125
9	The Government: Does the City Help?	138
10	Commodities: Who Are the Speculators?	153
11	Ships and Planes: The World's Charterer?	165
12	Foreign Exchange: Where Are the Gnomes?	174
13	Sterling: How Important?	191
14	Euromarkets: No Controls?	205
15	Who Controls the City?	221
16	Survival: Challenge from New York?	240
17	The City in the 1980s: What Lies Ahead?	259
	Glossary City Jargon: What Does It Mean?	273
	Index	283

List of Tables

1	Main Clearing Bank Groups	11
2	The Top Merchant Banks	12
3	Growth of Foreign Banks in London	16
4	Where Industry Can Find Finance	42
5	UK Insurance Premium Income: 1977	51
6	Insurance Companies Operating in the UK	55
7	The Largest Insurance Companies: 1978	56
8	Largest Insurance Brokers: British and American Groups (Gross Profits)	59
9	Insurance Operations Abroad	61
10	Turnover on World Stock Markets	74
11	Stock Exchange Dealers	79
12	London Stockbrokers Overseas, 1979–80	85
13	Foreign Security Houses in London	87
14	Growth of Unit Trusts	99
15	London's Money Markets	132
16	London Discount Market – Money Market Interests Abroad	136
17	International Market for Capital	214
18	Regular Returns Made by Merchant Banks to Bank of England	227
19	What the City of London Earns Abroad	244
20	Size of the World Eurodollar Market	248
21	Shares in the World Eurodollar Market	249

Chapter 1

What is the City?

The City of London, widely known simply as 'the City', is in reality a financial city within a city. It was once the centre, if not the whole, of London. At its peak, in the early seventeenth century, before the Great Fire, over 130,000 people lived there. Now only a few thousand can be found at night, though close on half a million still go there to work – in banks, insurance offices, broking houses and markets.

What do they do and is it worthwhile? Two simple questions, but ones that rouse fierce political passions. Part of the Labour Party wants to nationalise two of the City's basic industries – banking and insurance – and a Government-appointed Committee of Inquiry, under Sir Harold Wilson, has been looking behind the City's traditional façade. After a lifetime working in and around the City, I start with a bias in its favour. This is, therefore, essentially a book written from the inside looking out. I have been an observer, rather than a doer; a commentator, rather than a banker, broker or dealer, but a commentator from inside the City rather than from outside. I almost said 'inside the village', for the City has many characteristics of the narrow village life. It's only a mile square. People throng its streets. It thrives on gossip. It quickly detects the newcomer. It readily adopts an 'us' and 'them' approach to life. It trusts some and not others, though the recipients will hardly notice the difference. It is intensely loyal to its own kind. It needs and trusts its village policeman and abhors outside interference. Above all it can mistake polite criticism for outright attack. And as quickly regret it. In a word it has all the virtues and failings of a closely-knit community.

First I should explain exactly what the City is and what people generally mean by it. Just as 'Wall Street' operates from one of the oldest settlements on Manhattan, so the City's markets operate on the spot where Roman London developed nearly two thousand years ago. The foundations of Bucklersbury House, home of stockbrokers, foreign banks and insurance companies, contain a well preserved Temple of Mithras; and the City's International Commodity Clearing House is carefully built over the remains of the old Roman Wall. In effect the City extends from another section of the Roman Wall in the north (known as London Wall) to the river in the south and from the Tower of London in the east to Temple Bar in the west.

Within this square mile, the City's offices cluster in several specialisations: the banks and discount houses near Lombard Street and the Bank of England, the insurance companies (and Lloyd's) between the Bank of England and Leadenhall Street, the shipping offices (both the lines and the brokers) around Leadenhall Street and St Mary Axe, the commodity markets nearer the river, with the Bank of England and Stock Exchange (along with the old Royal Exchange – once the home of the foreign exchange market) at the fulcrum near the Mansion House.

In short, the City's financial district has grown up and developed on the oldest spot in London, while the government and the more prosperous residential districts have gradually moved westwards to the West End and beyond. But the City encompasses more than the physical square mile of offices and markets just east of St Paul's. It is the centre of the country's financial activities and, as such, acts as a magnet for the country's savings – from the thousands of bank branches, insurance offices and investment trust and unit trust investors up and down the land. Insurance offices in Liverpool, Norwich and Salisbury (each has the head office of a leading company), investment trusts in Edinburgh, banking offices in Manchester, Glasgow and Birmingham, the stock exchanges in Liverpool, Manchester and Birmingham – all maintain daily contact with and channel funds to, and from, the City. All are essential parts of the City's mechanism. 'The City' is in effect used as convenient shorthand for the hub of all the financial and commercial activities that go on in the UK, for a score of different markets and industries rather than geographically to describe a spot on the map.

Several functions and several characteristics need to be etched in at the outset. The City, as we have said, plays many overlapping roles. The following are, I believe, basic:

- It provides capital and services for industry and government.
- It channels and invests the country's savings.
- It operates leading domestic markets in commodities, securities and money.
- It operates *world* markets in Eurocurrencies, foreign exchange, gold, insurance, shipping and commodities.
- It provides advisory services in accountancy, investment, law and commerce.
- It attracts and communicates financial and economic information to and from the rest of the world.
- It earns valuable foreign exchange.

The main characteristic of the City is perhaps its compactness. You can walk from one side to the other in fifteen minutes. Most City people do just that: walk. Walking, meeting, talking – these are the habits of generations, and in many ways they have not changed much through the centuries. As in most villages, everyone seems to know everyone else. In ten minutes you can pass a bullion dealer in touch with Moscow; a shipbroker arranging the cargo for a ship in Hong Kong or Rio; a banker considering a loan for a chemical plant on Teeside; a bill broker dealing in millions daily (and often wearing a top hat); a Eurodollar dealer who has daily contacts with New York, Zurich, Paris and Frankfurt; an exchange manager who will still be dealing in dollars with New York from home at 10.30 that evening; or an insurance broker just off the plane from Seoul or Caracas. It is in essence a village with both domestic and international contacts. Internal communications, on the street or on the phone, are swift and immediate. Paperwork is kept to a minimum. One survey has shown that 500 people interviewed in the City had made no less than 28,000 contacts in the course of one day – by telephone, letter, messages or meeting face to face. More important, 70 per cent of the meetings were within the City and three quarters were ten minutes walk from their office.

International communications are almost equally common-place and equally fast. The City accounts for one in six of the country's total international telephone calls, and more than half of all the international private leased circuits provided by the Post Office terminate in the City. Moreover, the directors of one Lloyd's broking firm in a recent year made 220 overseas flights, covering $1\frac{1}{4}$ million miles between them. It pays the City to know what is going on in every corner of Britain and of the globe. And it is not by chance that Fleet Street, the centre of a similarly huge communications network, led by Reuters and aided by world-wide syndication through Britain's leading international papers and magazines, is within a stone's throw of the City's centre and well within its bound-aries. By using local and international communications the City can provide quick deals, often by word of mouth, covering millions of pounds and dollars, and a remarkable variety of services. Markets in gold, silver, rubber, ships, insurance and money are all within easy walking distance of one another.

As the City's contacts, particularly its involvement, with the outside world have grown, questions about the way it goes about its business have increased too. For example, have some of the gains in take-over bids, in special tax situations in the Cayman Islands, on the stock market, or on the commodity or foreign exchange markets been the result of manipulation or inside information denied to the rest of us, or are they simply the reflection of market forces? On some occasions – those high-lighted by Lonrho, Sir Hugh Fraser of Scottish and Universal Investments, and the Sime Darby affair, for example – the City has found its name dragged into the limelight, even when the action has been hundreds, if not thousands, of miles from the Square Mile itself. On others – the Bank Rate Tribunal of 1957, the unit trust operations of Sir Denys Lowson, the Slater-Walker affair – the finger has pointed directly at the City.

Some of the criticisms have been fierce and to the point. British bankers were described on a television programme some time ago as 'strong, arrogant, privileged, overweening and unpatriotic'. The money they deal in, across the exchanges, to the detriment of the pound, was 'mafia money, the cut off the top of the American gambling casinos'. The speaker was a union member of Sir Harold Wilson's Committee of inquiry into the City. Another critic, a member of the House of Commons, recently blamed 'currency manipulators, currency speculators, and currency dealers, most of whom are British and occupy desks in this country', for the plight of sterling and the British economy. The Stock Exchange, depicted extensively on a recent television programme, was described thus by a newspaper critic next morning: 'It was much as I remembered it. The pecuniary giants, in whose capable hands this island's economic destiny is juggled, still ran about the floor in undiminished schoolboy enthusiasm, shouting their amusing jargon, playing with their walkie-talkies, having enormous fun, and generally carrying on as if there were no tomorrow, which, in their case, is very possible'.

Some of the criticisms have had a broader, political or economic, base. The City can claim to do more international business in insurance, foreign exchange, shipping freights, Eurocurrencies, and several commodities than any other spot in the world. But it is also criticised for letting down British industry.

It earns no less than £1,700 million in foreign income every year and its foreign earnings per head are double those of British manufacturing industry. But it is also accused of deliberately speculating against the pound and pushing hard-earned British savings abroad as fast as it can.

It boasts of, and is admired for, its freedom from legal and government restrictions on its complex international deals, in contrast with New York, Tokyo and, especially, Paris. But statutory control and supervision are being urged by many people in prominent positions.

It is one of the few international centres where money can earn a rate of interest if left there overnight. But it is also said to attract needless millions of hot money from abroad, thereby adding to the instability of the whole economy.

These paradoxes highlight some of the main questions raised

by people outside the City, and need careful scrutiny. Some are based on misunderstandings. Some are sincere criticisms. Some derive from political conviction. But, as I hope to show, they are not necessarily the only issues the City should be considering as it prepares itself for the 1980s. Equally important, in my view, are the questions that arise from the growing investment monies of the pension funds and the insurance companies, from the revival of fierce competition from New York and Chicago, and from the way the Eurocurrency market may be controlled in future. Will there be a viable Stock Exchange in ten years time? Will New York replace London as the centre of the Eurocurrency system? Is government direction of funds the only way to curb the power of the investing institutions? What is the best way of protecting the investing public? Can the City survive with a weak pound? Should speculation be encouraged as a lubricant of the commodity, security and money markets or curbed as a matter of principle?

To write about these issues from the inside is to run the gauntlet of being mistaken for a partisan by the outside world and a fierce critic by those inside. At a time when outside pressures are changing the fabric of City life more rapidly than ever before, this is a major hazard. But I shall try not only to describe how the City goes about its business, but to offer a realistic assessment of the criticisms now being levelled at it and to explain precisely where I think the truth lies.

Chapter 2

The Banks:
A Vast Supermarket?

The streets of the City resemble some vast banking super-market: there are more banks in London than in any other spot in the world. At the last count 325 different banks were competing for the domestic and foreign business that daily accumulates in the Square Mile. There were more American banks than in New York. The daily fight for business even extends well beyond the banks, for the competition for deposits brings in the building societies, the life insurance offices, National Savings, and the more recently established National Giro.

Banking changes over the past couple of decades have been quite bewildering. In that period:

- The London clearing banks have seen the building societies' share of total deposits overtake their own for the first time. Their deposits now form less than a half of all funds held in liquid form.
- The number of foreign banks with branches or offices in London has shot up from under 100 to over 300 and the foreign bank share of total deposits has reached over £100 billion. The clearing banks have seen their share of total lending drop to well below half of the total, with the American banks alone carving out a 17 per cent share of total bank advances.
- With the London discount houses, British banks have created a vast new wholesale money market as a source

for their lending, alongside the money flowing from their thousands of branches. As a result the clearing banks have lengthened the terms of their lending to industry to such an extent that about 40 per cent of their loans are now medium-term.

- The clearing banks have provided some £1,200 million of their own money to help finance North Sea oil developments, and have begun a major banking revolution, extending banking services to a mass market and paving the way for a cashless society.

- They have been forced to become an instrument of government monetary policy, restricting loans to customers in accordance with government wishes.

- They have also been accused of letting down British industry and of having an over dominant position in the economy, and have been threatened both with nationalisation and with a new publicly owned competitor based on the existing National Savings banks and the National Giro.

In short, new markets have been established, foreign and domestic competition has increased, banking services have been transformed, and government controls have been tightened. In the process the kaleidoscopic array of banks in the Square Mile has been given a vigorous shake, leading to a new pattern of relationships which are still sorting themselves out. To understand what has happened, it helps to know what a bank is and does, how many different kinds of banks there are, and what competition, both inside and outside the banking world, they are now having to face. This is what I want to concentrate on first, before looking at the foreign and domestic climate the banks have had to grapple with.

What do we mean by a bank? Is it an institution which raises deposits from the public? Building societies do that too. Is it confined to those institutions which lend money to the man in the street or to British industry? Pawnbrokers do one and the capital market and the insurance companies and pension funds, indirectly, do the other. The truth is that, whatever the textbooks say, until recently a British bank was a bank when the Department of Trade or the Bank of England said it was. And their decision could have been in connection with the use of foreign exchange, the soliciting of public deposits or the use of a name in advertising. As I write legislation has been passed which subdivides banks into two categories for the purposes of supervision: those who can use the word 'bank' and those who, though licensed, cannot. But it still does not fully define what a bank is.

What a bank actually does is something else again. It borrows money. It lends money. It transfers money. It invests money. It advises about money. It will do these things for a farmer in Norfolk, a retired schoolteacher in Wigan, a millionaire Greek shipowner in Athens or a South American government in deep debt. Sometimes it will deliberately do none of these things, if it feels that it will not get paid or the borrower is unlikely to be able to repay the loan. You can find banks in the Square Mile who will have clients as diverse as those I have chosen as examples. You can also find banks who will specialise in one particular kind of customer. In New York they have taken this a stage further and have a bank run by and for women and one for those who clearly have everything: the millionaires' bank. So far as London is concerned, however, we can divide the banks we see in the City into four different groups: the large High Street banks, known as the clearing banks; the merchant banks; the British overseas banks; and, finally, the foreign banks.

The Clearing Banks

The familiar names of Barclays, Lloyds, Midland, National Westminster and Williams & Glyn's need little introduction. Their branches are on prominent corners in most towns and something like 12,000 of them are scattered throughout England and Wales. There are also three Scottish banks doing similar business in Scotland with 1,500 branches, and four Northern Ireland banks with about 400 branches.

It is easy to take the clearing banks for granted, but it is worth recalling that without them not only the rest of the City but even the rest of the economy would be unable to function as efficiently as they do.[1] Above all, they provide the basic facilities for transferring money from one person or company to another. It is estimated that well over 50,000 million payments are made in Britain every year, the equivalent of about four payments a day for everyone over the age of sixteen. Close on 95 per cent of these payments are made in cash and virtually the whole of this money is distributed by the clearing banks. Of the rest, that is money transmitted in the form of cheques and credit cards, the clearing banks handle some 80 per cent. The clearing banks thus dominate the domestic scene and have far outgrown the merchant and British overseas banks in foreign business. (Table I shows the extent of their foreign representation as well as their domestic coverage.) They cannot yet claim to be the all-purpose institutions that the German and the Swiss banks are; equally, they *can* claim to give a wider banking service to a larger proportion of the population than the leading banks in either of those two countries.

The Merchant Banks

To turn from the clearing banks to the merchant banks is to enter a different world. What kind of a world is still difficult to say. 'Too many chiefs and not enough Indians' is the view of more than one clearing banker about his merchant-banking rivals. 'They live on their deposits; we have to live on our wits' is a common rejoinder. The fact is that the merchant banks are difficult to describe – and more difficult to compare, for they all differ from one another. The older ones, however, were often specialists in goods and have become specialists in money. They were merchants turned bankers. Yet some still remain both. Originally they were essentially family businesses,

[1] It is also easy to exaggerate the role played by banks. Countries have done without them for short periods. Ireland managed to survive remarkably well without them for the six and a half months they were closed in 1970. During their closure, a highly personalised credit (and clearing) system emerged based on Ireland's 12,000 shops and 11,000 pubs. An encouraging experiment in many ways, but perhaps a lot depended on the number of pubs per head of population in the Republic (one pub to every 190 adults) and the Irish publican's acute assessment of the creditworthiness of his customers.

Table 1 Main Clearing Bank Groups

(Figures indicate main balance-sheet totals in £ millions)

MAIN ACTIVITY	BARCLAYS 23,884	LLOYDS 14,762	MIDLAND 15,550	NATIONAL WESTMINSTER 22,183	WILLIAMS & GLYN'S 2,078
Domestic banking[1]	Barclays Bank 10,981	Lloyds Bank 6,515 Lewis's Bank 22	Midland Bank 11,620 Clydesdale Bank 1,133 Northern Bank 965	National Westminster Bank 12,737 Coutts & Co 414 Ulster Bank 901 Isle of Man Bank 105	Williams & Glyn's Bank 1,920
International banking[2]	Barclays Bank International 12,000	Lloyds Bank International 5,995 Lloyds Bank California 1,052 National Bank of New Zealand 610		International Westminster Bank 6,397 Handelsbank NW 506 Global Bank 205	
Merchant and 'wholesale' banking Instalment credit, etc.	Barclays Merchant Bank 807 Mercantile Credit 805 Barclays Mercantile Industrial Finance Barclays Factoring	Lloyds Associated Banking Company 1,137 Lloyds Leasing 188 Lloyds Associated Air Leasing	Samuel Montagu 1,156 Forward Trust 425 Midland Montagu Leasing Griffin Factors	County Bank 566 Coutts Finance 437 Lombard North Central 1,492 Credit Factoring International	Williams, Glyn & Co St Margaret's Trust Williams & Glyn's Leasing
Other	Barclays Bank Trust Company Barclays Insurance Services Barclays Insurance Brokers International	Lloyds Bank Unit Trust Managers Exports Refinance Corporation Beehive Life Assurance Company	Midland Bank Trust Company Midland Bank Insurance Services Thomas Cook Group London American International Corporation	National Westminster Unit Trust Managers National Westminster Insurance Services Centre-File	Williams & Glyn's Trust Company Williams & Glyn's Insurance Consultants

[1] Deposit-gathering subsidiaries in Channel Islands and Isle of Man are excluded.
[2] In case of Midland and Williams & Glyn's international banking is undertaken by separate divisions of parent group. The National Westminster parent bank is also responsible for a substantial part of the group's international business.
Source: Evidence of London Clearing Banks to Wilson Committee.

specialising in some particular trade with a particular part
of the world. The original families are still prominent in the
affairs of many of them. There are still Kleinworts at
Kleinwort's, Rothschilds at Rothschild's, and Schroders at
Schroder's. It is still only a few years since the first non-family
director was appointed to the board of Rothschild's. But, as
taxation has eroded family fortunes and world projects have
grown in size, the financial power once wielded by these
banks has waned, though their influence remains high.

The status of a merchant bank is usually judged by whether
or not it is a member of the Accepting Houses Committee (see
Table 2). At present seventeen share this privilege and they
are the names that most people associate with a merchant
bank. Membership is not easy to achieve and, although controlled by the Committee, needs Bank of England approval.
The Chairman of the Committee has direct access to the

Table 2   *The Top Merchant Banks*[1]

		£m
1	Kleinwort Benson	1,621
2	Schroders	1,543
3	Hambros	1,340
4	Hill Samuel	1,180
5	Samuel Montagu	1,157
6	Morgan Grenfell	1,048
7	Mercury Securities (S. G. Warburg)	752
8	Lazard Brothers	569
9	N. M. Rothschild	528
10	Baring Brothers	386
11	Guiness Mahon	267
12	Singer and Friedlander	241
13	Antony Gibbs	222
14	Brown Shipley	208
15	Charterhouse Japhet	153
16	Arbuthnot Latham	129
17	Rea Brothers	93

[1]Members of the Accepting Houses Committee ranked by size of their latest
published balance sheet. The figures given are based, where possible, on the balance
sheet of the accepting house and its banking subsidiaries.

Governor of the Bank of England. The time when merchant banks were said to be financing both sides during the Napoleonic wars has long since disappeared. For a time during the 1930s, '40s and '50s it seemed that their foreign business had virtually vanished and that the era of foreign bond issues in London to finance governments, railways and industrial plants round the globe and of the 'bill on London' to finance trade on a world-wide basis had gone forever. But the birth of the Eurocurrency markets, which many of them were instrumental in developing in London, enabled them to return to their old haunts and to use their invaluable global contacts. Once again a merchant banker from London can be seen offering, or promising to find, money for governments and money for international projects. He will be found arranging finance for trade, using government guarantees (sometimes British, sometimes foreign) to buttress short-term credit. And he will often be the first person an industrialist turns to for help to ward off a take-over bid or proposed merger. Although their combined assets represent little more than 4 per cent of the country's total banking assets and their advances and acceptance credits only 6 per cent of total loans, they provide or, more important, procure loans for industry worth £12 billion.[1] They also manage funds – for pension funds, insurance companies, investment trusts and unit trusts – totalling about £7½ billion. Not for the first time in their remarkable history, the City's leading merchant banks have survived a lean period abroad and a testing time at home.

The British Overseas Banks

Whereas the merchant banks have offices largely operated from a London base, with individual forays into overseas territories, coupled with representative offices in strategic centres abroad, the so-called British overseas banks have worked through a combination of head offices in London and hundreds of overseas branches from the outset. Their network of branches remains unique in world banking, totalling over

[1]Billions denote thousand millions throughout the book.

5,000 retail and wholesale outlets round the world. The emphasis until quite recently was on local retail banking and trade financing. They were essentially a child of the British Empire, following and encouraging trade, providing banking services to British communities wherever they metaphorically pitched their tents. They still do. But they do a good deal more.

In the 1850s and 1860s the forerunners of the overseas banks were moving into Africa, South America, India and the Far East generally, at a time when the private banks, the forerunners of the present-day clearing banks, felt strongly that their main activities should be confined to Britain. It was a tough task, sometimes stimulated by the development of the overseas telegraph service, the opening up of the Suez Canal, the extension of steamship routes and the spread of the railway, sometimes hindered by war, famine and revolution. The remaining overseas banks of today – Standard Chartered, Grindlays Bank Group, Barclays Bank International, Lloyds Bank International (including the Bank of London and South America) and the British Bank of the Middle East (part of the Hong Kong and Shanghai Group) – would probably say that the risks have changed little. In the past fifteen years alone my own bank, Grindlays Bank, has had its branches nationalised or expropriated in five countries, survived civil wars in Cyprus and Bangladesh, withstood a siege in Aden and had an officer shot into the bargain, had another manager's wife hijacked in the Middle East, been unable to communicate with two of its territories for months at a time for political reasons, and seen its shares halve in value in six months and then treble again eighteen months later. Just after the First World War one of its managers was flung off the bank roof during a riot in Amritsar.

As the Commonwealth countries gained their independence, these overseas banks were forced to come to terms with the new-found sovereignty of the countries they were operating in and to share some of the ownership or direction of their branches. These moves coincided with the rise of the Eurodollar market and the expansion of banking outlets in the main financial centres. It was natural, therefore, for the overseas banks to join in these moves and to diversify their activities while trying to maintain a large share of their original business. It was also natural for them to move closer to the bigger banking groups, both at home and abroad, with different degrees of success.

The Foreign Banks

Finally, we must turn to the fourth category of banks found in the City, the ones that are now visually most prominent, the branches and offices of the foreign banks. They are thick on the ground between Cheapside and Gresham Street, along Bishopsgate and down Moorgate, and, with the new influx of Middle East banks, they are even beginning to flourish along Eastcheap. At the last count no fewer than 308 foreign banks were directly represented in the Square Mile. Add to this the involvement of foreign banks through consortium banks in London, as well as consortium banks with head offices elsewhere, and the total number of foreign banks with some kind of representation in the Square Mile could be pushed up to nearly 400. Little wonder that *The Banker*, which has been adding up the numbers annually for the past ten years, now finds it easier to stress which foreign banks are *not* yet in London. Table 3 shows cumulative totals of foreign banks represented in London.

Why they came is not hard to see. By the end of the nineteenth century London had firmly established itself as a centre for the 'bill on London', a simple monetary mechanism whereby accepting houses put their names to bills of exchange – promises to pay a certain sum on a certain date – and thereby enabled discount houses and other banks to buy and sell them with confidence. Foreign banks were naturally attracted to this essential, and profitable, means of financing trade with their own country. This trade financing continues today. So does foreign exchange business of all kinds. And foreigners still throng the streets of London and often seek help from their own bank in the metropolis. But these traditional activities are hardly enough to explain the phenomenal rise in the numbers of foreign banks over the past couple of decades, during which the port itself has finally decayed. To explain that, it is necessary

Table 3   *Growth of Foreign Banks in London*

	Directly Represented[1]	Indirectly Represented[2]	Total
1967	113	—	113
1968	134	—	134
1969	137	—	137
1970	161	—	161
1971	174	40	214
1972	213	43	256
1973	230	50	280
1974	262	87	349
1975	261	87	348
1976	262	93	355
1977	297	73	370
1978	308	87	395

[1] through a representative office, branch or subsidiary
[2] other banks represented through a stake in a joint venture or consortium bank
Source: *The Banker*

to talk of the Eurodollar market, the needs of the multi-national corporations and the Common Market. I shall be examining the Eurodollar market in more detail in Chapter 4, but its development in London in the late 1950s helps to explain why the number of foreign bank branches and representative offices rose from about 80 just after the war to the present 308 and why, in particular, the number doubled between 1967 and 1973.

Basically, the Eurocurrency market is a way of using surplus currencies held outside their country of origin. In the late 1950s, London banks – mainly the merchant banks, one or two of the overseas banks and, later, the newly formed subsidiaries of the clearing banks – began to seek out foreign currency deposits, especially dollars, to finance trade and projects in all parts of the world. But it was not long before it was realised that the branches of American banks in London could undertake the same business. They could do in London what they were prevented from doing in New York, for reasons we shall explain later. This ability of the American banks to tap a new source of funds in London also arose at a convenient time – when American multinationals were eyeing the growth prospects of the newly formed Common Market. Before long American banks in London were discovering another advantage: they could tap the Eurodollar market for funds when their own domestic market was being squeezed by the authorities. Thus London not only provided a new source of international money, it could also act as a convenient centre for the needs of American multinationals determined to penetrate the European market. Soon hardly any major American bank could avoid having an offshoot in the Square Mile, even if the main reason was to avoid losing valuable clients with European plants or subsidiaries. The total of American banks in London is now 65 – more than in New York.

The influx of foreign representatives and the establishment of foreign branches were not the only developments prompted by the growth of the Eurocurrency markets in London. Some foreign banks were incapable of plunging into these new techniques on their own, lacking both expertise and sufficient financial resources. Soon, therefore, specialised consortium banks were being set up, with several foreign banks as shareholders, to finance large projects through the Euromarkets or to concentrate on certain geographical areas. Some involved London clearing banks, such as Midland and International Banks (with Midland), Orion (with National Westminster) and European Banking Corporation (again Midland). Others were entirely foreign in origin. Their experience has varied. Some have been successful in that they have undertaken fruitful projects, made profits and provided a useful vehicle for their bank shareholders. Others have had a temporary success, providing foreign banks with valuable experience and capability until they were ready to undertake the same business independently. As a result there has been a gradual shaking out among the consortium banks, with foreign banks playing a form of musical chairs as shareholders. The American banks in particular have either moved out of the consortium arrangements or taken full control. Other American banks have achieved similar objectives by the establishment of merchant banking arms in London, undertaking investment business in the international Eurocurrency field still forbidden to them in the United States.

This foreign banking community now accounts for total assets in London of around £115 billion, no less than 58 per cent of the total assets of all banks within the United Kingdom. And, so far as foreign currency deposits are concerned, the foreign banks account for over 80 per cent of the total deposits of £125 billion. They now employ some 29,000 people in the City.

I have so far sketched in the main banking participants and what they do. I now want to turn to the various demands placed upon them and the kind of competition they have had to contend with. At home the clearing banks have had to meet increasing competition for deposits from other savings institutions, especially the building societies. They have also been reorganising the terms on which they lend money to industry, and preparing the way for the so-called cashless society. Overseas they have followed the American banks in setting up new networks in the main money centres of the world, geared to the changing demands of their international clients. I want to deal with their foreign and domestic business separately while bearing in mind that quite often the same bank will be doing both.

The foreign stimulus primarily came from the expansion of US corporations overseas, initially in Europe as the Common Market developed, then in Japan and elsewhere. American banks were forced to follow suit, seeking new sources of funds and providing better and swifter local services. At the beginning of the post-war period, American banks had only a few branches overseas, mainly belonging to a handful of New York banks and Bank of America in San Francisco. Three decades later the leading American banks had established a new network of banks in all the main money centres of the world and most American banks of note, whether regional or otherwise, had an office in London. In 1960 only eight US banks had overseas branches totalling 131. By 1973, 125 American banks had 732 branches overseas. American branches and offices in London rose from 15 in 1960 to 65 in 1978.

The post-war flow of American banks to London came in two main waves. The first, in the early 1960s, involved the large and medium-sized American banks from New York,

Chicago, San Francisco and Los Angeles. The second, at the end of that decade, was dominated by the arrival of the regional banks. Most of them, in both phases, came in order to provide their American industrial customers with the funds and guidance they needed. But it was not long before some of the more venturesome were casting their eyes around for domestic business too. Thus the British banks, prompted by similar demands from their own internationally-minded industrial corporations, were soon reassessing their foreign services, both at home and abroad. They were also having to look over their shoulder to see how far the American (and sometimes other foreign) banks were encroaching on domestic business too.

The subsequent shake-up among the British banks is still not over. It affected not only the way in which the clearing banks, the merchant banks and the overseas banks changed their approach to foreign business; it also transformed their relations with each other and with the Bank of England. At the outset of this decade and a half of intense change, the British banks had a remarkable opportunity. Between them they had a network of overseas branches unrivalled anywhere in the world. But it was not a network ideally suited to the new needs of the multinational businesses with factories and assets in growing numbers of countries. For one thing, hundreds of these overseas branches were primarily concerned with local business or financing trade between the territory and Britain. Secondly, the branches were not in the right places. They tended to be in Africa, India, Pakistan, Ceylon, Hong Kong, even Australia, and not in the money centres like Frankfurt, New York, Zurich, Milan, Paris or Brussels. On top of this the clearing banks tended to be inhibited in expanding into these centres, especially where they had established 'correspondent' relationships, which had resulted in substantial deposits being held in London. Moreover, the relationships between the various British banks (clearing, merchant and overseas) were not close enough to encourage swift moves to keep abreast of world developments.

What was clearly needed, as the leading American banks grasped quite quickly, was a network of wholly owned branches in the main money centres, which would enable them to switch funds from one centre to another, to offer immediate advice locally and, above all, to keep full control of anything being done, world-wide, on behalf of their clients. The British clearing banks started from different points. Barclays, through Barclays DCO, had a large network of branches, concentrating on trade finance and local banking. Midland depended almost entirely on correspondent relationships, plus an office in New York. Lloyds had stakes in National and Grindlays and Bank of London and South America and branches in parts of Europe. National Westminster (as it eventually became) had a small stake in a British overseas bank, a small presence in Europe and an office in New York.

Although the Big Four were not in a position to take advantage of the combined overseas networks of themselves and the overseas banks (with which some of them had loose, and even shared, links), they were always ahead of the other leading banks in the world in reacting to the American international challenge, though they had to await relaxation of exchange controls. They followed two main routes: either by establishing direct representation abroad through branches in the main centres; or by indirect means through co-operative groupings with other foreign banks. Some banks did both. Following the merger between Westminster Bank and National Provincial, the combined management moved swiftly to build up a chain of overseas branches and representative offices in all the main centres. Midland quickly covered itself by joining with its European partners in EBIC, the European Banks International Company, and by establishing one of the first clearing bank consortium banks, Midland and International Banks Ltd, and is now intent on establishing branches in the main centres. Barclays took full advantage of the overseas branches of Barclays DCO and brought the subsidiary fully within its control, at the same time filling in branches in vacant spots overseas and moving decisively into retail banking in California and New York State. Barclays also became a member of ABECOR (the Associated Banks of Europe). Lloyds too merged its European grouping with the Bank of London and South America (forming Lloyds Bank International), moved into retail banking in California, and soon had active representation in nearly fifty countries.

All the clearing banks have thus deliberately moved to the point where they can act decisively on behalf of industrial clients in the major centres of the world. But in doing so they have not yet resolved their final relationships either with British overseas banks or with the merchant banks. Of the overseas banks not yet fully absorbed into the fold of one of the clearers, both Standard Chartered (in which Midland Bank has a 16 per cent stake) and Grindlays Holdings (in which Lloyds Bank has 41 per cent, with First National City Bank holding 49 per cent of Grindlays Bank) can be regarded as international banks in their own right, ranking ahead of much larger foreign banks whose activities are confined to domestic business.

The clearing banks have also begun to encroach on the new issues, corporate financial advice and export finance traditionally provided by the merchant banks. They have had the 'financial muscle' and have been keen to use it in a wider area, particularly since the early 1970s when the Bank of England began not only to encourage competition but also to allow mergers with merchant banks. The result is that some clearing banks have formed their own merchant banking arms, while others have acquired existing ones. Barclays have formed Barclays Merchant Bank. National Westminster have built on the existing County Bank. Midland have bought Samuel Montagu, one of the members of the Accepting Houses Committee. There have been other cross-fertilisations too, with Grindlays Bank, one of the remaining overseas banks, acquiring Brandts and Bowring, a large insurance broking group, taking control of Singer and Friedlander.

The question to be faced now is whether the remaining merchant banks can sustain their independence for much longer. For a time in the early 1970s, as the world boom reached its peak and bigness seemed as important in banking as elsewhere, it seemed almost inevitable that the merchant banks would have to link themselves to one or other of the clearing banks or form bigger groupings among themselves. Even now some City people are convinced that this will have to happen in the end. Personally I doubt it. It is true that, as more and more merchant bankers join the clearing banks and as the clearing banks absorb the techniques of the merchant banks, the apparent difference in flair or style will begin to be blurred. Yet the characteristics that really matter – the closer relationships which can be forged with fewer business clients, the need for an outside 'independent' opinion, the swiftness of decision that comes from avoiding the more formalised decision making of a larger organisation – all these are bound to ensure the continuation of the larger merchant banks, especially in a period and a financial environment where specialisation is both needed and demanded.

We must now turn to the question of what the banks do at home. Personal services, of course, are almost entirely in the hands of the big clearing banks, though the merchant banks still have some rich clients, whereas industry will or should get help from the banking groups we have been describing so far.

The banking habit is probably as deeply ingrained in Britain, where 45 per cent of the adult population now have a bank account, as in any part of the world. If the Trustee Savings Banks, the National Savings Banks and National Giro are included, it is probable that up to 60 per cent of the adult population have an account. This leaves 40 per cent to go for, though about a half of this may turn out to be 'unbankable' for one reason or another. Basically the banks borrow money and lend money, transfer money and advise on money. Moreover, they have been attempting to do these basic things for more and more people. As a result, the way in which the banks finance their various services and how they charge for them has been changing too. Traditionally the banks have borrowed money from customers – from money placed on current or deposit account through their thousands of branches – and have in turn relent various proportions of this money to personal borrowers, industry, agriculture and government and kept agreed proportions in cash or in assets which can readily be turned into cash.

The difference between the rates of interest at which they borrowed and lent, and from which they made a profit, enabled them to decide what, if anything, to charge for their other services. In their efforts to widen their services to a mass public, they have naturally been forced to consider charging more for some of these other services. The introduction of computers, which in tackling the avalanche of paper and money transfer was inevitable, has brought difficulties of a different kind, though the high costs involved have again raised the question of whether they should not be passed on fully to customers. The cost of *not* introducing computers might have been even higher. And as the banks look ahead to 1985 and beyond, to an age when electronic transfer machinery will enable us to pay through a bank computer as we emerge from the supermarket, the question to be faced is whether the subsequent problems of impersonal service, the fears of fraud or computer errors will raise a public antagonism and a refusal to face and pay the true costs.

A few years ago, the rapid growth of credit cards in the US convinced the popular press in Britain that the cashless society here too was just round the corner. Yet at the last count in Britain more than 99 per cent of all payments over 50p by all people and organisations was also in cash. This, of course, is a measure of the volume of transactions only. When the *value* of transactions is measured the cash percentage drops below the 50 per cent mark. The move away from cash has been going on for generations; it was replaced first by cheques, then by credit cards and now by computerised payments systems. The truth, however, is that the change-over to these new systems has been far slower than expected. In America shops and restaurants have come to prefer payment by credit card to payment by cash. In Britain the reverse is still true, even though acceptance of the credit card in lieu of cash is now growing.

These new systems range from the computerised payments of wage bills, standing orders or direct debits, to the electronic machines capable of accepting deposits, providing cash or making payments when operated by a customer. Some of the machines capable of undertaking these jobs were pioneered in Britain, though currently some of the most advanced experiments are going on in different parts of the United States.

Publicity naturally focuses on the machines to be used directly by customers, but automated clearing houses (which will enable different banks to clear cheque payments automatically among themselves), the linking of automatic teller machines to each other and the introduction of telephonic banking systems loom just as large behind the scenes, for it is in these broader developments that the big investment will lie in the future.

It has been suggested[1] that, with a £35 million investment in terminals and central hardware, the banks might have established by the mid-1980s a system linking all banks to an operational centre which in turn would be linked to some 20,000 retail terminals (say, 20 per cent of the larger merchants already enfranchised to Access or Barclaycard). Such a system might attract up to 10 per cent of current cash transactions, and might equally encroach on some credit card transactions and cheque card payments. The new system would, of course, need a card of its own to operate. The proliferation of cards would then become the main irritation to customers and some rationalisation, such as the merging of the cheque guarantee card with the cash dispenser card, and the existing credit cards perhaps with the new debit cards needed for the electronic supermarket, would be essential.

How near then are we to this banking version of 1984? Experiments have been going on in several parts of the United States with the usual mixed results. In California a combined supermarket–bank system enabling customers to pay for their purchases at the point of sale has been discontinued because of lack of use. In Seattle the first telephonic banking system, enabling a customer to order and pay for his goods out of his bank account over the telephone, has also failed. But other experiments continue to thrive, in Massachusetts, Nebraska, New York State, Florida and California. Bankers on both sides of the Atlantic seem convinced that the new gadgets will gradually be accepted but that progress may be slower than once thought. The reasons are not far to seek. Customers' habits die hard. Customer convenience too needs to be con-

[1] In this analysis I have drawn heavily on the contributions of G. B. Hague, General Manager, Lloyds Bank, and J. M. Williamson, Inter-Bank Research Organisation, at International Conference on Payments Systems, Mexico City, June 1977.

tinually borne in mind; and so do customers' anxieties. Are the new gadgets foolproof? Can someone else raid his account? When standing orders, by computer, throw up more mistakes than the old hand-operated system, what hope is there for a whole new system? What happens when there is an electricity failure? Is it really impossible for a mass of people to know what our bank account contains and what we are doing with it? If there is fraud will we have to foot the bill and, if so, by how much?

The banks will have to move carefully. But it would be wrong to assume that the new systems are a simple way of reducing costs. The truth is that the cost of the existing system of payments has been outpacing inflation in recent years; the new system would simply help to contain some of these costs by greater efficiency based on turnover. Whatever they decide to do, the banks will have to consider charging customers more for these transfer payments or look elsewhere for the necessary subsidy. The place they have automatically looked in the past – the difference between the interest rate they charge borrowers and the rate they pay depositors – is no longer looking as profitable as it was, for reasons I now want to examine a little more closely.

The clearing banks have seen their thousands of branches as the basis of their personal services, attracting useful deposits, either on current account, on which no interest is paid, or on seven-day deposit account, on which there is a variable rate of interest. These branches have looked after their customers' varied needs – acting as executor or trustee, buying shares, receiving valuables for safe keeping, offering financial advice, as well as negotiating personal loans, overdrafts, hire purchase and so on. But behind these branch services has lurked a simple calculation: that the cost of some of these services could be subsidised from the so-called 'endowment element' that the banks receive from the ability to attract large sums of money on current account without paying interest.

In the past, therefore, the branch network was the catchment area for funds and so the backbone of the banks' lending policies. Private customers tended to place more money with the banks than they were borrowing. Companies, on the other

hand, tended to borrow rather more than they left with the
banks. Both kinds of customer generally borrowed on overdraft,
a flexible facility which in theory was repayable on demand but
which could be rolled over from month to month. But gradually
these habits, both of borrowing and lending, have been changing. Both the banks and industry have found snags with overdrafts, the banks because they could not always judge when a
borrower was going to use his facility and industry because of
the uncertainty caused by never knowing when the facility
might be withdrawn. Equally, on the borrowing side, the
banks have found, under increasing pressure from the building
societies, the Trustee Savings Banks, and the National Savings
Movement, that they could no longer depend to the same
extent on the inertia of their customers in leaving interest-
free balances with them on current account.

The competition from the building societies in particular
has been marked. In 1962 deposits (including shares) in
building societies amounted to 21 per cent of total deposits
throughout the country, whereas deposits in the London clearing
banks (that is excluding the Scottish and Irish banks and the
foreign banks) was as much as 43 per cent. By 1976 these
roles had been reversed, with the building society percentage
rising to 38 per cent, and the London clearing bank share
dropping to only 31 per cent.

The encroachment of the building societies can be explained
in several ways. The societies, of course, benefit from the composite tax arrangements they have with the Inland Revenue,
which enables them to offer a higher interest rate than the
banks can on deposit accounts. The increase in the volume of
total wages and salaries going to the lower-paid has also been
to the benefit of the building societies, whose customers have
tended to come from the classes which have suffered least from
the combination of taxation, inflation and the pay restrictions
of successive incomes policies. Moreover, the societies have
continued to open on Saturday mornings (when the banks are
closed) and have been encouraged to establish more branches
for their growing business.

The clearing banks also complain that the societies pay a
low rate of corporation tax, none at all on gains made by selling

government securities so long as they hold them for twelve months, and are safely outside the monetary controls operated, often to the detriment of profitable bank business, by the Bank of England. The societies have, of course, begun to attract the attention of the government in their influence on house prices, and have voluntarily curbed their lending. But the clearing bank view that the tax treatment of financial institutions is in need of urgent overhaul is understandable.

The result of this competition has been to reduce the proportion of the clearing banks' interest-free balances. One clearing bank has estimated that since the beginning of the 1970s the share of current account balances in the banks' total sterling deposits has dropped from over 50 per cent to about 40 per cent. Fortunately for the banks, this decline also coincided with the expansion of the City's parallel money markets, which will be explained in more detail in Chapter 8. These wholesale markets in money enabled the banks to bid for additional funds at a time when one of their main traditional sources of money was proving less dependable. There was, of course, a catch. Whereas the previous inertia of customers in leaving unwanted balances cost the banks little, except overheads, the cost of the new source depended on the demand and supply for funds, that is the current rate of interest. There was, however, an advantage to the banks. The traditional source of funds was based on the network of bank branches, whereas the new source was largely confined to the head office staff in London.

All these factors have led to corresponding changes on the lending policies of the banks. The flexibility of the overdraft (under which a borrowing limit is agreed with the borrower who himself decides when and how much of it he will use) has been replaced in some cases by term loans for specified periods. In spite of the comparative cheapness of the overdraft, a growing proportion of industrial lending is now done on a loan basis and I shall have much more to say about this in the next chapter. So far as the personal borrower is concerned, the introduction of hire purchase financing, personal loans and the use of credit cards have had the same effect. The first move of this kind by a London clearing bank, into hire purchase, was made in July 1958, when Barclays took a stake in United Dominions Trust, one of the leading hire purchase houses. Others quickly followed suit. Similar initiatives were subsequently taken in the personal loan business, where Midland just headed the field, and, ultimately, in credit cards, where Barclaycard was the pioneer and Access (in which the remaining banks have combined) the main domestic competitor, apart from the two major imports, American Express and Diners Club.

These various moves, both in lending and in borrowing, have recently coincided with sharply rising costs. The result has been a continuing questioning of traditional practices. And, not surprisingly, the cost of running an extensive branch network has come under sharp scrutiny. The so-called 'endowment element' (the flow of funds from current accounts in the branches) is not of course, costless. The banks calculate that the real costs of acquiring these funds are at least 7 or 7½ per cent. While interest rates remain above this level (as up to 1976 and more recently) there is little problem. When interest rates declined rapidly for a period in 1977, the cost of the 'endowment element' and thus of the branches became a more serious matter. It also coincided with the feeling that, as the banks tried to cope with increasing numbers of customers, a growing percentage of whom were more concerned with money transfers and routine payments, which could be separated from the more sophisticated advisory or commercial services, the role of the branches ought to be reconsidered. Was it not time to turn to the possibility of running smaller branch units, which would concentrate on the money demands of a mass market, leaving it to larger area offices to look after commercial, administrative and advisory operations? A number of experiments have already been conducted along these lines.

Thus change was already in the air, before the vision of 1984 banking supermarkets seemed poised to become reality. The banks, accordingly, are rapidly doing their sums. How should they charge for their various services? Should they go ahead and introduce the expensive electronic equipment needed to run a new-style payments system on the assumption that the customer will both want it and be willing to pay for it? Behind their calculations lies the knowledge that competition for the public's business could be sharpened by the merger of National Giro and the National Savings Banks to produce a publicly owned competitor. This we must now consider.

What the clearing banks are in effect competing for is the business of those people who at present do not have a bank account, or, perhaps more realistically, those who have the savings habit and are considered creditworthy for consumer finance. They are not alone. Both the Trustee Savings Banks and the two state-owned organisations, the National Savings Bank and the National Giro (set up in 1968 to run a cheap nation-wide money transfer system) are increasingly active in the same field. The Trustee Savings Banks, primarily founded on the Victorian habits of thrift which thrived in the north of England and in Scotland, have been spreading south for some time and, more important, have been providing services much closer to those of the high-street banks. Founded with a savings purpose, they have introduced money-transfer facilities, such as cheque books, and are said even to be considering a credit card of their own. The National Savings Bank, though it has lost ground over the past ten years, still has some 20 million accounts and deposits of over £3,000 million. The National Giro, which like the National Savings Banks, operates through the country's 22,000 post offices, has acquired some valuable private business accounts but is still confined to only about half a million private clients. It has some business from the nationalised industries.

Into this rather untidy jigsaw has recently been flung a new kind of challenge. The National Executive of the Labour Party has called for 'a substantial publicly-owned sector in banking'. This has meant different things to different people. Some have urged the merger of the National Giro and the National Savings Bank and the creation of a public rival to the privately owned banks. Others have simply supported the outright nationalisation of the Big Four. The motives behind the suggestion of a merger between the National Savings Bank and the National Giro are economic. They also come from the highest level. In an oft-quoted preface to a book published in

1973[1], Mr James Callaghan, before he became Prime Minister, put it this way:

> Such an institution would have complete facilities for the transfer of funds, the taking of deposits from the public and the lending of funds – indeed all the facilities of the clearing banks and on a comparable scale. Both the National Giro and National Savings Bank enjoy the overwhelming advantage of the Post Office being available in or near every high street and housing estate. Such a development would bring the advantages of banking almost to the doors of millions of people who now never cross the threshold of the clearing banks.

This is an attractive vision, but the pace of achievement might be somewhat slower than the enthusiasts tend to suggest. Union rivalries will have to be overcome, as well as the rivalry between Glasgow and Bootle for the privilege of becoming the joint headquarters. But, more fundamentally, there is the problem of turning the Post Office outlets from extremely busy agencies for both organisations into professionally run, and staffed, banking branches. Could they attract sufficient deposits to become viable quickly enough to avoid the inevitable subsidy? There is the further problem of switching what is an organisation for the small saver into a banking organisation capable of financing British industry – if some of the aims of the Labour Party are to be taken seriously. The clearing banks will watch these moves with more than casual interest. It would be one thing to encourage another domestic rival under normal competitive conditions; quite another if the full financial resources of the government were seen to be sudsidising such a rival.

One overriding threat now seems to have receded. The proposal to nationalise the Big Four banks never had the support of the main unions concerned. In any case, the arguments on which the proposal was based have largely been answered by events. It was argued that the economic power

[1] Glyn Davies, *National Giro* (London/George Allen & Unwin, 1973)

of the banks had become excessive and needed curbing. The banks were said to be inefficient and to have too many branches competing with each other. Their profits were said to be too high. They were also accused of starving industry of funds for expansion.

The conclusions I draw from my own brief survey of recent developments are rather different. Competition has been increasing for bank deposits and bank business at a greater pace in the past decade than at any time since the end of the war. The clearing banks no longer command the biggest share of the public's deposits. They are meeting stiffening competition from the American banks among their own domestic customers. London, in contrast with any other financial centre I know, opens its door to any bank worthy of the name. The services provided by the banks have been extended well beyond the traditional overdraft and the clearing banks in particular are on the threshold of the new electronic age. They are accordingly well aware of the costs of running branch networks and are poised to prune them in the interests both of efficiency and future profitability. They still irritate their customers by the lack of Saturday opening, by the withdrawal of detailed statements and by the inflexibility of computerised services. Yet a recent survey showed that 80 per cent of their customers were reasonably satisfied with their services. On the question of central control, an issue I want to look at in some detail in Chapter 15, the supervision exerted over them by government (through the Bank of England and the Department of Trade) is greater than ever before. As for the accusation that they have let down British industry, that now needs a chapter of its own.

Chapter 3

The Banks: Enough Help for Industry?

We must now turn to what the banks do for industry. Or rather what the City does for industry. The distinction, as we shall see, is vital in any comparison between London, on the one hand, and Paris, Frankfurt or Tokyo on the other. While the big all-purpose banks in Germany and Japan, for example, are said to be capable of providing their industrial customers with both money and management advice, British firms rely on a variety of City institutions, embracing the banks, insurance companies, pension funds, unit trusts, investment trusts and the Stock Exchange. All have been getting closer to industry for the past decade. Whether they have yet got close enough we must now consider.

Britain's economic record has been dismal, whether measured by annual output, productivity or capital investment. Output per head has risen more slowly than in all other main European countries and the UK share of world trade in manufactures has fallen by more than a half since the war. Above all, the increase in output achieved by the UK from a given amount of investment has been about half that of Western Germany and two-thirds that of France, Japan, the United States and Sweden. The question is why. Some critics put their finger on the role of the unions. Some blame management. Some suggest that we should have lost the war and should have started afresh with new capital equipment, like Germany and Japan. Some say that Britain is not a natural manufacturing country but still a country of shopkeepers, better at commerce than industry. Others again say we are lazy, perhaps even enlightened, preferring the quality of life to the rat-race.

Whatever the reason, the continuing spotlight on the lack of investment by British industry has in turn directed attention towards the providers of capital too. Has the City, in some way, been the real culprit, denying industry the wherewithal for expansion as well as the advice on which it should be based? This is certainly the view held by parts of the Labour Party, the TUC and a number of economists and commentators. British industry, according to these institutions, has not had the support from the City that French, Italian, German or Japanese firms have had from their financial sector. In these countries the banks have been far closer to industry, in some cases having equity stakes in the big firms, in others supplying technical and management experts when needed. It is also much easier, it is suggested, to borrow medium- and long-term money from Continental banks and institutions than it is from their counterparts in the City. Continental finance has also been cheaper. The British banks, it is alleged, are more concerned with earlier repayment and with short-term profit prospects, while the Stock Exchange puts far more emphasis on the secondary market in existing shares than it does on the new-issue market providing equity funds for industry.

What is needed, the critical argument goes on, is a clearer commitment on behalf of the City's institutions in channelling needed financial resources to British industry. The banks should be more concerned with directing funds to companies and projects which will show an adequate return in the long run. They should also have a closer day-to-day relationship with their industrial clients. To sum up, the City's banks and other investing institutions, it is suggested, have not only let down industry but now need to develop a new role towards it, as well as more imaginative investment criteria. The main solutions put forward have included a shake-up among City banks and institutions, if not outright nationalisation; a broadening of the new-issue market on the Stock Exchange; the establishment of specialised institutions to provide medium-

and long-term finance; more formal contacts between the City and industry; and, certainly, some formal direction of investment funds from the City to industry.

The easy answer to these charges is to stress that British industry, when asked about them by the Wilson Committee of Inquiry, promptly and virtually unanimously explained that their main troubles were not the supply of money but a lack of confidence. 'Industry', said the Confederation of British Industry, 'is not merely satisfied with, but often complimentary about, its relations with those who supply it with funds.' The reason why it was not investing lay elsewhere – in inflationary pressures, high taxation, high interest rates, and low productivity. But, even if British industry is generally satisfied with what the City does for it, the contrasts made with foreign banks and other institutions raise the fundamental questions of why the City goes about its investment business the way it does and whether any changes might not be needed. I propose, therefore, to examine the services provided by the City for industry and to consider whether they might be improved.

One of the persistent points made over the past decade has been that other countries have different, and supposedly better, relationships between finance and industry than we do. The first signs of these criticisms were seen during the wide discussions prior to Britain's final entry into the Common Market. After the first bout of euphoria, when talk hardly rose above the level of assuming London's clear destiny as the financial centre of a combined Europe, saner counsels prevailed and detailed comparisons of the different banking systems which existed in member countries were made. It was soon realised how much closer were the relations between banks and industry in Belgium, France, Germany and Italy than in Britain. It was only a small step from this to the assumption that perhaps the contrast in economic performance might owe something to the differences. When, as happened in 1974, the London capital market also dried up at a crucial time for industry, the contrasts with Continental markets were again drawn to London's detriment.

There is little doubt about the differences. In Britain money and capital move into industry from a variety of sources – from ploughed-back profits of industry itself, from the banks and from the various institutions and markets of the City. On the Continent, in contrast, with the possible exception of Holland, the necessary funds are generally provided by a few banks or financial institutions or by the state itself. Thus Britain (and the United States) tend to be market-oriented and the Continent is bank- or state-oriented. It is ironic that what was always regarded as a sophisticated advantage in London is now put forward as a major obstacle to Britain's economic development. Historically, British industry was in the vanguard of the industrial revolution and, as such, did not need the financial support required later by Continental firms. Britain's capital and money markets were allowed and encouraged to develop against a background of surplus capital in private hands. What industry could not provide for itself, the City in its various manifestations was increasingly able to supply.

Other countries had neither time nor money on their side. Few centres rivalled London and foreign industry had to be supported against fierce competition. Moreover, the inter-war depression and the subsequent industrial failures pushed Continental industry into the hands of the banks for immediate support. In the case of Japan it has to be remembered that the large industrial groupings, the so-called Zaibatsu, were instrumental in developing banking offshoots rather than the other way round. For all these reasons, Continental and Japanese industry has leaned heavily on its close relationships with the banks – sometimes for survival, sometimes for development – but only because they had no alternative. How far this relationship has contributed to the higher growth rates and investments in these countries is another matter. What to some eyes here has appeared to be an enviable system has looked quite differently in Germany, and France and even Switzerland. In Germany the banks are heavily criticised for being too involved in industry and for interfering in things they know least about. The Gessler Commission has recently strongly recommended a reduction in the power of German banks over industrial companies. It concluded that the so-called universal bank system led to conflicts of interest and that a limit of 25 per cent 'plus one share', should be imposed on German bank holdings in individual companies.

These historical developments also provide some explanation of the different sources of money and capital. On the Continent there is still a dearth of financial intermediaries which, in Britain, stand ready, alongside the banks, to tap personal savings and then, through the market mechanism, distribute them to borrowers, large and small. There are few Continental institutions, for example, enabling small savers to undertake contractual savings (that is regularly on their own behalf) on the scale regarded as normal in Britain. The relative absence of such institutions as life offices, investment and unit trusts and particularly pension funds (apart from in Holland) is striking. The result is that, while savers in Britain make about half of their financial investments through insurance companies and pension funds, Continental savers muster only about 10 per cent in that form. There are virtually no building societies on the Continent. As a result government and quasi-government institutions loom large in Continental primary markets (that is those raising new funds from the public), while the secondary markets (that is those concerned with the exchanging of existing securities and providing an opportunity for existing holders to obtain cash when they need it) are narrow and the equity markets are remarkably small. The market capitalisation of the London equity market, for example, is larger than that of the original six members of the Common Market put together.

In other words, Britain has a variety of *sources* of money at its disposal and, through the various markets in money, securities and capital, an equally varied range of lending *outlets*, while the Continent tends to channel its money through narrow institutional, usually banking, funnels. It is this contrast between systems that makes it difficult to compare one with another, weighing the advantages of one against the advantages of the other. It also makes it harder to handle in a book of this kind. Whereas a similar book in France, Germany and Japan might devote one chapter, like this one, to the way in which the banking system financed industry, we shall have to spread our treatment over several of the chapters which follow, covering the money markets, the Stock Exchange, the insurance companies, the pension funds, the investment trusts and the unit trusts.

Let me make one final general point about the British system, before we return to the role of the banks. In much of the recent discussion it has been too readily assumed that the non-banking institutions know precisely whom they are lending to in industry and exactly how the money will be spent. In some cases this may be true, as, for example, when a mortgage loan has been made by an insurance company to a firm to build a new factory. In other cases, however, an insurance company may have money on deposit at a bank; it may have bought shares in an investment trust; or it may have acquired existing shares in a manufacturing company. In these instances, the bank in its turn may use the money in a variety of ways; the investment trust too may buy new shares in a leading firm; and the shares of the manufacturing company may rise, enabling it to raise cheaper finance on the equity market. The permutations of such examples across the many institutions which form part of London's money and capital markets are both huge and bewildering. It partly explains why solutions which suggest the central direction of institutional funds as a simple way out of Britain's economic difficulties fit uneasily with the realities of the existing market-place in London.

It is time to return to the banks, and what they do and have been doing for industry. What will become clear is that both the conditions under which industry has been financing itself and the ways in which bank help has been provided have been changing profoundly in just that period when the criticisms have been loudest. It was in the early 1970s that industrialists first found it increasingly hard to rely on generating most of the funds for expansion by increasing profits within their own businesses. Throughout the 1960s, for example, retained earnings, net of stock appreciation, provided between 60 and 70 per cent of the total funds available for investment. By 1970 the share had fallen to 35 per cent and in 1974 dropped to only 19 per cent. The figure has since recovered, though not to the level of the 1960s. Over the same period new capital issues, another source of funds, first dropped dramatically – in 1973 and 1974 – and then recovered, while bank lending continued to rise, eventually overtaking the amount annually generated within individual businesses. To some extent these changes reflected the inflation of stocks and work in progress, but they also provided strong evidence that, contrary to some critics, the banks were providing the necessary funds. Moreover, as they were quick to explain, far from industry being deprived of funds, industry was not using borrowing facilities already agreed with the banks. Between 1975 and 1977, for example, manufacturing industry was using only between 47 and 51 per cent of the overdraft, loan and acceptance facilities of just over £10,000 millions agreed with the banks. This compared with a normal usage of between 60 and 65 per cent. In short, during a period when manufacturers were under growing pressure from inflationary costs, stagnant output and declining profit margins, making it difficult to finance any potential expansion from internally generated resources, the banks were providing a larger share of the needed finance. They were also, for reasons of their own, making significant changes in the way such finance was offered to industry.

The story of these changes, so far as the banks are concerned, goes back to the 1960s and especially to the autumn of 1971, when the Bank of England introduced a new monetary technique which was to become known as Competition and Credit Control. This was intended to increase competition in banking and to lead to a freer use of interest rates, a primary instrument of monetary policy. The opportunity was also taken in the following twelve months to sort out official policy in relation to mergers between one kind of bank and another – whether domestic or foreign. The upshot was that the big banks could and did begin to compete more vigorously with each other for deposits, having abandoned their agreement on uniform deposit rates. They were also coming under increasing pressure from the foreign, especially American, banks in the City to extend the range of services offered to industry. Thus, just at the time when industry was being offered attractive term loans from foreign banks, the clearing banks were enabled to shop around for deposits with a freedom not known for several decades. The result was a revival of and extension of banking services to industry. Some of these services were offered direct; some were done through specialised subsidiaries; some were provided by the establishment (sometimes the enlargement) of special institutions.

In order to appreciate what the banks have increasingly begun to offer, it is essential to realise the basis on which a bank, any bank, works. Since the bulk of deposits placed with banks are short-term, their lending too has traditionally been short-term. The banker is conscious that it is his depositors' money that he is lending and that it is returnable virtually without notice. So he must order his affairs, and particularly his loans, in such a way that when depositors want their money back he is able immediately to meet their demands. This is why, over the centuries, bankers have learned that it pays to have certain percentages of their money invested in liquid form, that is to say available to them too at a moment's notice. Those who have behaved differently, from the Baring crisis in the late nineteenth century to the secondary banks of the early 1970s, have suffered accordingly. 'Borrowing short to lend long', in City parlance, may satisfy industrial demands; it is not a practice that will ensure the undoubted safety of the depositors' money, and on that depends a bank's long-term survival.

As a result, and particularly because longer-term funds were provided in other ways – from ploughed-back profits, or loan stocks or equity issues in the stock market – British bank lending has been based on the overdraft, one of the most flexible short-term facilities available. An overdraft is an agreed line of credit that can be used by a borrowing customer through his current account. He uses as much of the credit as he needs, when he needs it, and pays the current rate of interest only on the amount borrowed day by day. It is also, by definition, repayable on demand. It is therefore an ideal instrument for the financing of debtors, stocks with a quick turn-round and work in progress which is approaching completion (and therefore delivery) and even for longer-term purposes in the context of temporary or 'bridging' needs pending more permanent arrangements. It would be wrong, however, to leave the impression that in practice it has always been used on a short-term basis. It has been usual, for example, for some overdraft accounts to operate permanently in overdraft with the outstanding balance fluctuating daily. This has meant that some firms have had a 'hard core' within their overdraft borrowing which has, in effect, been longer-term borrowing. Though theoretically payable on demand, the banks have invariably only pressed for repayment when a 'hard core' has become pronounced and have usually been lenient with borrowers. Moreover, throughout the 1960s, partly because the needs of industry were changing, partly because of American competition in London, overdraft facilities were increasingly accompanied by the extension of what is called 'term borrowing'. This is not necessarily medium- or long-term. It may be for no more than seven days. But it is usually for fixed periods and has the advantage that it can be moulded to fit a firm's expected cash-flow requirements.

The clearing banks initially began to undertake most of this type of lending, especially medium-term (between, say, 5 and 7 years), through their specialised subsidiaries which were able to borrow the funds through the new so-called wholesale money markets, which began to develop in London in the 1960s, first in Eurocurrencies and later in sterling itself. These additional facilities were also accompanied by specialised schemes, in which the banks participated, introduced by the government to provide medium-term credits for export and shipbuilding. With the introduction in 1971 of the Bank of England's new monetary technique, which allowed the clearing banks to bid aggressively for deposits and to manipulate their interest rates accordingly, the clearing banks were able to tap the inter-bank market (one of the new sections of the wholesale money market) in their own name and were able to base future medium-term lending on this new source of funds. It is, of course, a short-term market with most funds being lent on a 1–6 month basis. At the same time the American banks began to force the pace with similar services and to offer top companies their home-based experience in this particular kind of term lending. Both moves gained a ready response from British industry, which was beginning to suffer from an acute fall in its profit margins and a consequent liquidity squeeze, which in turn was accompanied, and partly caused, by a particularly fallow period for new issues on the stock market.

The upshot was that the volume of medium-term lending from the banks to industry rose significantly, and by 1976 had reached over £8 billion, no less than 47 per cent of their total loans to industry and commerce. Only three years earlier, in 1973, the total was nearly £4 billion and the share only 35 per cent. Over this same period other institutions either extended or introduced longer-term lending. Finance for Industry, generally known as FFI, was provided with additional capital by the Bank of England and the clearing banks and further loan stock by the life assurance offices and the pension funds, enabling it to offer medium-term loans to industry at both fixed and variable rates of interest. A new institution was also established called Equity Capital for Industry. Supported by the Bank of England and backed up by City capital, its purpose was to ensure that equity funds were available to industrial firms with a clear long-term future but whose needs were beyond the immediate resources of the markets, on the basis of current or prospective profits. It is still questionable whether such a gap in equity financing actually exists, but ECI now stands ready to fill it should it prove to be needed. Beyond these new institutions has been the development of a market in short- and medium-term corporate bonds, or at least a potential market for, as I write, the market conditions, especially interest rates, have not been conducive to such new instruments. But there is no reason why, in good time, such a market might not take over some of the longer-term borrowing from the banks.

These various developments in the financial area are additional to the investment lending also undertaken by the insurance companies, the pension funds and the investment and unit trusts, quite apart from the new-issue market on the Stock Exchange. The variety from the banks alone arises from the many different banks we outlined in Chapter 2 – the clearing banks, merchant banks, British overseas banks, consortium banks and foreign banks. And each, in turn, has its own variety of lending instruments. This is clearly brought out in

Table 4 *Where Industry Can Find Finance*

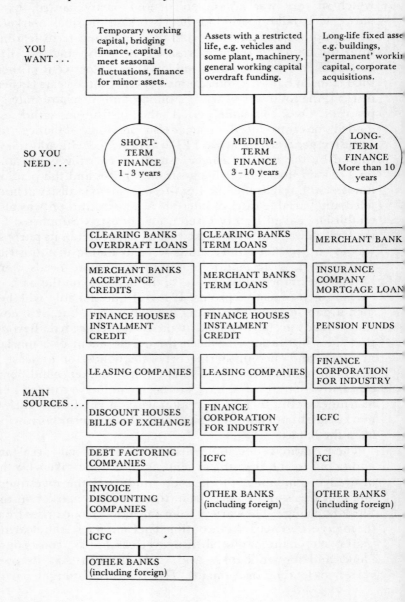

YOU WANT ...	Temporary working capital, bridging finance, capital to meet seasonal fluctuations, finance for minor assets.	Assets with a restricted life, e.g. vehicles and some plant, machinery, general working capital overdraft funding.	Long-life fixed asse e.g. buildings, 'permanent' workin capital, corporate acquisitions.
SO YOU NEED ...	SHORT-TERM FINANCE 1 – 3 years	MEDIUM-TERM FINANCE 3 – 10 years	LONG-TERM FINANCE More than 10 years
MAIN SOURCES ...	CLEARING BANKS OVERDRAFT LOANS	CLEARING BANKS TERM LOANS	MERCHANT BANK
	MERCHANT BANKS ACCEPTANCE CREDITS	MERCHANT BANKS TERM LOANS	INSURANCE COMPANY MORTGAGE LOAN
	FINANCE HOUSES INSTALMENT CREDIT	FINANCE HOUSES INSTALMENT CREDIT	PENSION FUNDS
	LEASING COMPANIES	LEASING COMPANIES	FINANCE CORPORATION FOR INDUSTRY
	DISCOUNT HOUSES BILLS OF EXCHANGE	FINANCE CORPORATION FOR INDUSTRY	ICFC
	DEBT FACTORING COMPANIES	ICFC	FCI
	INVOICE DISCOUNTING COMPANIES	OTHER BANKS (including foreign)	OTHER BANKS (including foreign)
	ICFC		
	OTHER BANKS (including foreign)		

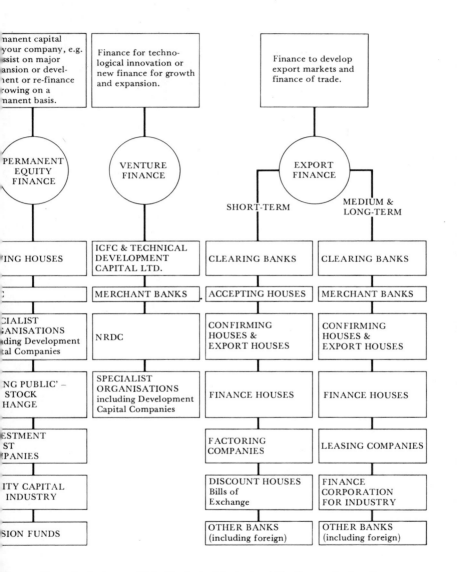

manent capital your company, e.g. ssist on major ansion or devel- nent or re-finance rowing on a nanent basis.	Finance for techno- logical innovation or new finance for growth and expansion.	Finance to develop export markets and finance of trade.	
PERMANENT EQUITY FINANCE	**VENTURE FINANCE**	**EXPORT FINANCE**	
		SHORT-TERM	MEDIUM & LONG-TERM
ING HOUSES	ICFC & TECHNICAL DEVELOPMENT CAPITAL LTD.	CLEARING BANKS	CLEARING BANKS
	MERCHANT BANKS	ACCEPTING HOUSES	MERCHANT BANKS
CIALIST GANISATIONS ding Development tal Companies	NRDC	CONFIRMING HOUSES & EXPORT HOUSES	CONFIRMING HOUSES & EXPORT HOUSES
NG PUBLIC' – STOCK HANGE	SPECIALIST ORGANISATIONS including Development Capital Companies	FINANCE HOUSES	FINANCE HOUSES
ESTMENT ST PANIES		FACTORING COMPANIES	LEASING COMPANIES
ITY CAPITAL INDUSTRY		DISCOUNT HOUSES Bills of Exchange	FINANCE CORPORATION FOR INDUSTRY
SION FUNDS		OTHER BANKS (including foreign)	OTHER BANKS (including foreign)

Source: *Money for Business*, published by Bank of England and City Communications Centre

Table 4, which I have borrowed from a recent publication by the City Communications Centre and the Bank of England. It is worth examining for it sets out more clearly than any detailed description the different kinds of help now available to industry. My own conclusion is that, with one or two exceptions which I will consider later, the City, in its various manifestations, is now providing, or at least offering, industry sufficient *financial* services to meet its needs.

It is a remarkable commentary on the debate about the City's financial help to industry that, at the height of the criticism, the banks were in fact quietly financing one of Britain's largest post-war investments. It was not surprising, therefore, that the Wilson Committee should look closely at this test case on Britain's own doorstep, or rather its own section of the Continental shelf. The Committee's working party under Professor Bain felt that a study of the financing of North Sea oil should shed some light on the question of whether the banks were capable of finding money when it was urgently required by industry. Its conclusion was clear: 'Investment in the North Sea oil and support industries does not seem to have been curtailed by a shortage of funds . . . In circumstances where business opportunities clearly existed and where there was a consequential demand for finance, the banks and capital market institutions came up with the money. To do so they had to break fresh ground. . . .' The money they found was not inconsiderable. It is not possible to identify all kinds of bank help since overdrafts to large companies involved in the North Sea are not specifically allocated for a particular purpose. But even the money that can be identified is impressive, totalling some £3,300 million. Of this the London clearing banks alone provided £1,200 million. Other banks involved included the Scottish banks, the merchant banks and the American and other foreign banks. The Bain report described the British banks' role this way: 'We note the way in which certain of the clearing banks, English and Scottish, have built up oil departments and moved into North Sea financing in a decisive manner. The British presence on our own Continental shelf would have been smaller but for these moves.'

Yet even this is by no means the end of the story. Two questions still need consideration. Does the City look after the small man as successfully as it does the ICIs of this world? Are the City's relationships with industry close enough? The experience of Rolls Royce, British Leyland and Alfred Herbert[1] are not easily forgotten; nor are the criticisms that City investment institutions would rather sell shares than get closer to industrial firms to help them to put right what has gone wrong. We shall be examining the role of the insurance companies and the pension funds in industry in later chapters, but I now want to look more closely at the attitude of the banks towards industry.

First, is there a distinction between the services given to large corporations and that given to small businesses? Such a difference is almost inevitable. The large firm can probably command a more direct personal service; the small firm needs, but does not always get, a similar but scaled-down service. The range of services may be similar – from leasing to factoring and from instalment credit to medium term finance – but the application quite different. ICI, for example, has over a hundred banks, world-wide, providing it with facilities; it relies on Barclays, Midland, Lloyds, National Westminster and Bank of Scotland for its main banking services in Britain; and it can use some 300 banking outlets for its attractive short-term deposits. Meanwhile, the small firm will be relying on its local bank manager and will hardly know its way round the City. On the other hand, both large and small have been getting more direct help from the banks over recent years as new divisions have been developed, specifically designed to co-ordinate finance for businesses. These changes have gone hand in hand with the moves away from the traditional overdraft. The large clearing banks, which have begun to operate through these new corporate divisions, to some extent matching American practice, in some ways striking out with methods of their own, have been enabled to do more direct selling of their services to industry, to co-ordinate the different services avail-

[1] Although these failures are often given as examples of the City's remoteness in time of trouble, the reason for disaster varied in each case and the government cannot escape blame in at least two of the three.

able to industrial customers and to make sure that one section of a bank knew what other sections were doing for a client. These divisions have also supplemented the more passive services available through local branches.

When all this has been said, however, it is still widely believed that the small firm is not getting the financial help it deserves. The point is put in different ways, but one set of statistics underlines some of the main anxieties. Proportionately there are fewer small firms in Britain's industrial population today than in North America, Japan or Western Europe and the rate of new business starts among small firms in Britain is half that in the United States. Why? Some argue that Britain's small firms (which account for 30 per cent of its labour force) have been squeezed dry by taxation and that the usual source of start-up capital – the small investor – has virtually vanished for the same reason. Others say that small firms are simply being strangled by red tape and the need to undertake too much paperwork on behalf of government. Inflation too has taken its toll by pushing development and working costs beyond the resources of the individuals running them. And, in any case, new and unproved firms are, by their nature, a high risk for lenders and investors alike. But one point remains; it seems to be easier to borrow £5 million from a bank than £50,000. The established firm will find it easier than the newcomer to find security for loans. So-called venture capital, whether for a completely new business or to finance a small technical innovation, will always be hard to come by. The City now has more institutions attempting to provide such capital than it has ever had. Yet the number failing to raise the necessary funds remains disturbing. Some, of course, are just not creditworthy. Some innovators have no financial sense. Others lack management expertise. Others again have no knowledge of how to seek the funds they need. Bank managers, on their side, though practised in assessing the character of the borrower, the amount he is willing to put into the project itself and his competence to run the business, may make mistakes. They may also lack the technical knowledge to assess the project. But the most common failing, I believe, is the lack of knowledge among small businesses of where they should go to seek the funds appropriate to their need, apart from their local bank. Whose fault this is is a matter of judgement. The Governor of the Bank of England believes that the fault does not lie wholly with the City: 'I am puzzled at the apparent lack of financial inquisitiveness of a number of would-be entrepreneurs. The information is there; the problem seems to be to get it disseminated.'

'Entrepreneurial cats', one City cynic once commented, putting the onus where he thought it belonged, 'can find their way to the dairy.' Even if they can't, there is rather less excuse than there used to be, for virtually everyone seems to be busy either analysing what to do or giving directions: the Wilson Committee,[1] the Department of Industry, the Confederation of British Industries, the Bank of England, the City Communications Centre, the Institute of Directors, the *Guardian*, Finance for Industry – the list of institutions who have produced booklets, opened up information centres or even suggested special guarantees for small businesses seems endless. But more information, even more bank finance, without the improvement in the economic and taxation environment suggested at the beginning of the decade by the Bolton Committee Report on Small Businesses, will do little to bring back the prosperity and encourage the enterprise still so sadly needed.

Finally, could the banks do more for industry by getting a little closer? Here again it is necessary to distinguish between the various banks, especially between the merchant banks and the clearing banks. The merchant banks have had close links with their industrial clients, partly because they have fewer. They are financial advisers, often procuring finance rather than providing it. As they themselves say, 'an accepting house, in its role as financial adviser, hopes to enjoy a continuing relationship over a long period with its client and has to justify and live with the consequences.' How close that relationship really is varies considerably. The Chairman of the Accepting Houses Committee put it this way:

[1] Among other things the Wilson Committee, in an Interim Report on the Financing of Small Firms, recommended: (a) the creation of a new institution, the Small Firms Investment Company (with tax relief for the purchase of the Company's shares); (b) an English Development Agency for Small Firms; (c) a publicly underwritten loan guarantee scheme.

There is a tremendous variety of relationships that we have with corporate customers, ranging from the sort of relationship which is almost a day-to-day one, a very personal relationship between an individual within a merchant bank and an individual within a corporate customer, maybe the chairman or the finance director, on to something much more remote where one would see the customer perhaps twice a year and be brought in on their financial thinking at that sort of interval.[1]

In some cases merchant bankers will be on the board of industrial companies. But, whatever the relationship, the problem remains – the struggle between loyalty to the bank and loyalty to the industrial board. If the merchant banker provides unacceptable advice he still runs the risk of losing his client. In any case, his advice is still likely to be confined to financial matters. Some merchant banks are beginning to feel that they should be capable of doing more for their industrial clients and some have begun to build up teams of experts on management consultancy and on particular industries. Yet, like the clearing banks, there is a general reluctance to go much beyond financial expertise and to become in any way responsible for technical or management developments.

The clearing banks too have been bringing in experts to advise them, especially, as we have seen, in their recent financing of North Sea oil developments. But these experts have been available primarily to advise the banks rather than their industrial clients. Their role in relation to industry has probably been passive rather than active. As in the past, the banks still feel that they should not interfere in the management of their customers' businesses. They should be available for advice; they should have experts of their own; but they should not try to run businesses. 'Beyond a point, a bank's involvement in the affairs of individual companies', the clearing banks told the Wilson Committee, 'must run the risk – now widely recognised in Germany – of creating conflicts of interest and of over-straining the managerial expertise available within

[1] The Hon. John Baring, evidence to the Wilson Committee, 6 December, 1977.

the bank itself. . . . The role of banker is different from the role of proprietor or manager, and it is dangerous to confuse them.' Yet the nagging thought remains that, when trouble hits a company, large or small, the passive role of the banker may not be enough. It is a thought that has also crossed the mind of the Bank of England. For in its own evidence to the Wilson Committee the Bank, picking its way delicately among the political and economic land-mines, put the issue in these terms:

> Attempts in recent years to encourage a closer relationship between finance and industry have provoked considerable controversy. The Bank, while recognising the force of some of the arguments deployed in defence of the arm's length relationship, and in particular accepting that it is no solution of industrial problems, came to the conclusion that some change was needed, and are not disappointed with the progress that has been made so far.

An enigmatic comment but one which could easily be interpreted to mean that both banks and other City institutions ought to do more. If so, what? My own view is that the City, in its different manifestations, should increasingly consider how far it can judge industrial management and, if dissatisfied, at least take steps to change it. In the early stages it may involve the use of more industrial advisers, or management consultants. This road bristles with obstacles – and potential mistakes – but 'hire and fire' may occasionally be a better formula than a polite silence.

Chapter 4

Insurance: World's Biggest Risks?

The London insurance market is a highly sensitive mechanism. It has to be. A crash on the M1; an earthquake in Guatemala; two jumbo jets crashing on take-off in Tenerife; a typhoon off Hong Kong; a robbery round the corner – all will mean something to a man at a desk somewhere in the Square Mile. And the City will mean something to the sufferer, whether in the rubble of Guatemala City or a hospital in Hertfordshire. For London's insurance market pays out over £15,000 in claims every minute, round the clock, year in year out. It also earns more in foreign exchange than any other sector of the City, and is the second largest source of finance for industrial expansion, after the pension funds.

The paradox is that what it does is known to millions; how it does it remains a mystery. A taxi-driver in San Francisco can greet the chairman of Lloyds Bank and immediately talk to him of the fire and earthquake in 1906, mistaking Lloyds for Lloyd's, but the point is well understood in insurance circles. If prompt payment in 1906 is still not forgotten, it must be important in their world-wide business. Yet Lloyd's is only one part of a complex and fascinating industry. The business of spreading risks of all kinds, and from all over the world, over a large number of insurers is now undertaken by three different sectors: the insurance companies, the reinsurance companies and Lloyd's underwriters. Servicing them all are the insurance brokers.

In essence, if enough people are prepared to pay a small sum to insure themselves against a similar risk (whether driving a car or carrying goods safely across the Atlantic), an insurance underwriter can be found to take the risk. Sometimes the underwriter will be in London – either an insurance company or at Lloyd's. Sometimes the underwriter will be a subsidiary of a London company overseas. Sometimes the business will go direct to the company. Sometimes a broker will bring the business to a company. In the case of Lloyd's, an accredited broker will *have* to bring the business and the underwriting will *have* to be done in London. As for the reinsurers, they stand ready to spread the risks still further, both at home and abroad.

Wherever the risks are accepted and wherever they are underwritten, the London market stands at the centre of this essential service to people, governments and industry and commerce. It is not, therefore, by chance that London insurance companies have more overseas offices and branches than others, nor that London has more foreign insurance companies in its midst than any other centre. Just as the centre of the world's Eurodollar market activity remains in London, the *international* insurance market is also in London.

A few figures will help to show the scale on which the

Table 5   *UK Insurance Premium Income: 1978*

	British Companies (members of BIA) £m	Lloyd's[1] £m	Total £m
United Kingdom			
General	3,104	396[2]	3,500
Life (new and renewal)	4,231	1	4,232
Rest of World			
General	3,861	1,185[2]	5,046
Life (new and renewal)	793	—	793
TOTAL	11,989	1,582	13,571

[1]Lloyd's run a three-year accounting method. Figures based on 1975 underwriting year
[2]Estimated on basis of 75% foreign business

London insurance market is now operating, as well as its international flavour. We can start with the inflow of premium, the money paid by policyholders of all kinds in exchange for the comfort of sharing their individual risks with others. As Table 5 shows, the world-wide premium income in 1978 totalled £13,571 million. Of this £11,989 million related to the companies and £1,582 million to Lloyd's. The total is roughly equivalent to the gross domestic product of Scotland and more than that of New Zealand or Portugal. This huge sum can be looked at in two ways; where it comes from, and the purpose for which it is paid. Both highlight significant features of the London market.

First, then, where does the premium income come from? Here the international trend is clear: Lloyd's derive some 75 per cent of their total business from overseas and the companies about 45 per cent. Since most life business is accepted and underwritten in the territory in which the insured live, only a small proportion of life business comes from abroad. If, therefore, life business is excluded from the analysis, the proportion of company business undertaken overseas rises to over 60 per cent. The proportions are even higher for some of the larger companies, with Commercial Union and the Royal reaching over 70 per cent. Commercial Union, the Royal and General Accident, for example, do more business in the United States than in Britain. With such premiums flowing from abroad, it is not surprising that the total London market's foreign earnings form such a dominant part of the City's total income. In recent years invisible income from insurance has been the City's biggest foreign earner, reaching £909 million in 1977. Of this the companies earned £345 million, Lloyd's earned £379 million and the brokers £185 million.

Secondly, as Table 5 also brings out, total premiums from life business, which is essentially contractual and long-term, in that policyholders agree to pay premiums regularly and the insurance companies accept long-term commitments, have reached over £5,000 million. This represents the country's second largest form of contractual saving, outranked in recent years only by the growth of self-administered pension schemes of companies like ICI and Unilever and public bodies like the Post Office and the National Coal Board. All in all, about 80 per cent of Britain's 18 million households, including 14 million families, benefit from life assurance protection in one form or another.

The insurance industry needs to keep large liquid resources and longer-term investments to meet both its day-to-day claims and its long-term obligations. The companies alone now manage invested resources totalling some £50,931 million, from which they earn some £3,718 million annually. These funds are the tangible substance, so to speak, of the peace of mind of millions of policyholders throughout the world, from the multi-million shipping magnate to the single-handed week-end sailor, from the hotel chain boss to the first-time home buyer. But by far the largest slice of insurance investments, amounting to some £39,319 million in 1978, basically represents the savings of UK life policy holders and members of pension schemes administered by insurance companies.

It is tempting to lump the different parts of the industry together, but it is easier to handle them separately. Let us take Lloyd's first. Lloyd's is essentially a market made up of individuals whom the Corporation of Lloyd's provides with common administrative services. Lloyd's has been transferred several times since it first grew up as a coffee-house in the seventeenth century – from Tower Street to Lombard Street and from the Royal Exchange to Lime Street – but the character and the strange echoing bustle of the great Under-writing Room remain. The 'waiters' (shades of the coffee-house), the Lutine Bell,[1] the Casualty Book and its quill pen, especially the narrow pew-like boxes at which the under-writers work – all leave something unique in the mind of the visitor looking down from the gallery above. What can be seen is probably the most successful eccentricity in the City. For

[1] The Lutine Bell is rung for silence for the announcement of important news (once for bad news; twice for good). The bell itself was salvaged in 1858 from the wreck of the frigate, HMS *Lutine*, which was originally French, then captured and used by the British during the Napoleonic wars and finally wrecked in 1799. The claim was paid out by Lloyd's and thus salvage from it still belongs to Lloyd's. There are still hopes that further gold salvage will be discovered.

nowhere else do members deal in such large sums on their own account, and in such cramped conditions. Rightly has Lloyd's been dubbed 'a market of unlimited liability for hazards unlimited'. It is in fact a collection of a wide variety of individuals, at present over 14,000-strong, who put their own individual resources at risk. Some are professional insurance men, leading syndicates; others are simply members of syndicates, ranging from doctors to housewives, from successful boxers to former civil servants. There are now 1,200 foreign members of whom 800 are American and 186 from Common Market countries. The common denominator is that they have all had to make a 'show of wealth' to the Committee of Lloyd's: £100,000 for British and Commonwealth members, £135,000 for other members and £50,000 for a new category of mini-member introduced recently. They have all also had to pay a non-returnable entrance fee of between £1,500 and £1,900 and to establish a separate Lloyd's deposit. A £15,000 deposit, for example, can allow a member to underwrite some £100,000 of business, The aim of course is to ensure that a member of Lloyd's has sufficient resources to meet any calamity. The layers of protection are impressive, starting with the premium trust funds (into which all premiums are payable) and going on to the special reserve fund, personal reserves, members' deposits and eventually members' personal fortunes, including the shirts on their backs. Even beyond this stand Lloyd's Central Fund, set up to protect policyholders, and the so-called guarantee policies.

The members are grouped into 367 underwriting syndicates, large and small, most belonging to more than one syndicate. Apart from 11 of these syndicates which concentrate on short-term life assurance policies, the rest are divided into four main categories: marine, non-marine, aviation and UK motor. Each of the syndicates is headed by experienced underwriters, many of them experts in quite narrow fields of insurance cover. They occupy the narrow 'boxes' on the floor of the Room and obtain their business from accredited Lloyd's brokers who shop around on behalf of their clients, at home and abroad, to get the best rate for the risk. Though acting for a syndicate of 'names', the Lloyd's underwriter is a principal acting on his own decisions and doing so quickly. Coupled with the comparative cheapness of the cramped quarters he works from and the centralised services he can call upon, this flexibility enables him not only to quote competitive rates but to modify policies in the light of world conditions. It is in fact an arrangement admirably suited to the underwriting of short-term, usually annual, risks. And it is hardly surprising that the unusual risks should find their way to Lloyd's under-writers, from the insurance of Betty Grable's legs for a million dollars in the thirties to the coverage of the odds against anyone claiming the £1 million prize from a whisky firm for finding the Loch Ness monster. Nor is it by chance that Lloyd's underwriters (and brokers) have been prominent in new areas of insurance, from credit insurance in the twenties to the oil rig, hijacking and communications satellite risks of the post-war period.

The insurance companies grew up alongside Lloyd's but, because of their limited liability status and their subsequent growth, have behaved and developed differently. They are far from homogeneous – either in terms of the work they do or the way they are constituted. As Table 6 shows, currently there are some 801 different companies operating in the London market, of which 169 are from overseas. Of the British total of 632, the majority, some 310, are engaged on non-life business only, with 150 involved in life business only, the rest doing composite business (that is both life and non-life) and reinsurance business. This is not the end of the complication, for these companies are formed in different ways. Some have shareholders; some do not. The 'proprietary'

Table 6   *Insurance Companies Operating in the UK*

	British	*Overseas*	*Total*
Life only	150	15	165
Non-Life only	310	80	390
Composite and others	135	30	165
TOTAL	632	169	801

Source: Department of Trade

companies have shareholders and pay out some of their financial surplus in the form of dividends. The 'mutual' offices are owned by the policyholders and the surpluses are allocated to them in the form of bonuses. While those with shareholders tend to undertake all kinds of business and those run by and for policyholders tend to concentrate on life business, there are exceptions on both counts. Again, while some companies concentrate on reinsurance (that is the process of spreading the risks taken by companies over a wide area, often on a world-wide basis), this is also undertaken by ordinary insurance companies, as well as by Lloyd's underwriters.

It is this variety that is the main feature of the London insurance market. It is also one of the reasons why it has not readily fitted into the preconceived Common Market legislation and why regulations which might suit companies do not necessarily suit Lloyd's and vice versa. Even among the large composite companies, some of the differences are striking. As Table 7 brings out, two companies dominate the list by size (Commercial Union and Royal), and especially by their concentration on general non-life business, whereas the third in the list, the Prudential, has a similar dominance in the life field. The top two, in fact, account for roughly a quarter of

Table 7   *The Largest Insurance Companies: 1978*

		Total Premiums £m	General Business £m	Long-term or Life Business £m
1	Commercial Union	1,381·4	1,100·7	280·7
2	Royal	1,347·0	1,220·1	126·9
3	Prudential	1,155·7	394·4	761·3
4	General Accident	831·4	745·8	85·6
5	Guardian Royal Exchange	778·5	619·7	158·8
6	Sun Alliance & London	641·4	520·7	120·7
7	Legal & General	608·6	131·0	477·6
8	Eagle Star	516·1	363·9	152·2
9	Phoenix	432·2	337·6	94·6
10	Norwich Union	416·9	154·4	262·5

the total premium income of all the companies, and receive more premium income from the United States than they do from the United Kingdom. The top six account for half of the total premium income of all the companies. It is hardly surprising that they also have an extensive network of branches and subsidiaries abroad and that their back-up in research and in investment is as impressive as that of any other institution in the City.

Beyond the large composite groups and the mutuals are other specialist companies: the marine, aviation and engineering insurers; the British subsidiaries of foreign companies; and the reinsurance companies. The foreign element has grown rapidly in recent years and has brought new capacity as well as new techniques to the London market. A flood of new foreign companies was encouraged by the combination of the UK decision to join the Common Market in 1973 and the ease with which they could enter the British market. Since then both the British market and the new entrants into it have become more closely controlled and the inflow has subsided. As for reinsurance, this basically arises when a company has decided what is the maximum amount it is prepared to lose on any particular risk: the liability above this limit is then reinsured with another company. The professional reinsurance companies concentrate on the reinsurance of business written direct by companies in the country where the risks are situated. They are, or should be, experts not only in assessing the original risk but also in gauging the professionalism of the companies from whom they receive such business. In some respects it has been said that they they are the insurance companies' insurance company. In addition to the professional reinsurers, both the composite companies and Lloyd's underwriters accept reinsurance business. It is because of this spreading of reinsurance risks over a larger number of institutions in London that British professional reinsurers account for a smaller share of the total reinsurance market than do their counterparts in other centres.

This complex mixture of underwriters in the London market has a correspondingly complex system for channelling premiums to them. The instruments include agents, brokers and inspectors. Each sector of the market has its own method as well as its own way of describing them. In the case of Lloyd's the appropriate channel is quite simple: business must be, and is, brought to the underwriters by accredited Lloyd's brokers. In the industrial life field, the backbone of Victorian life assurance, premiums are still collected at the doorstep on a weekly basis by agents. In the case of ordinary life, where premiums are paid regularly (monthly, quarterly or annually) out of bank accounts, both brokers and agents such as solicitors and other professional people seek out the business and leave it to inspectors to advise on and execute it later. Some companies, especially the offshoots of Commonwealth companies, use direct-selling methods with paid salesmen. More recently these direct methods have been introduced to back up the unit-linked type of life assurance. Yet, alongside all these different methods, stands the more traditional broker, and he too comes in all sizes, from a single operator to the large broking companies quoted on the Stock Exchange.

Close on 8,000 firms call themselves insurance brokers and, of these, some 4,100 had become members of the British Insurance Brokers' Association by the end of 1978. This recently formed national association has been directly charged with setting up a Registration Council to administer the Insurance Brokers (Registration) Act of 1977. The Council is expected to register up to 5,000 broking businesses and up to 15,000 individual insurance brokers. The work they do varies in the different sectors of the insurance business. They themselves estimate that insurance brokers handle 90 per cent of total pension business, 90 per cent of marine business, 74 per cent of commercial and industrial business and over 50 per cent of non-life business. On this basis the insurance brokers estimate that they handled premiums totalling over £7,000 million in 1977. Some of the insurance broking firms are run from corner shops with one expert and a few clerical staff. Some are among the largest in the world. One owns a merchant bank. Some have as many branches as leading international banks. Others have partners who are 'names' at Lloyd's.

Table 8   *Largest Insurance Brokers*

British and American Groups

Major US Brokers	Year to	US$ooos
Marsh & McLennan	31.12.78	148,000
Alexander & Alexander[1]	31.12.78	83,357
Johnson & Higgins[2]	31.12.78	n.a.
Frank B. Hall	31.12.78	48,487
Fred S. James	31.12.78	35,975
Corroon & Black	31.12.78	17,895
Major UK Brokers	*Year to*	*£ooos*
Bland Payne Holdings Limited[3]	30. 9.78	27,030
Sedgwick Forbes Holdings Limited[3]	31.12.78	25,042
C. T. Bowring Limited	31.12.78	37,657
Willis Faber Limited	31.12.78	19,141
Alexander Howden Limited	31.12.78	17,729
Minet Holdings Limited	31.12.78	15,279
C. E. Heath Limited	31. 3.78	14,681
Matthews Wrightson Limited	31.12.78	10,930
Stenhouse Holdings Limited	30. 9.78	10,300
Hogg Robinson Limited	31. 3.78	9,511
Bain Dawes (Inchcape)	31. 3.78	6,426
Wigham Poland Limited	31. 3.77	1,011
Brentnall Beard	31. 3.78	(556)

[1] Now includes R. P. Jones (acquired 1978).
[2] Known to be the third largest in the USA.
[3] Merged with effect from 12.2.79

At the top end of the scale, London's leading broking firms are bigger and more international than most. The biggest broking firm in the world is American. But of the next half dozen the majority are probably British (see Table 8). The London market estimates that, apart from the leading American broking firm, the remainder of the US top twenty insurance brokers control less premium income in aggregate than do the top twenty British brokers. Moreover, while British brokers earn over 60 per cent of their total premium income overseas, little more than 10 per cent of the American total comes from abroad. A recent survey of the top 11 Lloyd's brokers, showed that they covered 70 countries in their overseas trips in the course of a year, with 1,200 people spending some 20,000 man-days abroad. One broking firm's representatives made 623 different visits in a year, totalling some 4,000 man-days. Another firm's staff made 220 trips, travelling over one and a quarter million miles seeking business. Directly, these broking firms earn £185 million in invisible income in their own right.

In terms of pure domestic business the British insurance market is only third by size within the Common Market, is dwarfed by the American domestic market and accounts for little more than 5 per cent of the world's total. Yet, if international business is included, especially world reinsurance business, London still stands supreme. As Table 9 shows, British insurance companies, like British banks, have the largest network of offices overseas. It has been estimated[1] that of total world insurance premiums (excluding the Soviet bloc and China) of $140 billion, some $40 billion is not retained in domestic markets. Of this London accounts for some $7 billion, or about 20 per cent of the business needing international clearance or capacity. It is this international pre-eminence and the foreign earnings that accompany it that are plainly at stake when the threats surrounding the London market come to be analysed. This we must now attempt.

The problems facing the London market[2] are both international and domestic. Risks are increasing rapidly, partly because of inflation, partly because of technological changes. At the same time the whole global industry goes through regular cycles in which underwriting losses rise and fall, premiums follow, and spare underwriting capacity is followed by a contraction as marginal firms are squeezed out. During the most recent period of spare capacity, the companies have been facing outspoken criticisms of their services from domestic industry, and multinational businesses have continued to

[1] By Mr R. I. Sloan, executive director of Commercial Union & President of Britain's Chartered Insurance Institute.

[2] By this I imply the whole British insurance business, not simply foreign business undertaken in London.

spawn so-called captive insurance companies (set up to undertake their own insurance and usually run from an offshore
centre like Bermuda), while Lloyd's underwriters and brokers
have been grappling with the problem of foreign members in
London, as well as the growth of a rival market in New York.

Table 9   *Insurance Operations Abroad*

	Number of foreign countries in which insurance companies of the country of origin operate	Number of presentations of insurance companies from that country in other countries
Great Britain	54	861
USA	52	561
France	32	211
Switzerland	29	156
Germany (Fed. Rep.)	16	85
Netherlands	23	82
Belgium	9	68
Japan	17	59
Italy	23	54
Australia	16	53
Canada	13	42
New Zealand	18	34
South Africa	4	32
Hong Kong	9	28
Sweden	10	20
Singapore	3	18
Denmark	7	16
Ireland	5	15
Spain	6	11
Norway	5	10
Austria	4	10
Malaysia	3	9
Lebanon	3	7
Israel	2	7
Philippines	5	6
Brazil	5	5
Luxembourg	5	5
Finland	3	5
Greece	3	5

Source: Swiss Re, SIGMA, November/December 1975

Basically, the London market, like insurance in other centres, is facing an enormous growth in the size and complexity of its risks just at a time when the freedom on which it has grown and thrived is being threatened both at home and abroad. The complexity of the risks arises from technological developments of all kinds – in oil exploration, petrochemical plants, shipping and air transport, earth satellites and even the projected space platforms. The impact of even 'normal' occurrences such as fire, wind or earthquake on such large expensive equipment is pushing replacement costs to the limits of the world insurance market and beyond. Take the costs of building some of these new and complex pieces of hardware. The original Comets and Boeings at the outset of the jet age were running at around £4 million or £5 million apiece. The first jumbo jets were closer to £10 million, with additional liabilities of around £50 million. Now the replacements for these jumbos cost about £20 million with additional liabilities rising to some £200 million. With some 600 in service world-wide, the total risk is colossal. A major container ship with cargo will be worth all of £100 million. North Sea oil platforms come more expensive still; and so do industrial complexes, where risks have risen to as high as £250 million in a Mexican steel-mill and £280 million in a Middle East dry dock. And, when the market is in one of its schadenfreudan moods, it starts to contemplate the cost of a space platform running amuck, a collision of jumbo jets over New York, another big Californian earthquake at an estimated cost of £150 billion, or another Tokyo earthquake at a cost of some £80 billion.

The largest claims on the London market have hardly reached these levels, but recent disasters have been expensive enough. The crash of two jumbos on take-off at Tenerife airport is said to have led to claims of over £100 million. The first Tristar crash cost £20 million, the Flixborough chemical explosion £45 million, and the total loss of the Olympic Bravery oil tanker £25 million. And a recent huge fire in the Caribbean turned one of the islands into a significant earner of invisible income – from claims not premiums.

The challenge to the industry is not arising simply from the inflated sizes of the risks involved. Potential liabilities are growing for other reasons too. After the Tenerife disaster, other airport authorities were suddenly alerted to the potential risks they were running in allowing, or encouraging, thousands of passengers to use their facilities. The same is true when a jumbo jet is refuelling. But the new potential liabilities do not stop with aircraft. The danger of oil pollution by the break-up of oil tankers on the high seas is one which governments have already had to face and about which they may decide to take action by laying down compulsory rules. On an even greater scale, oil companies bringing up oil from the sea-bed, as in the North Sea, may have major mishaps with their oil platforms that lead to pollution on a scale hitherto unknown at sea. The blow-out of the Ekofisk Bravo platform in the North Sea, eventually staunched by the efforts of troubleshooters from Texas, was a warning to governments everywhere and ultimately to the insurance industry of the pollution dangers they were facing. And the drama of the rogue Russian satellite, with a nuclear device aboard, which burnt itself out partly in the earth's atmosphere and partly in the frozen north of Canada was a further reminder of the potential calamities ahead of us.

Moreover, commercial competition hardly diminishes, either at Lloyd's which now faces potential competition from New York, or within the companies whose efficiency has been openly attacked by some parts of British industry. Lloyd's in particular has been coping with American bids for some of its leading broking firms. When Frank B. Hall, one of the leading American broking firms, made its initial bid for the Lloyd's broker Leslie & Godwin in the spring of 1978, the Lloyd's response was to reject it on the grounds that 'no outside insurance interest may normally hold more than 20 per cent of the equity seeking recognition at Lloyd's'. Outside insurance interests were described as 'an insurance company, an underwriting agency or a non-Lloyd's broker'. Eventually a formula emerged which allowed the bid to go through, but the chairman of Lloyd's subsequently reiterated the view that it was essential that the 'control of firms operating in the Lloyd's market should rest firmly in the hands of people who have long experience with the workings of the Lloyd's market'. Since then further links between American and British broking firms have been

announced, bringing Marsh & McLennan alongside C. T.
Bowring, Alexander & Alexander alongside Sedgwick Forbes
and Bland Payne, and Willis Faber co-operating with Johnson
and Higgins. All had different motives, some industrial, some
geographical, though they all reflected the rising international
aspirations of the American brokers.

The basic problem arose from the fact that American brokers
channel large amounts of business to Lloyd's underwriters
usually through London brokers. (About a half of Lloyd's
business is said to be from the US.) They presumably wished
to get what they regarded as their appropriate share of the
commission business or, alternatively, to carve out different
relationships with Lloyd's brokers, as they had done in other
centres. It would be misleading to equate the Hall bid for
Leslie and Godwin too directly with the signing of the Bill to
set up a New York free-trade zone in insurance and the proposal
to establish a New York Insurance Exchange. The American
exchange, which is said to be closely modelled on Lloyd's,
has received the backing of the state authorities. Its initial
capital will probably amount to $60 million, with some twenty
syndicates putting up $3 million each, and it is hoped that it
will have an annual turnover at the start of some $200 million.
This is a modest share of the total American insurance and reinsurance market. The new exchange will also suffer initially
from its limited liability rules, compared with the unlimited
liability arrangements at Lloyd's. This may deter the placing
of large risks on the New York market. In any case, marine
business is not expected to be developed in the early stages.
Competition with Lloyd's will be slow to increase and a
switching of business between the two centres may well be one
of the early results. As one of the initiators of the American
scheme pointed out, in a candid interview in London, 'I think
there is room for us [New York and Lloyd's] to co-operate.
I think we will do more business with the London market than
some people fear we will take away.' In any case, London
insurance companies are likely to launch some of the first
syndicates in the New York exchange if the reciprocity rules
allow them. Thus, although it is easy to exaggerate the impact
the New York market will have on London, it is a clear example

of the competitive world Lloyd's and the companies are living in.

Another indication that it is not roses all the way came from the attacks on the London insurance company market from leading British industrial firms, such as British Leyland, Guest Keen & Nettlefolds, Rank Xerox, Glaxo and others. British Leyland complained that it could not get any UK company to submit outline proposals for its global products liability, basically insurance against the consequences of defective products. GKN went further and spoke of British insurance companies as 'the geriatric ward of world insurance'. Whether this was a reflection of the difficulties now faced by businesses operating on a global basis, the usual tug of war between insured and insurer about premiums (especially when underwriting capacity is close to its peak and rates are being cut to the bone) or simply a disgruntled customer, it is difficult to say. The British insurance companies made it clear at the time of the dispute that they were not prepared to take business at below cost price and would prefer to see it go elsewhere, putting their long-term interest against what they regarded as a short-term gain. The truth will emerge in the end. If the British industrial firms were right, foreign insurance companies will go from strength to strength and the London market will decline; if they were wrong in their assessment, the London market will survive yet again. This is what competition means in the end.

It is against this competitive background and the growing efforts of individual countries to undertake their own insurance that London's global role needs to be considered. The developing world naturally wants to control its own financial destiny. The list of countries which have nationalised their domestic insurance industry since the end of the Second World War has grown year by year. So has the number of governments controlling the activities of insurance companies in their territories. In some cases the aim has been to protect the public; in others governments have been tempted to direct insurance funds into government stocks; in others again the object has been to prevent premiums, payable abroad, being a charge on the country's balance of payments. Whatever the motive and whatever the underlying reason for government action, the operations of foreign insurance agencies and sub-sidiaries in foreign territories, especially those of the developing world, have been increasingly restricted, at a time when larger, not smaller, insurance capacities have been needed on a world-wide basis.

At the same time the developing world needs to rely on world markets for many of its needs and this applies to insurance as much as anything else. There is a limit to how far a country can cover the risk of catastrophe by its own insurance. This applies both to the size of certain risks faced by small countries and to particular kinds of risks, such as earthquake and hurricane damage. The latter cannot be covered in a narrow domestic market; the former could destroy the assets on which the local company was relying to pay out the claims. This strongly suggests that the world reinsurance market will be needed in some form, however much foreign insurance companies are nationalised or controlled. Yet the form of control can be crucial if adequate reserve back-up is to be pro-vided and if premium rates are not to rise beyond the capacity of those countries needing reinsurance services.

Quite apart from nationalisation, the increasing control over insurance funds in individual territories, coupled with the exchange control restrictions on the movement of funds from one country to another, is impeding the freedom of investment that insurance companies could once rely upon in their world-wide business. Reserves have to be held in individual terri-tories if only to match assets and liabilities in the same currency; at the same time insurance companies, undertaking risks round the world, want the ability to switch funds quickly from one place to another, to meet large claims at a moment's notice virtually anywhere. The difficulty is that governments increasingly insist on reserves being held in their territory and additionally insist on where and how those reserves should be invested. Some governments prohibit their own nationals from placing insurance with foreign companies. Others restrict foreign underwriters by prohibiting the remittance of premiums overseas. Others again insist on reinsurance being placed with a local (usually state-owned) corporation. The flexibility on which world insurance, or at least the international business undertaken by British underwriters, was originally based has thus been increasingly undermined by several newly sovereign governments of the developing world. This is not the place to outline the legal complexities faced by the different sections of the London market since Britain joined the Common Market, but suffice to say that, while Britain may benefit from the widening of its potential domestic market, those parts of the London market undertaking business outside the Common Market have hardly relished the fresh restrictions placed on their activities.

Yet the insurance industry hardly needs to look abroad for trouble. It faces enough at home. Some of the difficulties it has been facing arise from the risks themselves; some from the way in which the industry is administered and controlled; some again arise from the need to ensure that policyholders are protected from companies or brokers with inadequate experience and financial backing. Other difficulties have arisen from the size of the industry's investments and from the political desire to control the flow of insurance money into British industry, either by outright nationalisation or by the official direction of funds.

As for Lloyd's, it has recently been running into a particularly bad patch. The so called Savonita dispute, involving allegedly fire damaged Italian cars, and the subsequent official report produced remarkably outspoken criticism in the national press; this was followed by the announcement of heavy losses on computer leasing and the news that the Sasse Syndicate had piled up losses running into millions of dollars and needed help from the Committee of Lloyd's. At the same time the Corporation of Lloyd's has decided to look into its own way of running things by the appointment of a special committee of inquiry. It will have much to ponder, from the question of the relationships between brokers and syndicates to the arrangement of 'names', and from the self-discipline it ought to impose on members to the future structure of the Corporation itself.

The demand for the protection of policyholders came to a head following the failure of the Vehicle and General Insurance Company in 1971 and of other companies in 1974. This is now water over the dam but, at the time of the V and G collapse, the industry in general, and the British Insurance Association in particular, had a choice. They could mount a rescue operation for a company which was inside the Association and thus maintain the reputation of the industry in general; or they could do nothing. Views within the industry conflicted and the upshot was that V and G was allowed to fail. In effect, therefore, the industry abandoned any possibility of self-regulation and ensured stricter legislative control over its operations. This did not prevent active co-operation between the industry and the Department of Trade in producing a workable framework of legislation designed to safeguard the interests of policyholders, and the proposed changes were incorporated in the Insurance Companies Amendment Act of 1973, the Insurance Companies Act of 1974 and the Policy-holders Protection Act of 1975.

In effect the Department of Trade now controls new entries into the industry, lays down the capital and solvency margins of operating companies, demands detailed reports from operating companies, monitors the qualifications of people in insurance management and does not hesitate to intervene in the affairs of individual companies. It did so on 95 occasions in 1976. Further intervention in the life assurance field arose from the Consumer Credit Act of 1974. Its basic purpose was to achieve 'truth in lending' but the life offices are already suffering from the excessively detailed information required of them under the Act and costs are rising accordingly. At the other end of the industry, the insurance brokers have managed to introduce a welcome element of self-regulation by the establishment of a registration council, through the efforts of the newly formed British Insurance Brokers Association. Under the Insurance Brokers (Registration) Act 1977, firms wanting to call themselves insurance brokers will have to register and comply with the new regulations.

I have left the ultimate threat, nationalisation, until the end. This proposal was endorsed by the Labour Party in September 1976, though it was not adopted as part of the Labour Government's policy at that time. The distinction is important since Mr Callaghan immediately dubbed it 'an electoral albatross' round the neck of the Labour Party. The proposals were that the seven largest insurance companies – the Commercial Union, Royal, Prudential, Legal and General, General Accident, Guardian Royal Exchange and Sun Alliance & London – should be nationalised, along with the four leading clearing banks. The purpose was the same in each case. Both banks and insurance companies were accused of denying British industry its proper share of investment finance and were thus directly blamed for the weakness of British manufacturing industry. The Labour Party document argued that nationalisation was essential in order that banking and insurance funds could be directed to the needs of industry and particularly to help towards 'doubling the rate of manufacturing investment over the next decade' and to whatever else the Party perceived as being in the national interest. An alternative to nationalisation is of course the direction or partial direction of insurance company funds. Both proposals deserve a detailed assessment, especially of their impact on the London capital market. I shall be turning to this problem in Chapter 7 but now I want to look, briefly, at other repercussions of the nationalisation proposals.

In the first place nationalisation of the seven leading companies might well lead to the diversion of premium funds to the surviving privately owned parts of the industry, if public attitudes shown by a recent survey of the Opinion Research Centre are anything to go by. Only 13 per cent of respondents thought that nationalised insurance companies would do a better job for their customers. On the other hand, experience in France, where private and nationalised companies exist side by side, does not necessarily support this conclusion. The difference between Britain and France, however, and especially between London and Paris, is in international business. It is here that the nationalisation proposals might do most damage. The American market is a major source of foreign premiums both to the companies and to Lloyd's. Yet, in 31 states in the US, foreign insurers who are even partially government-owned are barred from carrying on business. Moreover, between them the seven British insurance companies have 26 and 20 per cent of the Australian and Canadian insurance markets, respectively. Neither country would be likely to allow the foreign nationalisation of a substantial sector of its domestic insurance market. In addition, foreign confidence in the future of the other major sectors of the London market, from Lloyd's to the leading brokers, might be undermined, threatening London's leading position as the centre of international insurance. As I write the nationalisation threat has receded once more, under union pressure, but it is a reminder of how easily, and quickly, a complex international market might be undermined by genuine political motives.

Chapter 5

The Stock Exchange: Still Necessary?

Yesterday's 'blue chip' has all too often turned into today's lame duck and the Stock Exchange,[1] where such former top-grade industrial shares are traded, has accordingly come under a murderous double fire – from private investors disillusioned by the failure of equity values to keep pace with inflation and from public figures criticising the City's record in providing finance for modernising and restructuring British industry.

There has always been a good deal of scepticism about the Stock Exchange, even in some of the boom years of the sixties. The layman has tended to feel himself held at arm's length by its specialist jargon and its cryptic procedures; the purists have looked on it as a kind of gambling casino where fortunes can be made without adding one iota to the nation's effective wealth. Some still do. But, while it is easy to understand some of these attitudes, virtually all of them show a fundamental misunderstanding of what the Stock Exchange is meant to do. The Stock Exchange was called into existence to bring together investors seeking a profitable home for spare capital and entrepreneurs seeking spare capital they could use profitably; to do so on the widest scale possible, both geographically and in the range of companies quoted; and to provide conditions in which deals in securities could be made with unprecedented safeguards against malpractice.

[1] Note that the Council of the Stock Exchange now refers to itself as 'The Stock Exchange' when it wishes to denote the inclusion of the exchanges in Birmingham, Dublin, Liverpool and Manchester as well as London.

It is not necessary to go back to the Seventeenth Century when the Stock Exchange was established to see why a place was needed where shares in companies could be bought and sold. Simply go to Kuwait, Jamaica, Singapore and similar places today and ask why, at the right moment in their development, a stock market became essential. As I write Trinidad is going through the same developing process. In virtually every case the time arrives when companies are being formed and private money is being invested in them, but, until a regular mechanism exists where holders of shares can easily and safely sell them, it proves difficult for such companies to raise new money from people prepared to put up capital. The Chairman of the London Stock Exchange has put it this way: 'Without the ability swiftly to realise their investments, the suppliers of funds would demand a substantial premium for the inconvenience of tying up their capital for long periods of time. New capital would thus become scarcer and more expensive.' Without such a market, the normal economic development process is hampered and, in addition, governments fail to achieve the wider share-ownership of private industry they would often like to see.

A market-place on which existing shares can change hands (known as the secondary market) and through which new issues of shares can be placed (known as the primary market) is thus an essential ingredient of development. But a market-place also has that uncomfortable feature – variable prices. When prices go up in unison the Stock Exchange and the City are said to be cheerful about something; when they go down the same institutions are said to be pessimistic. This is dangerous shorthand. The prices of shares are no more than a mirror of what people buying and selling them think is their true value. They are not what the Stock Exchange, or even the City, thinks they should be. Movements in prices should, if the market is reasonably efficient, reflect both present and future prospects of a company and enable successful companies to raise fresh capital on better terms than unsuccessful companies. That at least is the theory. But when, as happened in 1974–5, virtually all share prices were, with hindsight, seriously undervaluing most companies quoted on the

Stock Exchange, the practice proved embarrassingly different. To understand why this can sometimes happen, why London's particular jobbing system of putting buyers in touch with sellers is said to be under strain and why both London and New York stock markets have recently been described as distressed areas, we need to turn to the real world.

London's is not the oldest stock exchange. That distinction goes to Amsterdam. But, with New York and Tokyo, it now vies for top place on the world scene. In turnover, New York and Tokyo now clearly have the edge. London, however, claims to have the largest number of overseas securities as well as the largest number of companies. In fact about 9,500 separate securities are now quoted in London and just about as much business is done there as in all the other bourses of Europe combined, as Table 10 brings out. It is still very much alive and kicking, but facing challenges to its historic role and to its ability to survive in any presently recognisable form. These challenges come from a variety of quarters: from the dominance of institutional investors and the decline of the private investor; from an inflation that has wiped out three-quarters of the value of the pound in a quarter of a century; from the pressure of taxation and its direct impact on the capital resources of the jobbers; from the way in which overall supervision is being tightened further; from both commercial pressures and prices controls on brokers' commissions; and, as we have already indicated, from those who want the Stock Exchange to perform functions, often in the national interest, it was never intended to perform. The London Stock Exchange is not alone in these challenges. New York has been facing many of them in a more acute form for close on a decade and London can hardly like what it sees across the Atlantic.

The Stock Exchange is, in the first instance, a meeting place for buyers and sellers of securities, providing a secondary market where investors are assured they can resell shares they have purchased either in a new company or in an existing company. In short, it provides them with immediate liquidity. Whatever the form in which buyers and sellers are brought together, this is the main advantage of the market process. There are various ways in which such a market can be

Table 10 *Turnover on World Stock Markets*

(Turnover to Calendar Year 1978 and valuations at year end)

| Exchange | FIXED INTEREST | | EQUITY | | |
	Nominal Value £m	Turnover £m	Market Value £m	Turnover £m	Total Turnover £m
New York	240,284	2,240	493,299	103,150	105,390
Tokyo	84,426	15,233	167,641	82,237	92,470
London (a)	71,859	59,777	63,342	9,607[1]	69,384
Zurich (b)	21,001	(b)	18,653	(b)	28,759
Germany (All Exchanges)	124,471	—	41,026	10,402	n.a.
Amsterdam	15,485	5,535	13,012	5,100	10,635
Paris	40,678	4,292	22,246	5,295	9,587
Brussels	22,716	1,224	6,131	650	1,874
Toronto	not traded	not traded	32,837	1,840	1,840
American	2,214	192	19,231	7,547	7,739
Kuwait	not traded	not traded	5,455	2,545	2,545
Milan (1977)	45,610	—	4,807	445	—
Copenhagen	34,465	1,600	1,164	29	1,629
Johannesburg	10,323	373	15,169	539	912
Madrid	9,145	295	8,796	324	619
Stockholm	26,110	—	5,012	208	—
Hong Kong	200	6	6,339	540	546

a. Market Valuation for London includes all UK and Irish Stocks.
b. Turnover figures for Zurich include over the counter transactions in unlisted securities. They also combine fixed interest and equity turnover.

organised. In some cases brokers can try to match a buyer with a seller. In others specialists emerge who concentrate on and sometimes have a monopoly in certain kinds of shares. In others again, regular auctions take place, through newspapers or in an actual market, in parcels of shares. It is not always the method chosen, nor the range of securities, which ensures smooth changes in prices, but sometimes the volume of business generated daily. Kuwait, with a high turnover in, say, forty shares, can probably boast of less volatile price changes than several European markets. Even in London half the market capitalisation in equity shares probably arises from 200 companies. The way in which buyers and sellers are brought together, however, can have a significant effect on the volatility of prices.

London goes about this in its own peculiar way, or has done since 1911, with advantages to investors that, until recently, most people rated highly. This is the jobbing system, under which deals are done by brokers, acting as agents of the investing public, with jobbers, acting as principals in their own right. The brokers make their money from the commissions they charge, the minimum level of which is laid down by the Council; the jobbers quote different buying and selling prices, which is known as their 'turn', and make money both by trying to make a profit on this small difference and by trying to arrange their holdings of securities, like wholesalers, without loss. The jobbers can deal only with brokers, and in almost every share there is more than one firm of jobbers operating, thus ensuring competition on prices. If the time came, as some are beginning to fear, when only one jobber was operating in the most active sections of the market, then the jobbing system would lose one of its chief safeguards on prices. Until then (and we shall be discussing this threat in a moment), the jobbing system provides a useful cushion to the market made up of the wholesale stocks of shares held by jobbers, and, in theory, provides a more continuous market than a system where buyers and sellers are simply brought together by a broker. The other safeguard provided on prices is that when a broker in London approaches a jobber about a certain share, the jobber immediately quotes a spread of prices, say 242–246, indicating that he is willing to buy at the first and sell at the second, though at that stage he will not know what the broker's client wishes to do. Other jobbers will be approached and, again, will quote a spread of prices, thus offering the broker a choice of prices (either buying or selling) for his client. When the deal is completed with one of the jobbers, it is no more than a verbal agreement; notes are made but nothing is signed.

I have already hinted, however, that all is not well with this system and we must turn to the character of the creaks and groans now to be heard throughout Throgmorton Street. I must also add in haste that such criticisms, though more vocal, are not entirely new. Even thirty years ago, when I first began to call on stockbrokers' offices, I was told with some conviction that the jobbing system's days were numbered. It still survives, but the pressures on it today are greater than they have ever been. They are worth setting out in some detail for, I believe, change and reform are in the air.

Although it is the drama of the trading floor that catches the popular imagination, this is only one aspect of the vast City complex that one refers to by the term 'Stock Exchange'. The London market alone has a telephone exchange which could handle a town of 50,000 people. The apparently simple operation of buying and selling shares, and determining a price for them in the process, also requires a formidable logistic back-up provided by the brokers and jobbers. Like everyone else, they have been subjected to cost pressures, intensified by the inflation of the 1970s. But the problem has been even more acute for brokers and jobbers than for industry at large. The traditional customer, in the form of the private investor, has become rarer, and money is piling up in the hands of institutions like the insurance companies, pension funds, and unit trusts. Taxation and inflation are the twin causes of this shift in investing power. It does not necessarily imply any drying-up of the sums available for investment, rather the contrary, but the impact on London's peculiar jobbing system has helped neither jobbers nor brokers. Brokers have awakened to the fact that they have been making a loss on smaller deals and, much as they might personally welcome the widest possible catchment area of investors, they are certainly not in business to subsidise a share-owning society out of their own pockets. The break-even point for a share deal varies considerably over the country as a whole, depending on the size of the total business, what particular business is undertaken and many other factors. But even if it varies between £500 and £2,000, the small investor has already become a costly client for many broking firms.

At the other end of the scale, the large institutions have been causing difficulties of a different kind. The size of individual deals, for example, has escalated to a point where jobbers may find it difficult to assemble the required parcel from their own 'books', let alone finance the operation. An institution may have assets of £18 million, like Debenham's pension fund, or equity holdings of £1·5 billion like the Prudential. It will in either case think of buying and selling on a scale which would have daunted even the wealthiest private investors of the past. The old informal encounters between broker and competing jobbers, which may have been perfect for minimising the size of the 'turn' on a couple of hundred pounds' worth of Great Western Railway stock, are no longer so completely appropriate for meeting a sudden demand for a couple of hundred thousand shares in a large company. The institutions can hardly be blamed for wondering why they should be charged minimum commissions for such transactions when they would be quite capable of going straight to the jobber making a market in particular shares. Nor are they likely to be persuaded that the research undertaken by leading stockbrokers is sufficient recompense for the agent's commission they have to pay. It is questionable whether such research services are as essential to the institutions as the simpler form of briefing was to the old-time private investor. A family stockbroker was after all an honoured and permanent feature of the Victorian middle-class scene, like a family lawyer and a 'family doctor. All had symbolic status, as well as practical usefulness, rather like the human figures who flatter and glorify the central saints in medieval pictures. Naturally, the institutional investor is canny enough to welcome any advice that could be useful, particularly when it comes served up on a plate and without cost. But he is less happy when the broker expects him to pay a commission based on the value of the transaction rather than the amount of labour involved in putting it through. After all, it takes a broker little more trouble to handle several thousand shares at once than a single share bought by an environmentalist who wants to ask awkward questions at a mining company's annual meeting.

The thought of bypassing the Stock Exchange, which has no monopoly in security trading as in France, has been a natural next step. Not surprisingly, two ways of doing so have developed. One is a small market in shares of particularly small companies which are not listed on the Stock Exchange. The other is the computerised system called Ariel, set up by the merchant banks to inform fund operators of both transactions and prices. But it would be wrong to exaggerate how much business is at present bypassing the central exchange. Ariel probably accounts for 1 per cent of the total turnover and it is doubtful, if allowance is made for transactions done directly between institutions, whether as much as 5 per cent of business is even now bypassing the Exchange. Britain (and France) are so far unique, at least in Europe, for the degree to which stock and share transactions do pass through the Stock Exchange. In Italy, which stands at the other extreme, the figure is as low as 20 per cent, and we have lately seen the bizarre spectacle of Milanese stockbrokers going on strike in protest against the habit of trading better-quality shares privately, and leaving the stock market with a miscellaneous collection that no one seems keen to invest in.

The jobbers have been even harder hit than the brokers. They act as principals, keeping their own 'book' of shares, and inflation has posed acute cash-flow problems for them. They have to finance the holding of their shares as well as many other running costs. Some jobbing firms have attempted to cope with their new financing problems by mergers and by widening the spread of their business, thus enabling them to raise fresh funds for their growing needs. Between 1960 and 1979, the number of broking firms on the London Stock Exchange fell from 305 to 106 and the number of jobbing firms from 100 to 14, though there are a further 6 firms of jobbers on trading floors outside London (see Table 11).

This reduction in numbers had led to the accusation that competition has been diminished too and it is estimated, for example, that five of the remaining jobbing firms now account for 90 per cent of the total business. But the figures are slightly misleading since, out of the thousands of quoted company shares, under 50 are dealt in by only one jobbing firm. For the rest competition continues between what are now much larger units. Whereas each of the 100 jobbers in 1960, for example, had an average of eight dealers, the remaining 14 firms in 1979 had an average of 40 dealers. As the Stock Exchange Chairman recently put it: 'Today, just as we have retailing supermarkets we also have jobbing supermarkets. Does anyone deny that price competition in retailing is more

Table 11   *Stock Exchange Dealers*

(a) *Brokers and Broking Firms*

	No. of Firms	No. of Partners	No. of Associate Members	No. of dealers other than Members	Total
1960	305	1,886	794	379	3,059
1965	270	1,893	863	495	3,251
1970	192	1,810	909	529	3,258
1975	124 (284)	1,531 (2,129)	1,060 (1,360)	399 (489)	2,990 (3,978)
1977	110 (260)	1,403 (2,083)	1,121 (1,302)	404 (457)	2,928 (3,842)
1979	106 (256)	1,432 (2,106)	1,150 (1,410)	410 (511)	3,098 (4,283)

Note: The figures in brackets for 1975, 1977 and 1979 include the country units of the Stock Exchange, other figures are for London only.
Source: The Stock Exchange

(b) *Jobbers and Jobbing Firms*

	No. of Firms	No. of Partners	No. of Associate Members	No. of Non-member Dealers	Total No. of Dealers
1960	100	545	166	88	799
1965	60	417	198	135	750
1970	31	273	219	130	622
1975	16 (21)	149 (231)	274 (331)	103 (207)	526 (769)
1977	14 (20)	203 (219)	226 (249)	99 (116)	528 (584)
1979	14 (20)	173 (199)	287 (301)	95 (111)	569 (631)

[1]Figures in brackets for 1975, 1977 and 1979 include both London and Country units. Other figures are for London only.

[2]A large jobbing member firm, which was a limited corporate member in 1975, reconverted itself into a partnership during 1976.
Source: The Stock Exchange

intense now with fewer, but larger, units than it was twenty years ago?' The jobbing system has been coming under scrutiny from other directions too. The Monopolies Commission has examined the proposed merger of two large jobbing firms. The Prices Commission, until its demise, showed interest in any changes in the scale of commissions. And the Office of Fair Trading, following the registration of restrictive practices, has been closely examining both the Exchange's fixed minimum commissions and the ban on jobbers acting as brokers, that is, the basis of the present London system. In addition, some institutions have not hidden their desire to see the end of fixed commissions, though it is a moot point whether they would really like to see the end of the fixing system or simply to share in the fixing process.

If the present system of fixed minimum charges were to be changed to negotiated rates, whether through the initiative of the Office for Fair Trading or voluntarily by the Council of the London Stock Exchange itself, would it have any fundamental effect on the workings of the market? The experience of New York suggests that it would. There commissions have been freely negotiable since May 1975 and in that time no fewer than 150 brokerage houses have gone out of business or merged with others. The Securities and Exchange Commission have also estimated that the reduction from the old commission rate has been about 40 per cent on average for institutional investors. Moreover, discount brokerage houses have started to spring up, offering sizeable discounts to small investors who want nothing more than a simple bare-bones service, without research or other elaborate advice.

The final result, in terms of the broking industry itself, however, may well be to leave the big business in the hands of a few large firms, surrounded by cut-throat competition among a host of smaller firms. If, at the same time, the SEC eventually introduces an international computer system, with the implication that the dealing monopoly of the floors of the recognised exchanges, like New York, is no longer assured, these trends may be accelerated. The danger is that the stock market as we know it might disappear just as investors, big and small, seem to be getting a cheaper and cheaper service. Competition may turn out to have a self-wounding cutting edge.

The Chairman of the London Stock Exchange, in trying to sum up the American experience, put it as follows:

> The separation of principal and agent would most likely be affected and we would see a great disruption of the dealing system. The second thing is you would see the disappearance of quite a lot of research services and the burden for research thrown to the institutional investors who at the moment are relying largely on brokers. You would see a very great reduction in the number of broking firms as a result of this. The fourth thing is that the price of investing for the individual investor would go up. The risk is that you would end up with a less competitive market rather than a more competitive one.

Thus the introduction of negotiated commissions might strike at the heart of the present system and enable brokers to act both as agent and as principal. The dangers of this dual capacity are not lost on investors, for a broker would be tempted to manipulate prices in his favour whenever he held, or had an interest in, the shares he was asked to deal in. This has persuaded some critics of the present system to consider a compromise solution, maintaining the use of brokers as agents for small investors, while allowing professional or institutional investors to trade directly with jobbers. Under such a scheme a broking firm would be allowed to act as a market maker, that is as a jobber, provided that the two functions were kept separate within the same firm. Equally, a jobbing firm would also be allowed to act as an agent. Thus any firm, broker or jobber, would be allowed to act as principal or as agent but would not be allowed to mix the two businesses. Dealings in foreign securities, as we shall see in a moment, would be another area where dual capacity might be introduced.

There remains the question of the protection of the small, private investor. If New York experience is anything to go by, a move away from a minimum commission scale of charges

could lead to a cut-price service being offered by some brokers –
a cheap service that would simply enable people to buy and
sell shares and would rule out any possibility of advice or
research. The new Talisman system for computerising settlements should, of course, help brokers to reduce commissions
on small deals. Once again, however, the question is whether
these lowered costs, coupled with increasing competition
among brokers, would lead to a further thinning out of the
ranks of brokers, through failures or mergers, as in New York.
Moreover, would the remaining brokers be willing to finance
the Compensation Fund, set up specifically to protect the
public against failures among Stock Exchange firms? The
Talisman system also depends on the mutual guarantees of
all member firms and raises the further question of whether
they would wish to continue these guarantees when commission price-cutting was rampant.

The demise of the small investor is plainly having an impact
on the fate of the small industrial company too. The big
institutions tend to concentrate on the top 100 or 200 quoted
companies on the Stock Exchange, largely because of the need
for marketability. This, coupled with the pressure of taxation
and inflation, has made it increasingly difficult for small firms
to raise the necessary financial backing, especially through
the stock market. Is the Stock Exchange helping enough
to resolve the problems of these small businesses? Some people
think not. The Stock Exchange, the argument runs, could help
a little more by allowing what is called an 'over the counter'
market in these newer and smaller companies. Why does it not
do so? Is it because, as the critics say, the Stock Exchange is
blind to recent changes and still acts as if the big institutions
do not exist and is so intent on protecting the small investor
that it prevents the trading of large numbers of small, though
admittedly risky, shares? Moreover, the critics go on, the
compromise of using Rule 163(2), under which smaller companies can obtain a stock market quotation but cannot raise
fresh capital, and under which members may deal in unquoted
securities, is no effective answer.

An 'over the counter' market, which would allow shares of
small companies to be dealt in without having to adhere to

the strict information regulations of the Stock Exchange, has some clear attractions. But anyone comparing London practice with that in New York, often to the detriment of London, needs to remember that some companies with a full quote in London would be too small by New York standards and would be a natural for the 'over the counter' market there. One danger to the Stock Exchange remains, however. Since the Stock Exchange does not have a monopoly of dealings in securities, other rival markets could spring up, especially in the field of small companies. One such operation exists at present. A firm called M. J. H. Nightingale and Company, is operating a type of 'over the counter' market in the shares of small companies and believes strongly that other dealing firms should be encouraged to do the same and thus produce a wider market in an area that, they feel, is still being neglected by the Stock Exchange. Although Nightingale simply matches buyers and sellers and cannot be compared with the US 'over the counter' market, they can certainly point to a healthy turnover and to the fact that they have raised at least £3 million for small companies through public offerings in recent years. Whether others will be tempted to follow their lead, helped by the Wilson Committee's ideas that official fiscal obstacles should be removed, remains to be seen. If nothing else, Nightingale's operations have already led to pressure from within the Stock Exchange itself for the Council's own Rule 163(2) to be developed and extended to a wider range of companies, giving them access to the stock market several years before they are ready for a quote. The Stock Exchange, in response, has begun to publish weekly details of dealings done in unquoted securities and to highlight such dealings in other ways. It can already point to the fact that the total value of such transactions is running at about £1 million a week, and that over £160 million has been raised over a six-year period for unlisted companies through stockbrokers.

Even if further such changes are delayed or indefinitely postponed, the methods of dealing with foreign securities are plainly ripe for change. Once this kind of business was a significant proportion of the total turnover of the London market and London prices were a major influence on other stock markets. At the turn of the century the financial pages of *The Times* were full of the prices of overseas stocks then quoted on the London Stock Exchange. The names tell their own story: Union Pacific Railroad, Illinois Central & Atchison, United Havana Consolidated Debentures, Ottoman Railways, London & San Francisco Bank, London & Hanseatic Bank, Imperial Russian Bonds, Russian Petroleum, Anglo-Argentine Tramways and loans for Brazil, Uruguay, Greece and Mexico. Since the last war the number of new foreign issues has been deliberately restricted and, for a time, priority was given to Commonwealth borrowers. Yet in spite of this reduced flow of new issues, a number of secondary markets in foreign securities remained active throughout this period. Moreover several foreign companies gained a quotation on the London Stock Exchange. Exxon, IBM and, more recently, American Express all have a London quotation which facilitates the buying and selling of their shares in London. Until the early part of 1978, such dealings were badly restricted by the operation of what was termed the dollar pool, and the 25 per cent surrender rule. Whereas the first, which prevented the amount of currencies available for investment in foreign shares from growing significantly and thus had the effect of imposing a premium on the price to be paid by a British investor in foreign securities, the second (the 25 per cent surrender rule) effectively imposed a penalty when such shares were sold. The impact of both restrictions was to drive out of London, or at least seriously reduce the activity of, several of the markets in foreign stocks. As I write the hope is that the abolition of the 25 per cent surrender rule will lead to a rapid revival of the London markets in foreign stocks and that London-based stockbrokers and jobbers will again manage to earn a growing amount of foreign exchange as a by-product. There are also hopes that the Council will allow the introduction of dual capacity in dealings in foreign securities.

London's interest in foreign securities and the interest of foreign security houses in British and European securities have naturally led to some cross-fertilisation in London and else-where. London brokers have been particularly active in making 'agency' arrangements and in setting up offices overseas and

thus becoming expert in foreign security transactions. They
have also had an eye on the investing needs of the British ex-
patriate communities in many of these territories. Some
London broking firms have undertaken this dual business by
frequent visits to the countries concerned: others, as Table 12
makes clear, have simply set up shop in the country and the
total number of offices abroad is now between 30 and 40. Hong
Kong, Japan, the United States and Europe have clearly
been the most popular. Foreign security houses have correspondingly flooded into London and there are said to be some

Table 12   *London Stockbrokers Overseas 1979–80*

	Australia
Sydney:	CAZENOVE & CO.
	Bahamas
Nassau:	VICKERS, DA COSTA & CO. (Bahamas) Ltd
	Bermuda
Hamilton:	CAZENOVE & CO. (Bermuda)
	France
Paris:	STRAUSS, TURNBULL & CO. (France) SA
	Gibraltar
Irish Town:	CHARLES STANLEY & CO.
	A. J. BEKHOR & CO.
	Holland
Amstelveen:	STRAUSS TURNBULL & CO. BV
	Hong Kong
Hong Kong:	ASTAIRE & CO. (Far East)
	JAMES CAPEL FAR EAST NOMINEES Ltd
	JAMES CAPEL (Far East) Ltd
	W. I. CARR, SONS & CO. (Overseas)
	CAZENOVE & CO. (Overseas)
	HOARE GOVETT (Far East) Ltd
	ROWE & PITMAN (Far East) Ltd
	JOSEPH SEBAG & CO. (Far East) Ltd
	VICKERS, DA COSTA & CO (Hong Kong) Ltd
	Japan
Tokyo:	W: I. CARR, SONS & CO. (Overseas)
	VICKERS DA COSTA & CO. Ltd
	ROWE & PITMAN (Far East) Ltd
	GRIEVESON GRANT & CO.

Malaysia

Kuala Limpur: LAURENCE, PRUST & CO.

Luxembourg

Luxembourg: JAMES CAPEL (International) SA

Philippines

Rizal: W. I. CARR, SONS & CO. (Overseas)
VICKERS DA COSTA & CO. Ltd

Singapore

Singapore: JAMES CAPEL (Far East) Ltd

South Africa

Johannesburg: CAZENOVE & CO.
ROWE & PITMAN (South Africa) (Pty) Ltd

Switzerland

Geneva: ROWE RUDD SA
W. I. CARR, SONS & CO.

United States of America

Los Angeles: JOSEPH SEBAG Inc.
New York: CAZENOVE Inc.
San Francisco: CAZENOVE Inc.
ROWE & PITMAN Inc.

---

55 foreign broking offices in the Square Mile. Over a half are American with Canadian and Japanese firms accounting for most of the rest. The details are set out in Table 13.

This cross-fertilisation has also been seen in the recent developments of traded option markets, first in the United States, primarily in Chicago, and later in Toronto, Montreal, Sydney and Singapore. Not surprisingly, London too has felt the need to open such a market, more or less simultaneously with Amsterdam. Tokyo and Hong Kong have a similar intention. Options, alas, have had a bad name almost before birth even though they simply represent an entitlement to buy or sell an underlying share at a fixed price at any time within a period before the option expires. Chicago's successful launching of an active market in options was unfortunately accompanied by attempts to rig market turnover, apparently without fraudulent intent, in order to attract business from other markets. Thus the Securities and Exchange Commission became involved at an early stage in its development. Above all, the combination of moving prices with no underlying assets is, to many people, a pretty good definition of pure speculation.

In fact, traded options are a means of spreading or curbing risks, not creating them. But the surrounding controversy is perhaps enough to explain why the London Stock Exchange took so many tentative steps in introducing (or rather, re-introducing, for London was the largest conventional option security market between the wars) what is by international standards a fairly modest operation. The Chicago options

Table 13   *Foreign Security Houses in London*

	Date of entry into London
Australia	
Bain & Company (Securities) Ltd	1970
Potters Partners	1970
J. B. Were & Son	1928
Canada	
A. E. Ames & Co.	1925
Burns Fry Ltd	1956
Dominion Securities	1905
Greenshields Inc.	1957
Mead & Co. Ltd	1973
McLeod, Young, Weir & Co. Ltd	1968
Merrill Lynch, Royal Securities Ltd	1961
Midland Doherty Ltd	1969
Nesbitt, Thomson & Co. Ltd	1969
W. C. Pitfield & Co. (London) Ltd	1959
Richardson Securities of Canada	1959
Wood Gundy Ltd	1910
Japan	
Daiwa Europe NV	1964
New Japan Securities Co Ltd	1970
The Nikko Securities Co. (Europe) Ltd	1964
The Nippon-Kangyo Kakumaru Securities Co. Ltd	1971
Nomura Europe NV	1964
Okasan Securities Co. Ltd	1974
Wako Securities Co. Ltd	1972
Yamaichi International (Europe) Ltd	1964
Switzerland	
Tradition Securities Ltd	1972
United Arab Emirates	
Sharjah Group	1977

	Date of entry into London
USA	
Bache Halsey Stuart Shields Inc.[1]	1934
Becker Securities Inc.	1971
Brown Brothers Harriman & Co.	1974
Dean Witter International Ltd	1968
Dillon Read Overseas Corp	1968
Dominick & Dominick Ltd	1956
Drexel, Burnham Lambert Inc.	1965
Fahnestock & Co.	1936
The First Boston Corporation	1965
Fox-Pitt, Kelton Inc.	1971
Goldman Sachs International Corporation	1970
E. F. Hutton & Co. (Securities) Ltd	1973
E. F. Hutton & Co. (London) Ltd	1973
Kidder Peabody & Co. Ltd	1956
Kuhn, Loeb & Co. International	1967
Lehman Brothers Ltd	1971
Loeb, Rhoades & Co.	1934
Merrill Lynch Holdings Ltd	1960
Morgan Stanley International	1977
Moseley, Hallgarten & Estabrook Inc.	1912
Oppenheimer & Co. Ltd	1971
Paine Webber Jackson & Curtis Securities Ltd	1973
Reynolds Securities Inc.[2]	1931
Salomon Brothers International	1971
Shearson, Hayden, Stone Ltd[3]	1937
Smith Barney Harris Upham International Inc.	1968
Thomson & McKinnon International Ltd	1960
Weeden & Co. Inc	1963
White, Weld & Co. Inc.[4]	1931
Wobaco Investments Ltd	1974

[1] Bache Halsey Stuart Inc. merged with Shields Model Roland Co.
[2] Formerly Baker Weeks & Co.
[3] Formerly H. Hentz & Co. Ltd
[4] The White Weld Group has two representatives in London.

market, by contrast, which opened in the spring of 1973, is not only well established but has an enviable turnover with some 1,500 options being traded on about 150 underlying securities, and Chicago also has one of the largest security turnovers in the world.

A call option simply gives the right to buy a specified share at a fixed date in the future and at a fixed price. When these options are also traded, it means that this entitlement can be bought or sold like any ordinary security. The maximum length of the option is normally nine months. It is in effect akin to paying an insurance premium for a certain kind of cover which, also like insurance, runs out at the end of a specified period. It can therefore be used in two ways: either as a form of protection for an investor's portfolio or as a limited form of gambling.

When an investor buys an option on a specified share he acquires the privilege of buying the underlying share, at the current price, say, nine months ahead. If, therefore, the share price remains unchanged or falls, he will hardly exercise his option and will therefore lose the whole of the premium he has paid. If, however, the share price goes up, he stands to gain the difference between the present price and the future higher price since he will be entitled to exercise the option and receive the dearer shares at today's prices. This means that the risk of loss is limited to the loss of the premium, whereas the gain is simply limited by the potential rise in the underlying share. When options are sold, the gains and losses will depend on whether the seller owns the underlying shares or not. In short, buying or selling options can be incorporated into an existing share portfolio in a way that provides greater or less safety, depending on the wishes and intentions of the individual investor. He can in fact make what he will of the option market: use it to protect himself or to heighten his risks still further.

The Wilson Committee, the Monopolies Commission, the Prices Commission and the Office of Fair Trading have all been concerned with Stock Exchange practices. But one question recurs most frequently: how best should the public be protected in its dealings not only on the Stock Exchange but on all City markets? Should this protection be imposed by government or government agency, as in New York, or should it continue to be left in the hands of the various City markets themselves? I shall be exploring the City's general response to these questions in Chapter 15, but at this juncture I want to look briefly at the Stock Exchange's own involvement. The Stock Exchange Council's regulatory function is concerned primarily with two areas of activity: the buying and selling mechanism provided by its own members to the general public; and the information and operations of the various companies whose shares or fixed-interest stock are quoted and dealt in on the Exchange. Both are directly concerned with most of the cases that have been prominent in recent years: the circumstances in which take-over bids have been made and won; the leaks of information about individual shares; the use of company funds by chairmen and directors; the loss of share-holders' and depositors' money when fringe banks have gone bust; and the charges of casual auditing and accountancy.

It would be wrong to think that there is still a free-for-all within the City. The Stock Exchange itself, with the 46-strong Council, supervises activity on the floors of the London, Birmingham, Dublin, Liverpool and Manchester exchanges and lays down precise rules about the relationships between its members and the investing public. It runs a Compensation Fund, with cash of over £1 million and virtually unlimited overall liability, to protect the public from the default of any of its members. In 1978, for example its Quotations Department monitored some 1300 share price movements, leading to 41 preliminary inquiries by its investigation unit and eventually to 11 formal share investigations. Above all, it lays down strict regulations about the behaviour of, and especially the provision of information from, the companies whose stocks and shares it quotes. In short, it does not pretend to hold the hand of the investor all the way to the market, nor even after he has plunged in by his own volition. But it does try to protect him from the dangers of false information and sharp practices of all kinds. In addition, since 1968, the Stock Exchange has had a valuable ally in the growing area of bids and deals by the establishment of the Panel on Take-overs and Mergers, and its increasing supervision of companies and their financial advisers. Beyond these two bodies have stood the ethical codes of the three professional bodies primarily concerned with stock market business: the auditors, accountants and solicitors.

Yet, in recent years, two points have become clearer in assessing the public's growing interest: one is that the City's self-imposed regulations, curbing the activities of its own members, are no longer enough in a world in which its activities are spread well beyond the City and its professional classes. The other is that it is no longer enough for the Stock Exchange to look after one area, the Bank of England another and the various professional bodies others again. The public interest has become much wider and more involved.

Hence the understandable demands for Government action in a statutory way and the subsequent establishment of the Council for the Securities Industry. This raises the broader question of how the City in general, as well as the Stock Exchange, should be controlled, which I will be returning to in some detail in Chapter 15.

Thus the Stock Exchange is moving through turbulent waters. Economic and fiscal forces, over which it has no control, are producing conditions in which big institutional investors are threatening to swamp, or at least to transform, existing conditions. At the same time official agencies have been probing at the Exchange's very foundations. Yet over the three years 1976–8, the Stock Exchange, through its normal market mechanism, still managed to launch £28,000 million of government securities and £3,000 million of new industrial stock. Whether it will continue to operate so efficiently in future or will simply, in Sir Harold Wilson's phrase, become 'no more than an electric scoreboard at a cricket match', recording large transactions though not servicing them directly, will depend on the future power of the institutional investors, and the future role of the small investor. I turn to these issues in the next two chapters.

Chapter 6

Private Investors: A Vanishing Race?

The private investor has become a threatened species. Twenty years ago he owned more than four-fifths of all United Kingdom ordinary shares. Today the big financial institutions – pension funds, banks, insurance companies, unit trusts and the like – own over half and their share is expected to rise to two-thirds by the mid-1980s. The private investor in fact is selling more shares than he is buying – at the rate of about £1,500 million a year. The institutions, on the other hand, find themselves with about £6,000 million of new money a year to invest; and one City estimate puts their annual disposable income in 1985 at no less than £20,000 million.

These dramatic changes are already having a profound impact on the way in which the public's savings are invested, on individual City institutions and the way they go about their business and particularly on the current debate about the City's future relations with industry. But, before we try to analyse what further changes may be ahead, we need to be clear about the precise nature of the recent changes and what brought them about.

Although the individual investor still accounts for approximately 70 per cent of the number of stock market transactions and 60 per cent of deals have a value of £2,000 or less, in value terms the institutions now account for 60 per cent of total turnover. Thus the private investor is either on the way out or at least settling down to an existence which is a far cry from the unique role he played in the middle and later stages of the

Industrial Revolution. For anyone with a sense of history, this is an inglorious end to what has been an honourable record. For it was largely the private investor, working through the newfangled stock exchanges in London and the provinces, whose frugality and shrewd judgement enabled early industrial Britain to become the workshop of the world.

The railway network alone had an enormous capital hunger, amounting at the height of the boom in the 1840s to nearly 7 per cent of the national income, or about £4,000 million a year in today's terms. At the same time, huge sums were being absorbed by textiles, shipbuilding, engineering, and manufacturing industry at large. The scale of capital accumulation in the Victorian heyday was prodigious. The degree of saving by individuals is hard to imagine in the changed political and social climate of today. And the direction, size and emphasis of this vast and profitable commitment was in the hands of the private investor, Walter Bagehot's 'Man on the Clapham omnibus'. He had no doubt his full share of human greed and social prejudice, alongside his common sense and unquenched optimism. He thought that anyone who worked hard enough and lived modestly enough might become as wise and well-heeled as himself.

His knowledge, even of his own long-term self-interest, probably never matched the near-omniscience assumed on his behalf by the classical economists. But, as a result of running his own business, he had a pretty shrewd notion of what was commercially viable, and his practical intelligence could judge the technical prospects of a project put up to him.

Companies on the look-out for his money sprang up in their thousands, like mushrooms. It was not always possible to identify the toxic ones before tasting; and Victorian fiction is obsessed with the predators who robbed widows and orphans, meeting retribution in either the bankruptcy court or, like Dickens's Montague Tigg, from a victim's melodramatic dagger.

But the rise of the joint-stock company, and the creation in the Stock Exchange of a reputable market where its shares could be traded, helped to create a class of alert, well informed, and, on the whole, reasonably responsible investors.

Until recently these private investors dominated the stock market. Even in the early 1960s they still accounted for well over half of total shareholdings. But the latest estimates of the Stock Exchange show that the market share held by personal investors fell from 55 per cent in 1963 to 48 per cent in 1969 and to 32 per cent in 1977. Institutional investors on the other hand have seen their share double from 26 per cent to 52 per cent over the same period.

The most obvious reason for the private investor's decline has been the growth of income tax from a few shillings in the (undecimalised) pound to a level starting at around a third of income and rising to a virtually confiscatory level. As a consequence, there has been a steady redistribution from higher to lower incomes, and with it a corresponding shift from private accumulation to consumption. The private investor, squeezed between taxation and the rising cost of maintaining traditional living standards, has typically tended to realise past savings to meet current expenses.

Taxation levels apart, the general economic climate has also worked against the private investor, and mounting inflation has virtually given him the *coup de grâce*. During the 1950s and 1960s equity investment did have a new lease of life. The risk which justifies its rewards seemed to have been ironed out in practice by new and refined methods of economic management. Bull markets seemed to be the order of the day; and it came to be assumed that, bar the occasional 'hiccup' in the graph, the trend of share values would be upward, thus providing in effect an inflation-proof asset.

This could not last. The world economic boom of the sixties and early seventies eventually brought mounting inflation in its wake and, while the sudden increase in oil prices in 1973–4 gave an added impetus to rising prices, it also punctured the economic boom itself, leaving both individual economies and stock markets highly vulnerable. In Britain the pound plunged to new lows and the *Financial Times* share index fell sharply, wiping out two-thirds of the nominal value of shareholdings, throughout 1974 and 1975. Although share values recovered later, both inflation (which was to reach increases of close on 30 per cent in 1975–6) and taxation put further pressures on individual investors. Moreover, government policy made it harder for investors to catch up with inflation. Dividend control, introduced as a quid pro quo for wage restraint, meant that the return for the ordinary shareholder fell further behind. Between 1971 and 1976, for example, retail prices rose by 141 per cent, wages by 126 per cent and dividends by only 87 per cent.

The private investor has thus been under a variety of economic and political pressures for over a decade. The country's savings, meanwhile, have increasingly moved through other channels towards the stock market – through unit trusts, investment trusts, insurance companies and pension funds. For a time the unit and investment trusts seemed to be the obvious outlet for small investors, since they enabled the small man to spread his risks and to lean on professional investment ability at one remove. They still are. But both kinds of trusts are battling with the competitive impact of contractual savings, with built-in tax advantages, offered by insurance offices and occupational pension schemes, as well as the corresponding tax advantages of the building societies.

The investment and unit trusts, though they have similar aims in spreading risks, have developed and are still developing differently. The investment trusts have a history going back a century and more, and there were already 58 investment trusts operating by the turn of the century. The last burst of activity was in the early 1970s when some 40 new companies were formed and attracted close on £500 million of extra money. The new companies concentrated largely on overseas shares in America, Europe and the Far East. At about this time the numbers of investment trusts reached their peak of about 300. Following recent mergers, the number is back to the 200 mark. Since 1960, however, the total assets of these trusts have risen from close on £2 billion to about £6 billion. Of this just under a half is invested in overseas shares.

The investment trusts were the first specialised instruments designed to provide investors with a collective approach to the stock market. They were joint-stock companies which invested their closed-end funds in a diversified portfolio of securities.

The primary objective of each trust was to give shareholders, over the medium and long term, a secure and increasing return on their capital, as well as some increase on the capital itself. The purpose of each individual trust could vary. Some offered a high income return; others were more concerned with capital growth. While some concentrated on foreign investment, others specialised in investment in British industry. The advantages to investors were clear. The trusts were able to give the small investor a spread of investments he could not hope to match from his own small resources, as well as professional management. Institutional investors have increasingly come to appreciate the same advantages, and have particularly recognised the concentration of some trusts on overseas investment and their use as a hedge against the depreciation of the domestic currency.

Yet, in spite of these clear attractions, the underlying asset values of the investment trusts have, in recent years, tended to move away from the corresponding market price of the trusts' own shares in the stock market. City people with long memories of half a century and more can recall investment trust shares standing at a premium over their underlying assets. But in the last decade the shares have tended to stand at a discount, and since the early 1970s the discount has widened significantly, rising from 5 per cent in 1972 to a peak of over 40 per cent towards the end of 1976.

This discount is not quite as great as the figures immediately suggest. For one thing it is not a discount on a break-up value, but rather on a going concern basis. In other words, if a trust were to be wound up, several costs, including tax costs (on capital gains, for example) would have to be borne. These extra factors might reduce the going concern discount by anything between 15 and 20 per cent.

Nonetheless, several different factors have combined to push investment trust shares into disfavour. For one thing, the private investor has not been adding to his investments; rather the reverse. And, in any case, the unit trust movement has been providing a similar service and highly publicised competition since, unlike the investment trusts, unit trusts are by their nature open-ended, and can expand and contract in line with market demand. Moreover, investment trusts are not permitted by law to advertise their shares. As for institutional investors, they have hardly needed to buy trust shares for their professional management since they have that themselves. Finally, while at present the profit on the sale of an investment trust holding is taxed at a favourable rate, any loss is liable at the full capital gains tax rate. This leads to a natural temptation to sell investment trust shares before others. On top of which the large volume of new issues made by the trusts in the early 1970s has continued to depress share prices.

This was the situation up to the end of 1976 or thereabouts when the investment trust movement was faced with a number of options. It could try to draw attention to its virtues in a more positive way. It could decide to liquidate individual trusts and release the underlying assets. It could decide to unitise individual trusts, that is to make them open-ended like unit trusts. Or it could consider mergers from within and take-over bids from outside. As I write virtually all these options are being considered – even utilised – by one trust or another. Liquidation, of course, is a particularly ruthless, and expensive, solution, akin to curing toothache by chopping off someone's head, in the view of one chairman. But unitisation, mergers, reorganisations and, especially, takeovers have begun to bring some renewed interest to investment trust shares, and to reduce the share discount. Some of these solutions were bound to come sooner or later, though the costs of unitisations and even liquidation have often been ignored, but, if the movement as a whole is to survive in anything like its recent shape, attempts to attune the movement to the needs of the institutional investor (by merging into bigger units, for example) and to encourage the survival of the private investor will need constant support by the movement as a whole.

The unit trust movement, with a much shorter history, offers similar advantages to investment trusts but has so far proved to be more flexible. Nevertheless, it too is beginning to feel the encroachment of the larger investing battalions – especially those with built-in tax advantages, such as the building societies, life offices and pension funds. Traces of unit trusts have been found by diligent City historians about a hundred years ago in the survival of the Submarine Cables Trust from a round of legal tussles in the courts. But the real start of the movement dates from the early 1920s in the United States and the early 1930s in Britain. The First British Fixed Trust was established by Municipal and General Securities in 1931. Within three years nearly twenty trusts had been established, though they still had a fixed portfolio of shares. Then came the so-called flexible trusts, in which managers were enabled to vary the constituent shares.

Unit trusts continued to expand at a modest pace, both before and after the war, but not until the 'bull' markets of the late 1950s and the 1960s did the movement really boom. The small investor was still being widely cultivated, the cult of the equity was in full swing and the spread of investment risks offered by unit trusts was highly attractive. Existing trusts boomed and new ones proliferated. The new trusts served a variety of purposes – some offering growth, others income; some a geographical vehicle, others an industrial one. Some trusts concentrated on domestic shares; some on foreign shares; and others again were deliberately 'offshore'. In the late 1950s there were about 40 unit trusts. At the last count there were no less than 100 separate groups running 395 separate unit trusts with 2 million unit holders. The movement's total investments are now valued at £3,873 million (see Table 14).

A unit trust has been described as an 'investment co-operative'. It is in fact a fund fed by individual investors who, in turn, receive units in return for their money. The money is invested in stocks or shares through a trust, in which there are three partners: the investors, the trustee and the managers. The advantage to the small investor, as in the case of the investment trust, is that he can obtain a much wider spread of investments than he could on his own and can be assured of professional management. It is also cheaper to invest a sum below, say, £700 through a unit trust than through an individual security. Unit trust managers have also shown remarkable ingenuity in introducing trusts for specialised purposes. They have also been alert to new areas for expansion, such as the linking of life assurance with units. These are simply conven-

Table 14 *Growth of Unit Trusts*

Year	Value of Funds (year end) £m	Sales £m	Repurchases £m	Net Investment £m	Holdings millions	Repurchase Ratio[1]
1959	200.0	n.a.	n.a.	n.a.	0.52	n.a.
1960	201.4	26.88	13.37	13.51	0.66	6.7
1961	236.6	21.57	14.21	7.36	0.67	6.3
1962	272.5	45.01	11.07	33.94	0.82	4.4
1963	371.2	77.46	17.78	59.68	1.05	5.5
1964	428.9	99.64	22.60	77.04	1.31	5.5
1965	521.9	80.80	21.78	59.02	1.42	4.6
1966	581.8	129.69	24.26	105.43	1.64	4.3
1967	853.6	126.56	42.64	83.91	1.71	6.0
1968	1,482.4	328.93	70.45	258.48	2.15	6.0
1969	1,411.9	262.70	76.53	186.17	2.39	5.4
1970	1,397.7	171.15	73.35	97.80	2.40	5.3
1971	1,991.2	204.10	127.45	76.65	2.32	7.6
1972	2,647.5	436.86	195.59	241.27	2.29	8.3
1973	2,060.4	357.90	171.75	186.15	2.24	7.0
1974	1,310.8	194.87	110.17	84.70	2.20	6.5
1975	2,512.4	321.21	130.90	190.31	2.20	6.2
1976	2,543.0	333.40	165.80	167.52	2.12	6.5
1977	3,461.3	372.32	257.90	114.42	1.99	8.4
1978	3,873.4	529.68	294.08	235.60	1.95	7.9

[1]The repurchase ratio is the total value of units repurchased in each year expressed as a percentage of the average value of funds at the end of each month of the year.

tional life assurance contracts, under which the normal premiums are invested in unit trusts. The advantage is that the premiums still attract tax relief. The disadvantage is that, since the early 1970s, many unit holders in these unit-linked assurance schemes have seen their investments fall as well as rise.

One of the reasons for the post-war success of unit trusts has been the professional way in which they have been marketed. The methods vary. Some are sold by press advertising; some through professional intermediaries such as stockbrokers, accountants, solicitors and banks; and some, specifically the unit-linked assurance, through direct selling. Selling methods are strictly controlled and, apart from unit-linked insurance, the direct selling of units is forbidden. Investment in unit trusts arises either from lump sums or from regular, often monthly, payment arrangements. For a time the industry sought small regular payments, often as low as £1 a month. But the costs of marketing and administration, as well as the growing habit of using the facilities for short-term saving only, eventually persuaded the industry to raise the limits. At the same time, the linking of unit trust sales to life assurance pushed the industry in a direction which resolved several of these problems. As a result some 1,400,000 policies have been issued, linked with unit trust sales, contributing some £7 million a month to the inflow of new investments.

The stark question the unit trusts now have to face is whether, given the present political and economic climate, their recent period of expansion, perhaps even investment usefulness, has not come to an end. The small investor, whom unit trusts were ostensibly set up to cater for, has been under pressure from a combination of high taxation and high inflation and, at the same time, has seen his equity investments eroded in real terms too. From the beginning of 1967 to the end of 1976, for example, the *Financial Times* ordinary share index rose a modest 15 per cent, whereas the cost of living soared more than two and a half times. On top of this, the movement, like the clearing banks, has also been coping with increasing competition from the building societies, which the unit trusts believe have been capturing long-term investment money in the shape of shorter-term deposits. For all these reasons the unit trusts have perhaps done well to attract as much as they have in recent years. Even so, some critics rightly ask, if the movement had not embraced the link with life assurance, would not the industry by now have been showing net losses, that is bigger repurchases than new sales, month by month? In other words, without the tax advantages of the life premiums, the movement might easily have entered a period of net disinvestment.

Against this sombre background, however, all is not lost. The movement continues to show flexibility; it has moved alongside the insurance companies and has also shown an interest in providing specialised units for special situations. Some within the industry have even begun to wonder whether, in the light of the market conditions of the past seven or eight years, the long-term emphasis may not be in need of amendment. Thus two original beliefs have come under increasing scrutiny: the emphasis on both the small man and on long-term investment. Should either be changed and in what way? As the Chairman of the Unit Trust Association told the Wilson Committee, units are 'marketed as a long-term investment and we do not want people to get the impression that they are anything but a long-term investment'. Some people in the industry, however, are convinced that they should come to terms with the dilemma of small investors, faced with the recent sharp fluctuations in the stock market, and advise them to use unit trusts on a short-term basis and to use professional help in doing so. The reasoning behind this is that, while over the past decade equity shares as a whole have shown little increase, especially in comparison with inflation, there have been some sharp fluctuations in the shorter term which investors might have taken advantage of had they been a little more ready to move into and out of the market.

At the same time the proliferation of unit trusts has led to increasing bewilderment among the general public. Are there in fact too many trusts specialising in particular sectors of the market? Some trusts of course were never intended for the ordinary investor and serve the special needs of certain institutions. But it has been estimated that a reduction of at least

50 per cent in the number of trusts might be to everyone's advantage. It can certainly be argued that the increasing specialisation of recent trusts has run counter to the original aim of the movement to provide small investors with a broad cross-section of the market which, in the long term, would provide both security and income.

Does this indicate perhaps that, in attempting to meet new needs – sometimes from the institutions, sometimes in response to market movements, sometimes in response to the change in the character of the 'small investor' – the movement is in danger of losing touch with its original aims? Who in fact is the typical unit trust investor and who is he likely to be? Statistically, the Chairman of the Association has stressed, the average unit trust investor 'is the small investor, as you can see from the figures. On the other hand, I think most of us would agree that our clientele is much better informed than most people imagine. The unit trust investor may be small but he is not the cloth-cap investor of popular mythology, not by any means.' The truth is probably that, while the old-type small investor, who had some investment knowledge or at least some contact with professional advice, is now under constant economic pressure, the more affluent workers do not automatically think of unit trusts when they have money to spare at the end of the week, and turn more readily to the familiarity of the building society offices. Meanwhile the large institutions prefer the specialised trusts to the larger general trusts, though their unit holdings are not yet significant in terms of value or volume. Unless the political and financial climate changes in favour of the small investor, the unit trust movement will have to decide whether to try to cater for the new kind of small investor or for the institutional investor, or perhaps both.

While the investment and unit trusts have been doing as best they can in these changing circumstances, other City institutions have been benefiting on a remarkable scale. Direct personal thrift has been gradually replaced by contractual savings, through public and private pension funds and insurance endowment policies, encouraged by the tax incentives they offer. As a result both life insurance offices and pension funds have had growing amounts to invest in the stock market and elsewhere. The cash flow available for investment by pension schemes and long-term insurance funds rose from £1,166 million in 1966 to £2,023 million in 1971 and to £5,398 million in 1976. By 1980, it has been estimated, the annual cash flow will have reached nearly £10 billion and, if inflation continues at around 10 per cent and real growth in the economy maintains a rate of 3 per cent a year, the total by 1985 could double again to £20 billion. It is difficult to be precise about the competitive positions of the long-term insurance funds and the pension funds, since in some cases pension arrangements are done through life offices. But, while the total assets of the insurance companies at £39 billion are well above those of the pension funds (though there is some double-counting in the figures), the flow of new money to both has recently moved in favour of the pension funds and this trend seems likely to continue.

The purposes of insurance companies and pension funds are different and the aim of their investment policies naturally reflects this. The insurance companies make a distinction between two kinds of insurance contracts: those that pay a sum of money if a misfortune occurs within a specific period of time and those that pay a sum of money when a predictable event occurs after a definite lapse of time. The first largely concerns protection, while the second covers savings of all kinds for retirement, for mortgage repayments and other pre-dictable financial obligations. Most of the insurance contracts in the second category, especially life assurance and pensions, lead to the need for longer-term investments by the insurance companies undertaking them. There is a time-gap between the receipt of the premiums and the obligation to pay out certain sums in the future. They have to so arrange their investment funds that their maturities and potential liquidity match the liabilities they have undertaken with policyholders; that is to say they have to ensure that cash will be available as and when policyholders need it. The insurance companies have in any case to maintain what are known as 'solvency margins', that is to say they have to ensure under insurance law that their assets exceed their liabilities by a certain margin. It is within these parameters that the insurance companies invest their funds in the stock market and elsewhere. These contractual savings funds are considerably higher than in most other countries. Funds from life assurance premiums in Britain, as a percentage of gross national product, for example, are more than three times as large as in Belgium and France, over one and a half times as large as in West Germany, Sweden and Canada, and larger even than in the United States or Japan. The net amount of new funds available for investment arising from UK insurance operations increased more than fivefold between 1962 and 1976 from around £500 million to £2,800 million. These investments have been naturally long-term and have gone into the longer end of the gilt-edged market, into debentures and, of course, into equities and property. At the last count the proportion in gilt-edged stock was over 25 per cent and that in ordinary shares slightly higher again. The current investment in industrial stocks and shares alone comes to between £12 and 15 billion.

The pension fund investments have arisen for different reasons but they too are essentially long-term. Pension schemes can trace their history back to Victorian times, but it was not until after the First World War that modern-style occupational pension schemes received preferential tax treatment and started to develop along modern lines. Following the Second World War, the provision of pensions by, and through, employers spread to manual workers, as well as to professional and clerical staff. By the mid-1970s the clash between state and occupational pension schemes was beginning to be resolved and their relationship was eventually set out in the Act of 1975. All occupational pension schemes are now 'approved' for tax purposes and can be based either on schemes which invest their funds direct in the stock market or on those which invest through a life assurance office.

Someone joining a pension fund at, say, the age of twenty-five assumes that he will be retiring forty years later. The pension fund would, therefore, look for corresponding investments of that maturity to match the employee's future pension liabilities. As investors they are, therefore, less interested in short-term fluctuations than other investors and are keen to maximise the rate of return on their investments in the long term. Because most pension schemes provide benefits which are geared to the income of the recipients just prior to retirement, pension funds are concerned to maintain a high return as well as to keep pace with inflation. This means that they invest both in government securities and in ordinary shares and are influenced by the changes in yields between one and the other. This is an oversimplified version of their general investment policies but it partly explains why, at present, with inflation such a dominant force, they have close on a half of their funds in ordinary shares (and another 15 per cent in property) and around 25 per cent in government stock.

The expansion of occupational pension schemes can be said to have become a marked feature of the stock markets since the beginning of the 1970s. Throughout the 1960s their acquisition of assets represented about 2·5 per cent of the country's total wages and salaries. By 1975 it had risen to over 4 per cent and should reach 5 per cent over the next few years. The acquisition of these assets is, of course, a feature of what are termed 'funded' schemes, whereby most employers in Britain, apart from the government, put aside funds sufficient to meet the liabilities in the future. The basic advantage of this is that, should the employer go out of business, the pension rights are still secured. This is the basis on which most schemes are financed in Britain, though pay-as-you-go schemes operate successfully in France. As a result, the amount of money arising for investment within British pension funds has been increasing at a rate of close on 12 per cent compound in recent years and the total assets of these funds (including the overlap through life offices) is now over £20 billion and still rising. These funds are in the hands of pension schemes of all sizes and vary from those with assets under £1 million to one or two large funds with assets of over £1 billion. The National Association of Pension Funds has 1,600 members. The biggest are the pension funds of the Post Office, the National Coal Board, British Rail and the Electricity Supply Industry.

These then are the new colossi of the stock markets, pouring thousands of millions of pounds yearly into government securities, ordinary shares, debentures, property and even works of art. As one television programme put it, 'In the span of a decade, they have toppled the great traditional landlords: the Crown, the Church, the Oxbridge colleges. Since 1971, City money has increased its land-holdings from 50,000 acres to more than half a million, greater than the landed wealth of the monarchy.'[1] In the art world too, this financial power has been seen. Whereas a few pension funds have confined their investments in the art world to stakes in art-dealing firms, the British Rail Pension Fund has some £28 millions' worth of antiques, porcelain and paintings, including, it is said, Cézannes, Renoirs and Picassos. Sotheby's act as advisors. These investments began in the autumn of 1974, and, in the spring of 1979, the general manager arranged that, once he had spent a further £12 million 'rounding out' existing collections, he would be investing no further funds in the art world. These investments were clearly aimed at a capital appreciation and the income foregone has been estimated at some £2 million a year. In an art world with a turnover of £1 billion, an annual investment of £7 million has been a drop in the ocean, but, like so many other examples of the new power of the City's institutions, it has raised many questions of accountability and control and their growing impact on the City's stock markets. We must turn to these issues in the next chapter.

[1] BBC *Money Programme*, June 1978. Even so, according to the Northfield Committee's report, the financial institutions only own 1·2 per cent of Britain's agricultural land. The Committee contemplated a rise to 10 per cent over the next forty years with equanimity.

Chapter 7

Investing Institutions: Too Much Power?

The bogy of financial power has haunted Wall Street for longer than it has the City. 'The hands on the levers of control of giant private corporations must be visible to the public for its own protection,' concluded a recent study by a US Senate sub committee into the voting rights of financial institutions in American business. It is a conclusion which has been reached by countless other investigative bodies in the United States since the mid-1930s. In essence the issue is whether a handful of investment managers in Lower Manhattan could – and, more important, should – control the industrial and economic destiny of the whole of the United States. It is a question that is being asked, with rather less drama though with equal seriousness, of the City's institutional investors. If they already have £6 billion to invest yearly and if, as some in the City estimate, they may have up to £20 billion to invest annually by 1985, is this in the country's interests?

With this growth of a new financial power in the land it is not surprising that some critical questions are being asked about the way institutional investors are organised, the way they invest and the impact they have had, and can have, both on the stock market and the economy. In the words of Sir Harold Wilson, the pension funds 'are so powerful that they do not know how powerful they are. They could very well be transforming the nature of our society more than any govern-ment would dare to do.' The large City institutions are also blamed on the following grounds:

- They have led to a large increase in the volatility of stock market prices, because large institutions tend to think alike and go in and out of the market at the same time and for much the same reasons.

- They concentrate on no more than 200 companies in their stock market investments and this is pushing the prices of these shares too high, particularly in relation to the thousands of smaller companies who are thereby deprived of new capital on such favourable terms as in the past.

- The weight of money they have to invest is forcing them to seek out strange new outlets for their funds, from doubtful property at one end of the scale to doubtfully valued Picassos, Renoirs and the like at the other. Some of the pension funds have power without adequate expertise or accountability.

- While they can have, and do have, enormous influence over the refinancing of large areas of British industry, the institutions do not have any corresponding responsibility for the actual running of the large firms and in fact sell their shares at the first sign of trouble rather than act as partners in a shared enterprise.

- Above all – some politicians and trade unionists are saying – the kind of financial power now in the hands of the institutional managers should be subject to state direction of some kind, if the institutions are not to be nationalised outright.

These charges go to the heart of the relations between the City and industry. The basic impact of the growth of large institutions and of the decline in the small investor has naturally been detected first in the stock market. But there is a dispute about what form it takes and how it has come about. The Stock Exchange itself is convinced that the main result is a bigger volatility in stock market prices. It does not say that the institutions are the main culprits. As the Chairman of the Stock Exchange has put it: 'I doubt if there is any stock market in the world that would not have been volatile when faced with an increase in Minimum Lending Rate [the equivalent of the old Bank Rate] from 9 per cent up to 15 per cent and down to 9 per cent again in the year to April 1977, or with a fall in Minimum Lending Rate from 15 per cent to 5 per cent during the last year.' He was speaking at the end of 1977. Nevertheless the Stock Exchange still believes that the activities of the institutions are a contributory cause of undue stock market fluctuations, because, whereas a few years ago investment decisions were in the hands of $2\frac{1}{2}$ million people with varying views, nowadays a larger part of the market is in fewer hands, with correspondingly similar views. The decline in the smaller, individual investor has, in the view of the Stock Exchange, led to a decline in the active two-way market which in earlier days led to smoother share price changes. These changes have also led to a fall in the day-to-day liquidity of the market in that buyers and sellers are now less evenly matched. The current loss of liquidity thus naturally produces greater daily stock market movements, according to the Stock Exchange, because in a narrow one-way market buyer and seller cannot be matched so easily.

The institutions take a different view, or at least some of the larger ones do. They believe that any volatility that has been detected owes far more to the political and economic uncertainties surrounding the stock market in recent years than to structural changes within the investing public. And they point to the bewildering changes in fiscal regulations, in exchange rates, and in interest rates, quite apart from political changes or potential political changes, which also sway markets. They also argue cogently that the word 'institution' covers a multitude of activities and that thousands of investment bodies with widely differing objectives and of widely differing sizes are unlikely to form a collective view of stock market prospects and of market strategy. As for volatility, they point to the fact that the ratio of securities bought and sold annually to the total value of those listed on individual exchanges worked out at 0·21 in London compared with 0·26 in Amsterdam, 0·18 in Brussels, 0·20 in Germany, 0·25 in Milan and 0·16 in Paris. In other words, London share-dealing activity is hardly out of line with other bourses in Europe.

Where then does the truth lie? It depends, I think, on what is meant by volatility. Does it imply the speed of reaction of the stock market to new events? Or does it indicate the sharpness of such changes, whether measured daily or yearly? Reaction to new events, given the professional back-up available to the bigger institutions as well as the technical improvements in all kinds of communications, should be far quicker than it used to be when the individual investor was the dominant force. This can only improve the quality of the stock market as a means of reflecting underlying economic and political forces. But what is worrying to investors on the stock market, to the jobbers trying to make a market and to industrial companies with shares quoted there, is the evidence that price changes have been sharper than they used to be. Over the longer term, that is from the peaks to troughs of individual bear markets and from the troughs to peaks of individual bull markets, the sharpness of price changes is in my view a clear reflection of the uncertain economic and political conditions we are living in. But on a day-to-day basis I believe that the Stock Exchange's conviction is right and that, while the existence of thousands of different institutions rules out any possibility of a 'collective' view, the *similarity* of views expressed by the large institutions through their buying and selling decisions has become a growing influence on the pattern of day-to-day price changes. In addition, the purchases and sales of the large institutions are much bigger, and lumpier, than they used to be and this, in turn, has already increased the financing problem of the jobbers and, hence, the sharpness of some price changes.

We must now turn to the more important impact of institutional investing habits on industry itself. Sometimes the impact is through the stock market; sometimes it is direct. The overriding fact is that the institutions, in contrast with most private investors, have tended to concentrate their investments on a narrow range of shares, partly because of the difficulty they would face in trying to buy or sell large amounts of shares in small companies – although some pension funds, such as that of the Imperial Group, have actually concentrated on smaller companies. Either such sales or purchases would move the share price disproportionately, up or down, or the institutions would find it difficult to find a ready buyer or seller. In other words only a narrow range of shares have the kind of marketability that the institutions need for their operations. Another factor narrowing their investment range is the difficulty in managing (and, above all, of monitoring) more than a certain number of shares in individual companies. For both reasons the institutions tend to concentrate their equity investments on the shares of the top 200 companies with assets over the £40 million mark, which in total account for close on 80 per cent of the London market's equity capitalisation. Even with the concentration of their investments on the shares of large companies, it is not always practicable for large insurance companies and pension funds to make substantial switches in their equity holdings and they are usually reluctant to dispose of many of their basic holdings. Many of them, therefore, have substantial 'core holdings' in the shares of the large industrial companies. This brings some stability to these particular share dealings and, in addition, usually implies that the institutional holders are keen to acquire further holdings through 'rights issues', the issue of new shares to existing shareholders.

On the other hand, it is strongly argued, this concentration on a narrow number of shares in large companies leaves smaller firms at a relative disadvantage. For one thing, the share prices of the larger companies, it is said, will be higher than they would otherwise be and those of smaller companies lower. As a result the larger firms will be better placed to get new capital on the stock market and will also be able to get it on cheaper terms. In addition, whereas private investors tended to put their money, on occasions, in small local firms which they knew something about, the large institutions do not follow the same habit and certainly not in the same way nor to the same extent.

In other words, the rise of the large institutions has given the City's capital market a tilt in favour of the larger borrowers. This is true as far as it goes. But the tilt itself is bound to bring some self-correction with it. By this I mean that if the yield on the top 200 shares, for example, drops low enough several institutions will be tempted towards the shares of the smaller and medium-sized companies whose yields will become increasingly attractive as the institutions continually pile up the shares of the large companies. There is evidence to suggest that this may already be happening.

This process, however, takes time and meanwhile the smaller companies, already deprived of the fresh flow of risk capital as a result of the decline of the private investor, have been meeting troubles enough from taxation, inflation and the general encroachment of government into day-to-day decision making. But a response is clearly visible from the City as we detected in Chapter 3 in discussing what the banks were doing for industry. The Bank of England and the City Communications Centre have published a guide, *Money for Business*, for the smaller businessmen. Virtually all the institutions now have their own particular form of help for the smaller businessman. Local bank managers deal with small firms on a day-to-day basis. The unit trusts, recognising that while risks are higher with smaller firms returns may be higher too, now have holdings in 1,000 of the 1,840 firms on the Stock Exchange with a capitalisation below £20 million. The insurance companies usually prefer to invest their funds in smaller firms through intermediaries, rather than direct. Intermediaries used by other City institutions are of different kinds, ranging from Industrial and Commercial Finance Corporation (within the Finance for Industry Group), the Charterhouse Group and Electra House Group to joint ventures with banks and pension funds. The pension funds themselves have, among other things, established five units to invest in the equity of smaller companies, four of which are run by merchant banks and one internally by the pension funds. One or two of the larger funds have even begun to invest directly in small firms.

In short, City institutions are hardly unaware of the problems facing small firms seeking finance. In making sure that the right kind of finance is available to the right borrowers, and in trying to make sure that small businesses seeking money know where to go and even how to ask for it, the banks, unit trusts, insurance companies and pension funds have done a great deal. Whether they, or indeed the government, have done enough is still debatable. Given the overriding obligations of institutional investment managers to their policyholders or pensioners, it is difficult to avoid the conclusion that risk taking, in the sense that private investors were prepared to undertake it, for an adequate reward, is unlikely to be replaced by any of the institutional schemes now being introduced to help the small man. In any case it will be hard to assess the City's reaction to the problem until the political and economic climate is again welcoming enough to the small man with a viable enterprise needing money. But even if the political clock were turned back and the taxation and bureaucratic pressures on small businesses were also, in some way, relaxed overnight, would the problem of the small firm disappear too? I doubt it. The starting up of a business and its nursing through the early stages of its development are fraught with anxiety and a lack of experience which add to its natural vulnerability. These are natural risks, which no amount of City or governmental help can totally eradicate. I suspect that when the next inquiry into the City is launched in another couple of decades, the problem of finance for the small man will be rediscovered all over again; and whether it is caused by government, the City or simply by the small man himself will again be debated with renewed vigour.

The future power of the institutions, and especially of the pension funds, has naturally raised the question of whether they should continue to be 'funded'; that is should pension funds be secured, as they accrue, by investment in appropriate assets held in trust for future pensioners or should pensions be paid out of current income? If they were not 'funded', such large amounts of money would not pile up in their hands. There is little pressure to place private pension funds on a 'pay as you go' basis, if only because the security of future pensions, it is felt, should not depend wholly on the survival of the individual firm concerned. Equally, it is felt to be appropriate to finance civil service pensions out of current government income. The real issue is whether the pension funds of the nationalised industries should continue to be funded or not. This is a complex question, which has been analysed by the experts in some considerable detail. The upshot of a switch to 'pay as you go' for the nationalised bodies, we are told, would be to produce immediate substantial savings. Thus the government's public sector borrowing requirement (the amount the government needs to borrow to balance its budget) would be significantly reduced, this in turn allowing some fall in interest rates. Whether this would also have a disturbing effect on equity prices and yields and on wage demands is still in dispute. But the Treasury at least is in no doubt what should be decided: 'There would seem to be little, if any, economic advantage in the switch to "pay as you go" and indeed some possible disadvantages.' On the other hand, such a switch would at least reduce the almost embarrassing flow of funds into the hands of the investing institutions, and temper political reactions to such so-called 'power'.

If the estimates of future funds are taken at face value, however, are the investment managers of the insurance companies and pension funds likely to be as all-powerful as some people say? They themselves do not think so and point to the enormous variation in size of the pension funds, some with assets of over £1 billion, some with assets below £1 million. Each fund and each insurance company is in competition with all the others and, as a result, cannot form a corporate view. Even the largest pension funds are small in relation to the total flow of money moving in and out of the City's capital markets. They estimate that no one fund has a cash flow for investment of even 3 per cent of the total of institutional funds for investment in any one year. It is true that the institutions increasingly form similar views and that the money they invest moves in a more rigid pattern, in and out, than was usual when thousands of private investors made up the bulk of the investing public. But this is not the same as investing power or financial manipulation.

It is also sometimes suggested that, in some way, these growing institutions, especially the pension funds, lack the professionalism their new-found wealth requires. This is more difficult to assess, for, while some of the largest pension funds have full-time management staff and a large number have member trustees elected or appointed, others do not. Yet even in the case of the smaller funds it would be wrong to think that they are unable to call on professional City advice. The merchant banks have, for some years, accepted the role of investment managers for pension funds and continue to do so. The total funds under management by the merchant banks, including all kinds of City and foreign institutions, totalled £7½ billion at the end of 1976. Many of the American banks in London provide similar investing help to the pension funds. And, as the pension funds grow, management rationalisation grows too. They recently, for example, set up a new Institute of Pensions Management with the aim of conducting examinations and providing agreed qualifications to those running the funds.

Several nagging thoughts still remain in the public's mind. Are all pension funds safe? Is there sufficient representation on the boards of trustees? Are the funds providing enough information about their activities? Are there still too many reports of funds investing in their own company to an unhealthy degree? Are they in fact sufficiently accountable for their own actions? The answers are not entirely reassuring. *The Economist*,[1] for example, has published evidence of (1) a major British company embarking on transactions with its pension fund whereby the fund pumped cash into the company when the company's finances were under severe pressure; (2) the pension fund of a large British group being obliged to participate in the rescue of a former group subsidiary in circumstances which involved a clear conflict of interest; (3) numerous examples of unusually heavy investment by pension funds in ordinary shares of, or loans to, their own companies; and (4) trustees placing themselves in a position which could, in the last resort, force them to choose between protecting the pensioners' interests and damaging their family fortune. The point being made was not that all kinds of self-investment by pension funds were necessarily risky or wrong, but rather that, at present, no one knew where the line should be drawn; and above all that such transactions were not generally known and that funds were not accountable for such actions.

Not all pension funds have had the detailed airing of a House of Commons standing committee, as did the British Rail Pension Fund early in 1978 in connection with its investments

[1] 4 November 1978

in the art world. But public pressure for more disclosure, more representation, more accountability and, in some areas, more legislation is clearly growing. It is fairly clear that the pension fund movement itself is convinced that adherence to trust law, where appropriate, is not enough.

The pressure for wider representation on the management bodies of pension funds has added to the political sharpness of the debates, especially the proposal that trade unions should be given the sole right to appoint half the management bodies. But a CBI survey of fund members has established that 83 per cent of those interviewed believed that members' interests would be better served by allowing all members of pension funds, rather than just trade-unionists, to be represented. So far as additional disclosure is concerned, pressure there too is rising. Some funds already reach high standards of disclosure; others do not. The Stock Exchange has made some clear-cut recommendations and has called for the establishment of a 'code of best business practice' for pension funds, which, it stressed, might form the basis for a future Pension Fund Act.

It went further and suggested that such a code might include the responsibilities of pension fund trustees and managers, and their accountability to members and the public, as well as the details of an audited annual statement. The Stock Exchange also called for some means of comparing fund performances on an annual basis, and put forward the idea that its own Listing Agreement (under which firms have their shares listed on the Stock Exchange) might perhaps include a requirement for a company to comment on the adequate state of its pension fund. The pension funds hardly welcomed the Stock Exchange's initiative (or perhaps the way it was done), but, coupled with the pension funds' own discussion papers about the contents of fund annual reports, the debate has been given a much sharper edge. If a further tightening of the law is to be avoided, an agreed code laid down by the movement itself is clearly the first essential step.

Many critics, however, are not concerned with the success or failure, in market terms, of the professional investment managers. Their real concern is whether financial power of this kind should be left in private hands at all. To talk to such critics about 'financial weight' rather than 'financial power' is to miss the thrust of their argument. What is being suggested is that, while financial decisions are left to investment managers who have to base them on the long-term needs of their potential pensioners, national investment requirements may be being ignored. Some argue that the new-found power of the insurance companies and the pension funds should be used positively in rebuilding Britain's industrial structure. Some believe that the institutions are not using the power they already possess in the interests of industry and argue that, instead of selling the shares of individual companies at the first sign of trouble, they should work out a more permanent and flexible relationship within which they could be regarded as partners in a joint enterprise rather than somewhat distant providers of risk and loan capital. Others say that only outright nationalisation will ensure that the country's main economic objectives will be achieved. Others again stress that the same ends could be met by the direction of the investible funds of the institutions, either fully or partially. A variation on this theme was suggested by the TUC to the Wilson Committee. In this version it was proposed that the government and the City institutions should set up a special fund under which the institutions would receive a guaranteed minimum return. The fund would then invest its funds in areas that served the national interest. This particular formula, it was suggested, would provide a reasonable guaranteed return to the institutions while enabling national economic goals to be met. Unfortunately, as the institutions were quick to point out, it all depends on what is thought to be 'reasonable'. If it means that the return from such a fund, while guaranteed, is going to be below the market rate, then it amounts to a subsidy from the institutions (and ultimately their policyholders and pensioners) to the borrowing companies. Any subsidy of that kind, the City institutions feel, should be supplied by the government direct. In other words, the government has enough ways of influencing the investment and economic climate, as well as the power to direct its own tax revenue to needy areas, without persuading the private sector to provide subsidies too. Moreover, if the government did not have sufficient funds for its industrial purposes, it could always raise money in the gilt-edged market, where competitive market rates exist, and where the institutions would provide the funds in the normal way. The difference between this and the TUC proposal is that in this case no private subsidy would be involved.

The idea that these large funds should be directed towards national ends takes many other forms, and, as we have discussed earlier, is supported by two or three different arguments. One is the conviction that, since British industry has a worse investment record than most, it must have been starved of essential funds. Secondly, there is the view that City institutions take too short-term a view of investment prospects and that industrial firms with longer-term potential have difficulty in raising capital. Thirdly, it is suggested that the institutions, because of the obligations to policyholders, are unwilling to provide basic risk capital, other than to major established companies, in the volume once provided by the private investor. The weight of industrial evidence to the Wilson Committee has, I believe, already disposed of the argument of a few years back that the City institutions could be blamed for the lack of investment by British industry. The remaining arguments, therefore, mainly concern the way in which City institutions provide funds for industrial companies and the terms on which they do so.

The view that they take too short-term a time-scale crops up again and again. In some versions it is a reflection of the way an efficient stock market works, since in an active market it is always possible to dispose of shares in companies that are not performing as well as the institutions would like. We shall be considering shortly whether there is an alternative to this in terms of nursing a company back to health. But what of companies, it is sometimes asked, which are healthy in the longer-term but take time to reach their full potential? Should not the City treat them as they do property developments, providing funds in stages? A fair point, though any insurance company or pension fund would immediately counter by talking of a partly paid-up share capital, under which a proportion of the basic risk capital would be provided immediately and the balance sought at a later stage when needed.

The ingenuity of the City in providing a financial mechanism of this kind to meet individual needs should hardly be in dispute. The real clash of interests lies elsewhere, mainly in assessing why it is felt that some parts of British industry are not getting the funds they ought to get. Is it, as some City institutions suspect, that inefficient companies need to be buttressed by national policy? If so, are they likely to be made more competitive by providing them with money on uncommercial terms? To the institutions this smacks too much of subsidising the inefficient business with policyholders' money. In any case the process of directing institutional funds into British plant and machinery on the factory floor is not one simple process. The word 'investment' is used in two different ways. To the institution it is a matter of providing funds to industrial firms, either directly or indirectly. To the individual firm it is a matter of spending money on machinery. One is simply the exchange of a piece of paper or certificate for cash; the other, the actual purchase of equipment. Too often it is assumed that the process of persuading or forcing the institutions to invest in British industry is the same as persuading individual firms to buy modern plant and equipment. It is not. The first may enable the second to take place; it does not and cannot ensure it. As one insurance expert told the Wilson Committee, 'if we are put under a statutory obligation to invest more money in industry we do not even physically know how we do it if industry does not, behind the word "investment", physically go out and want to use up more national resources'. One reply is to suggest that the TUC proposal, in which a joint fund would be set up, would resolve this problem for the insurance companies and pension funds. To some extent it would, but the fund itself would then be left with the problem of how to persuade or force industry to use its funds. Sir Harold Wilson probably summed up the position best, in rounding off a discussion with the same insurance expert: 'Could we summarise your position in rather similar terms to that of the banks: that if industry comes to you and wants the money you will supply it; but you cannot, as it were, force people to take it who do not want it?'

There are two further, and wider, issues to be considered in connection with the possible direction of institutional funds. Both raise dangers for the institutions themselves. The first concerns the insurance companies which are discussing the future framework of the regulations to be imposed by the Common Market. If British companies are to be given the same kind of freedom in the investment of their funds in the future as in the past, the EEC rules should exclude any possibility of the direction of funds. It would be dangerous to their world-wide operations to have restrictive regulations imposed upon them at this juncture. Were directives given to them by a British Government during these European negotiations, their case for a freer European insurance regime would be undermined from the outset. The other anxiety, a domestic one, is that the experience of those countries which have introduced direction of investment suggests that the amount of the directed investment tends to become a ceiling to further investment in the same direction. More important, policyholders and savers generally, worried that their funds were being used uncommercially, could easily decide to switch their funds elsewhere to outlets which were not being forced to provide government subsidies. It is difficult to assess how far people would wish to switch their funds in this way, but the danger cannot be shrugged aside. As the insurance companies put it, more brutally, why tinker with, or even destroy, a successful savings industry in order to buttress an inefficient manufacturing one?

Are we then to conclude that the official direction of institutional funds is unnecessary and that institutional relations with industry are as good as they should be? While acknowledging the first, I hesitate about the second, for the insurance companies and especially the pension funds have hardly had time to adjust to their growing financial power and to the changes this may imply in the way they behave.

Shareholders, whether private or institutional, are the legal owners of companies in which they invest and, as a result, many people these days feel that they have obligations to employees, to customers, to the people supplying the company and to the environment in which the company operates, as well as rights to a return on the money they have invested. The obligations are usually fulfilled by delegating the task to management and by appointing a board of directors. It is worth setting all this out, rather painstakingly, if only to compare it with current reality. The fact is that shareholders, though they have the ability to dismiss boards, rarely do so, partly because their ownership is fragmented and they find it difficult to adopt a united front and partly because they often prefer to take advantage of the efficiency of the stock market and sell their shares. As a result company boards have been given more freedom than company law originally intended. At least that was true so long as private investors, in their hundreds of thousands, dominated the stock markets. Now that institutional investors are becoming more influential and shares are being concentrated in fewer hands, it should become easier not only to establish communications between boards and their share-holders but also to encourage continuing dialogues. There are some grounds for believing that this is happening. Whether it is happening quickly enough and in the right areas is another matter.

The institutions do not entirely dismiss the choice they have of selling shares in inefficient companies. Many of them remain unconvinced that it is wrong to allow the stock market to play its customary role in the allocation of resources, and as a spur to management. A company's share price is in essence a measure of a company's past and expected performance relative to other companies. If a company's share price slumps, it immediately becomes subject to a possible take-over bid. And, even if it can protect itself against this eventuality, the fall in the share price makes it more expensive to raise fresh capital. As the British Insurance Association has put it, 'For many years now industrial managements have shown them-selves to be sensitive to the message of their relative ratings in the stock market. Far more managements of public companies have taken this message and put their houses in order than have ever been taken over, and far more are taken over than go into liquidation or need to be rescued.'

Thus the stock market has its role to play in monitoring the efficiency of individual companies. What is beginning to worry some people, however, is whether this can continue to the same extent when institutional investors dominate the markets more than at present and when sales by such investors become increasingly difficult as a result. It is this possibility that focuses attention on the relationships between institutional investors and individual companies. Contacts already take place on several levels. Investment managers and analysts from the institutions have regular contacts of their own and, according to a recent survey of close on 1,000 companies by the British Insurance Association, of the top 600 companies with a market capitalisation of £8 million and over, 43 per cent were covered at investment manager level and 72 per cent at analyst level. As the Chairman of Shell Transport & Trading, Mr C. C. Pocock, has put it: 'We in Shell, and many other companies I know, welcome the interest of financial analysts and try to keep live contact with them.' Occasionally meetings are arranged by third parties such as stockbrokers, issuing houses or the Association of Investment Analysts. In fact one of the complaints increasingly heard in industry is the time spent dealing with junior investment analysts from the institutions.

Although these contacts provide the opportunity for an institution to be alerted to trouble at an early stage, they do little to ward off trouble and are concerned primarily with assessing and monitoring the institutions' share portfolios. The real questions are whether an institution should act alone, or jointly with others, and what action if any should be taken. The answer naturally depends on the nature of the difficulties faced by the company, but often an informal joint approach by a limited number of institutions brings the best results. But it is a process that bristles with snags. If management has to be changed, what role will the existing board play? When should other shareholders be consulted? If special information is made available to the small group of institutional investors, should share dealings be suspended until *all* shareholders have been similarly informed? Since action behind the scenes is sometimes more effective than in the full glare of publicity, institutional investors often have a particularly difficult task on their hands. This is why the real fire-fighting often takes place jointly elsewhere, especially within the Investment Protection Committees of the British Insurance Association, the National Association of Pension Funds, the Unit Trust Association or the Association of Investment Trust Companies, or within the more recently formed umbrella organisation, the Institutional Shareholders' Committee. These are essentially for joint use by the institutions concerned. The IPC of the BIA, for example, have generally acted by appointing special subcommittees and in recent years 210 such subcommittees have been formed each year, largely to discuss debentures, loan stock, equity shares and the capital reconstruction schemes of individual companies, as well as broader issues such as company law reform and inflation accounting.

The broader-based ISC was formed at the end of 1972 by the insurance companies, pension funds, investment trusts and unit trusts, all of whom have their own investment protection committees, following prompting from the Governor of the Bank of England. Its purpose was to provide a mechanism through which institutional investors could co-operate with industrial managers in improving industrial efficiency. It operates by setting up what are termed case committees to study individual problems. In its first four years of operation, the ISC examined about 20 cases and 6 case committees were formed and 6 other cases dealt with in other ways. It was a slow beginning, but the Committee has recently taken steps to widen its dialogue with industry by encouraging company directors, with the prior knowledge of their chairman, to discuss their company's affairs with it on a confidential basis. It has also suggested that it would act as a channel of communication between boards and shareholders in cases where criticism of management was not involved, and would be available to help boards appoint non-executive directors.

Beyond these joint mechanisms, which are confined largely to the treatment of large industrial companies, insurance companies have much closer involvements with medium-sized companies to whom they have lent substantial sums by way of loan or mortgage. In such cases they often have directors on the board. So far as the smaller companies are concerned, the insurance companies have so far preferred to lend indirectly, through specialised agencies, again on the grounds that they could not hope to provide the expertise necessary to management if their investments in this area were to be monitored efficiently. The industry, however, is clearly far from certain whether enough has been done for small businesses. I would draw the same conclusion about the industry's relationship with industrial management in general. It has started to feel its way towards a new, and closer, set of relationships, within the parameters provided by its obligations to its policyholders.

Individually, and jointly, the institutions are already heeding the advice proffered by the Governor of the Bank of England, reminding them of their responsibilities as shareholders, that is their ultimate right to 'hire and fire' boards of directors. He told them recently that:

> Institutional shareholders should take trouble to ensure that directors of companies in which they have important investments are doing a good job. If they are doubtful or uneasy, they should ask for explanations and expect to receive them. Thereafter the nature of the appropriate action will depend on the circumstances of the case. But if in the end they are dissatisfied, they should, individually or collectively, take steps to change the composition of the board.

The list of examples in which the big institutions have intervened in this way is growing monthly. In some cases they have been instrumental in changing management. In others they have opposed management policies concerning the future of the company, the future use of its funds, or its proposals for acquisitions. The list of firms which have thus felt the pressure of institutional feeling is lengthening and already includes Distillers, Burton Group, Allied Breweries, Rank, Barclays Bank and S. Pearson. Others are bound to follow. The institutions will of course be accused of interfering with the future jobs of thousands of workers. They will make mistakes. They will also gradually learn how to balance the needs of their pensioners and policyholders with their wider responsibilities. How far they may be forced to go down this interventionist road and how far they ought to go, I will be exploring in Chapter 17.

Chapter 8

Money Markets: A Billion a Day?

A market in money is what it implies: a place where the demand for, and supply of, money can be satisfied – at a price. In the City, spare cash can be lent overnight or for several years and, unlike yours or mine, runs into millions, even billions. Our spare cash will go into a bank or a building society, but a bank's spare cash, or that of a local authority, a big company or a foreign government, will as often as not go to, or through, one of London's traditional discount houses or their broking offshoots. It has been estimated that the discount market handles between £6 and 10 billion a week, or, on average, something like a billion pounds a day.

Twenty years ago these strange left-overs from the Victorian era were dismissed somewhat disparagingly by the Radcliffe Committee of Inquiry into the City's operations. It's report concluded: 'It would not be beyond human ingenuity to replace the work of the discount houses; but they are there, they are doing the work effectively, and they are doing it at a trifling cost in terms of labour and other real resources.' The report described the use of the discount houses' facilities in discounting bills of exchange as 'vestigial' and gave a figure of £152 million as the total outstanding on bill finance for industry and commerce. Now these same houses can point to a twentyfold rise in the volume of commercial bills and to the fact that the total of bill finance is approaching £3 billion. They can also claim to have been at the centre of one of the most remarkable developments in the City: the parallel wholesale markets in money. Two decades ago, they still relied on the leisurely 'calls' on banks to bring in the millions of their stock in trade, overnight money. Now they have spawned computerised dealing rooms and a professional aggression that still fits uneasily with their more traditional habits.

The lending of spare cash for the use of others is hardly a new occupation in the City. Over a century ago, Walter Bagehot, in his classic exposition of the money market, *Lombard Street*, claimed that England was 'the greatest moneyed country in the world' and had 'much more immediately disposable and ready cash than any other country'. The point he was making then is still true today. A money market is a concentration of ready money and is quite different from the same amount of money tucked away under mattresses up and down the country. The French peasant was and probably still is wealthier than his counterpart in this and many other countries.[1] But his money remains idle and unused. In contrast London money markets were, and are, based on the concentration of spare cash in London and other large institutions. A century ago the money reflected the concentration of wealth in English and Scottish banks; now it reflects the cash in the hands of hundreds of foreign banks, international companies, local authorities and foreign governments. Then it was entirely in sterling: now it is in both sterling and the leading currencies of the world.

A market in money on such a large scale can provide help in many different ways. In London it has been benefiting three main participants for a century and more: first, it has helped the banks to maintain their cash reserves in a convenient form and has acted as a buffer between the banks and the Bank of England; second, it has provided financial help to industry and commerce; third, it has provided temporary help, on a huge and growing scale, to the British Government and has enabled it to manipulate interest rates and so control monetary policy.

The discount houses, and their predecessors the bill brokers, go back to the early nineteenth century, when by the use of

[1] Even today private gold holdings in France are estimated to be the equivalent of 4,000 to 5,000 tons, worth, say, $20–5 billion or a quarter or a fifth of the world's total gold. Since they are not concentrated or readily available, they remain of little help to the French Government.

money bills they played a vital role among the private banks in smoothing out the surpluses in money generated in the country areas, especially at time of harvest, and the shortages in the growing industrial areas. The bill brokers acted as inter-mediaries, as one of them put it, 'taking from those who have a surplus and distributing it to those who require it'. These latter-day Robin Hoods have continued to do the same thing, though the method of doing so has changed considerably over the years. Initially, in the early days of the Industrial Revo-lution, manufacturers in the north of England started to finance their holdings of raw materials on a short-term basis by the use of bills of exchange, which were in essence post-dated cheques. The bill brokers began to buy these bills, either from the importers of the raw materials in London or from the northern banks, and to sell them to the cash-surplus banks in the south. Over the years these relationships developed in different ways. The banks began to lend money on a short-term basis to the discount houses which in turn continued to buy bills of exchange, and the Bank of England, learning the hard way as it went from crisis to crisis, increasingly began to stand behind the discount houses as 'lender of last resort'.

As we shall see, the discount houses began to use these domestic techniques on a wider international scale as British trade expanded throughout the nineteenth century, eventually establishing the so-called 'bill on London', still in essence a post-dated cheque, which was acceptable virtually anywhere in the world as the basis of international trade for close on a century. Private industry was not the only beneficiary. Just over a hundred years ago, following the advice of Walter Bagehot, the Treasury introduced its own bill of exchange, the Treasury bill, which the discount houses continue to buy and deal in on a huge scale to this day. Other government instruments have been added to the discount houses' repertoire since then, such as the wartime Treasury deposit receipt and short-dated government bonds.

It was, however, the discount houses' relations with the banks, initially the private banks and later the present-day joint-stock banks, that served as the basis for their growing activities. They still do. In the early days the bill brokers acted as middlemen between private banks in different parts of the country. But as amalgamations took place among the banks, spurred on by the introduction of limited liability, the transfer of savings from the cash-starved north of England to the richer south began to take place within the banking system, especially as branch networks began to evolve on the modern basis.

The discount houses, however, while continuing to buy bills for domestic and, increasingly, international trade, were themselves moving closer to the banks (and to the Bank of England) and before long they were providing the banks with a convenient outlet for their spare cash, what was to become known as 'call money', that is money which could be called back at any time. This had several advantages to the banks. Call money was more convenient than the holding of bills, whose capital value could fluctuate, since it had no fixed maturity and could be recalled at any time. Since the Bank of England was acting as lender of last resort to the discount houses, the banks were also in effect indirectly relying on the central bank for their short-term funds. In short, the discount houses had built up a useful monetary buffer between the banks and the Bank of England, which suited everyone, for the central bank too was provided with a much smoother and more delicate monetary instrument than that operated by most other central banks, who simply use bill holdings to maintain control over monetary policy.

In the next chapter we shall be looking more closely at the way in which the Bank of England (and thus the government) uses the discount market, but in the rest of this chapter I want to concentrate on the way in which the banks benefit from them and on the remarkable new ways in which both commerce and industry have been benefiting.

The use of call money is the key to the liquidity of the banking system. A banker becomes a real banker when he begins to use other people's money as well as his own in lending funds to industry and commerce. But in doing so he has to remember that the people he borrows money from may want it back. Bankers have learnt from experience that it is wise to keep some of their money readily available to meet such calls from their creditors. 'Readily available' can mean actual cash, or short-dated bills of exchange or government securities, or call money extended to the discount houses. The banks have usually found it prudent to have about a third of their money in what are known as liquid assets, that is in assets which can be turned into cash within a reasonable time, say within three months. The government, in its efforts to control the banking system and to manipulate monetary policy, has in any case usually insisted on a certain percentage of bank assets being in cash or near-cash and has set out clearly what form these should take. Since 1971, for example, the banks have had to maintain a minimum of $12\frac{1}{2}$ per cent of·their 'eligible liabilities' in certain reserve assets, which include Treasury bills, commercial bills, government securities with less than a year to run to maturity, and call money with the London money market. In addition to this the Bank of England can instruct the banks to place a certain percentage of their assets with the Bank as 'special deposits', especially when the authorities wish to curb further bank lending.

Thus call money, placed with the discount houses, is at the heart of the control of the Bank of England over the banks, since it can be used by the banks as a highly flexible balancing item in their total reserve assets, and on occasions can account for up to two-thirds of the banks' short-term liquid assets. The size of the surplus funds deposited with the discount houses varies from day to day, largely depending on the flow of funds between the banks and the government (that is, whether it is the tax gathering season or not) and between the banks and private industry. If the banks think that they will be running down their cash resources too low, they will ask for the return of some of their call money from the discount houses. If their cash reserves seem likely to rise during the day, they will add to their short-term funds in the discount market. As we shall see in the next chapter, these potential shortages or surpluses play a significant part in enabling the authorities – the Bank of England – to encourage changes in the level of interest rates.

Up to about a decade and a half ago, these relationships between the Bank of England, the discount houses and the banks made up what the textbooks regarded as the classical money market. It was unique to London, but it worked. Yet, even as some of the peculiarities of this system were being exported to developing money centres abroad, such as Toronto, Johannesburg, Salisbury, and Singapore, significant changes were beginning to be seen in the City itself. The inflow of foreign banks, eventually pushing the number of international banks in London to over 300, was one important factor; the expansion of the banks' operations themselves provided new strains of their own. The upshot was that the traditional call by top-hatted representatives of the discount houses on the money managers of the leading clearing banks, in which millions were offered or withdrawn over a cup of tea, was slowly replaced by the more active use of an embryo interbank market and by the introduction of telephones, computers, television screens and a virtually new electronic market in money. The old conventions, under which banks wanting to withdraw money from the discount market had to do so before midday, were slowly undermined, first by borrowing surpluses from non-clearing banks, later by the extension of this peripheral market to all the big banks. Before long sterling money-brokers had emerged with the specific object of acting as intermediaries between banks. It was the start of the new interbank market in money.

This development meant that the narrow money market had at least broken its bonds and embraced new sources of money, both within the banking system and outside. The banks in London, both large and small, now lend spare deposits to each other through specialist brokers and the total market is estimated at over £11 billion, over a fifth of all bank deposits in Britain. Yet, in spite of the size of the market, daily deficits can still occur in banking demands for funds and the discount market's access to official funds at the Bank of England remains both an essential source for the banks and a means of moulding official monetary policy.

It was a natural extension of the interbank market when certificates of deposit, known as CDs, were provided as an additional option for lenders of funds. These were introduced, because of their convenience, about a decade ago. A lender may not be happy simply lending an agreed sum of money for an agreed period, since his funds will be tied up for the period of the loan. But, if he gets a negotiable instrument such as a CD in return for his money, he is being given the option of selling the instrument in the market should he suddenly need the cash. Issues of sterling CDs have reached over £4 billion over the past couple of years. They are dealt in by the discount houses, which not only hold them (according to their view of future market rates) but also make a secondary market in them for the convenience of others.

The vast interbank market was not the only new development in the late 1960s and early 1970s. Estimates of this and other markets are set out in Table 15. The provision of spare bank and other institutional money for local authorities and finance houses, the development of a market in spare cash among large industrial corporations, as well as corresponding markets in foreign currencies (again including appropriate certificates of deposit) – all blossomed in this period. The local authority market arose, largely because of the restraints imposed on local borrowers by the Public Works Loan Board, once the main source of public funds, and the growing opportunities opened up by the freer lending habits in the Euro-currency markets (especially the ability to borrow Eurodollars and switch to sterling) and the growth of spare funds among insurance companies, pension funds and the like. With the growth in the amount of money, in the number of banks involved (they doubled in a decade), and especially in the number of local authorities wanting to participate (something like 1,400 in total though not all were borrowers), the discount houses began to find that their habits had to change radically. The result was the establishment of brokers willing to bring borrowers and lenders together, either the branching out of existing brokers into local authority debt or the introduction of new broking firms.

Apart from local authorities, the private commercial sector has also benefited from these developments. Markets in deposits for finance houses and in short-term funds on offer between larger industrial companies have grown significantly in this period. The discount market has also continued to provide its traditional commercial bill finance, on a remarkably bigger scale. The finance house market simply developed from the way

Table 15   London's Money Markets

£ millions

	Interbank Market	Markets in Sterling Certificates of Deposit	Discount Market Borrowed Funds	Finance House Deposits	Local Authority Temporary Debt
1965	366	—	1,381	654	1,740
1970	1,694	1,089	2,259	688	1,879
1974	8,582	4,318	2,616	459	3,925
1975	7,415[1]	2,979[1]	2,536[2]	415	3,758
1976	8,610	3,340	2,546	703[3]	4,349
1977	11,497	4,641	3,610	809	3,013

[1] Excludes one contributor after 1975.
[2] Includes two money brokers and the money trading departments of several banks from 1975 onwards.
[3] Includes some other consumer credit companies from 1976.
Source: Bank of England Bulletin: 'Financial Statistics', HMSO.

in which instalment credit companies normally financed part of their business by bidding for public deposits. A market in large deposits from institutions, banks, industrial companies and even foreign investors quickly developed in the early 1970s. Over the same period large companies, with spare cash to invest, gradually became aware of short-term possibilities in the City's money markets. Money brokers deliberately helped to put one company in touch with another. Some company treasurers got in touch direct. The upshot was that surplus funds which might otherwise have been used to reduce overdrafts or bank charges were put out to the money market. The restrictions on bank lending were a final spur to this comparatively new market.

This has meant that a company treasurer, with spare funds, can put a call through to a discount house or its broking off-shoot and be offered a range of different homes for his money. Money can be left 'overnight' (this can be accepted up to three o'clock in the afternoon and will be available again next day), on a day-to-day basis (when it can be called back any day before noon), on several days' notice, or for a fixed period. Rates of interest will vary, as they do in the additional range of investment instruments now offered by the money markets, extending from Treasury bills to bank and trade bills and from certificates of deposit to local authority bonds. The risk element varies too. Some, like Treasury bills and short-term government bonds, have a government guarantee. Bank bills are 'accepted', that is underwritten, by a bank and certificates of deposit will have been issued by a bank. But banks vary, and so does the underlying risk.

Industry has also made growing use of the discounting of commercial bills in the money market. The 'bill on London' was the backbone of the discount houses throughout the nineteenth century and, before the latest expansion, the amount outstanding tended to rise and fall according to the cost of borrowing in other ways, particularly on overdraft. The total has risen twentyfold in two decades and has reached £3 billion. Commercial bills of this kind are guaranteed, or accepted, by banks, indicating that the bank will pay a certain sum on a certain date. They enable an importer waiting for delivery of his goods, or a manufacturer temporarily holding large stocks, to finance his operations. The bill, once accepted by a bank, can be rediscounted by a discount house. This means that the discount house buys the bill from the recipient, paying out the full amount less an appropriate discount, the equivalent of interest, say, on a three-month loan.

This method of financing is ideal for what are called self-liquidating transactions, such as importing or the short-term holding of stocks. Although they are normally used for three months, one- and two-month bills are increasing in volume. A six-month bill is usually the maximum facility financed in this way. The import trades and the commodity trades have all been traditional users of these credits. Increasingly, under the persuasion of some of the leading City houses, big industrial firms have been issuing bills with their own name attached. These are called 'trade bills' in contrast to 'bank bills'. The nationalised industries, which now account for some £150 million of outstanding acceptance credits, have used them to finance sales of steel, the industrial use of gas, electricity and coal, and the purchase of natural gas from the oil companies by the Gas Corporation. The timber trade, always a traditional user, has extended bill finance to the conversion processes in the furniture trade. Sales of synthetic fibres to the textile trade, the import of meat, monthly purchases by dairy groups from the Milk Marketing Board – these are all typical examples of processes financed by commercial bills. In all these ways the discount houses, in conjunction with London's banks and Britain's leading industrial enterprises, have been co-operating in providing a growing volume of short-term finance as working capital.

These various domestic developments, from the early 1960s onwards, coincided with and sometimes were encouraged, perhaps even caused, by the other phenomenon of the period, the Eurodollar market. I shall be exploring that vast new market in Chapter 14, but its involvement with the new wholesale markets in money that we have just discussed and with the discount houses and brokerage firms needs touching on here, if only for completeness. Eurodollars are confined neither to dollars nor to Europe, but the name describes how they developed. They are currencies, held outside their country of origin, used to finance trade, industrial projects, and even sovereign governments. In early days, when London banks first began to bid for the surplus dollars then accumulating in Europe, New York banks were unable to offer higher interest rates because of official restrictions there. The dollars were generally used outside Britain but, when interest rate differentials made it profitable, some were converted into sterling and lent to local authorities and other institutions. This had two effects. It meant that the brokers involved in the currency and Eurocurrency markets began to move into the sterling money markets. Secondly, since at this time foreign banks were moving to London in droves, it became increasingly difficult for the discount houses to keep in daily touch with these banks as principals. The problems of direct dealing increased and more specialised broking firms started up, some in local authority business, some in interbank business and some in foreign currency deposits.

The result of this intermixing of the growing Eurocurrency and sterling parallel markets was that the discount houses were forced back into the broking business. Many of them now have broking subsidiaries involved in both the sterling and currency deposit markets. Others have involvements in similar operations overseas, either through representative offices or subsidiaries. Only five of the eleven members of the Discount Market Association do not have overseas interests, and three of those have had such interests (see Table 16). Thus once again the traditional City structure has been shaken into new shapes and new directions by the brutal interplay of market forces.

The question that crops up time and again is whether the discount houses really have an independent role to play or whether they are, in essence, simply doing what the banks would do just as well without them. Are they really necessary? This was the question the banks asked themselves many times in the early thirties, when the relations between the two became remarkably strained and the banks were tempted to sidestep them in applying for Treasury bills. The Radcliffe Committee asked a similar question in the late 1950s, and

Table 16   *London Discount Market – Money Market Interests Abroad*

Alexanders	Nil
Allen Harvey	Representative Office – Amsterdam. Minority interest in a Dutch foreign exchange broking company.
Cater Ryder	Nil
Clive Discount	Minority interest in a discount house – Singapore.
Gerrard & National	Majority interest in Astley & Pearce (international money brokers) with subsidiaries or affiliates in Singapore, Denmark, USA, Switzerland, Hongkong & Tokyo. Minority interest in First International Money Markets, Inc., in USA.
Gillett Brothers	Minority interests or affiliation with money market companies – Rhodesia & Singapore. Wholly own Kirkland-Whittaker (international money brokers) with subsidiaries (or affiliates) in Holland, Malaysia, Hongkong, Luxembourg, Jersey, USA, Germany, France, Switzerland & Bahrain.
Jessel Tonybee	Nil.
King & Shaxson	Minority interest in a discount house – South Africa.
Seccombe Marshall	Nil.
Smith St Aubyn	Minority interests or affiliation with money market companies – South Africa, Rhodesia.
Union Discount	Nil.

almost answered 'no'. But, since the discount houses were apparently doing no harm, the Radcliffe Committee clearly felt it would be wrong to disturb them. It was a short-sighted view then. It is even more so now, two decades on.

Leaving aside their involvement in the remarkable growth of the wholesale money markets we have been describing, the buffer provided by the discount houses between the banks and the Bank of England has features which they would find it hard to reproduce between them. The prime role the discount houses play is clearly in operating a market in call money and in providing the banks with fully secured alternatives for their cash reserves. Without them the banks would have to carry much larger cash reserves, which would earn them far less, and, more important, the system would not give the Bank of England such a grip on monetary policy. Under present arrangements cash resources can be kept to a minimum, which enables the Bank of England to use the occasional shortage to impose its will on interest rates. In providing a market in both Treasury bills and short-dated government bonds, the houses enable the banks to take the bills they want, especially the shorter maturities, and relieve them of any obligation to 'cover the weekly tender'. They provide a useful market in short-dated bonds and they give the banks an alternative to going to the central bank as a lender of last resort. They also discount commercial bills of exchange, an activity the banks would find both risky and not automatically profitable.

These advantages, however, are not easily exportable and money markets which have been modelled on London lines in such countries as Canada, Australia, South Africa and Singapore still lack the complex relationships seen in London. But some of them at least seem to be moving in similar directions. The lessons to be learned are usually the same. In the first place, it is wiser for discount houses to take deposits from banks and not to compete with the banks for public deposits. Secondly, money brokers need to be introduced with more than usual care, for they can, if not supervised, begin to deal indiscriminately between unregulated institutions. Above all, the relationships between the banks, the discount houses and the central bank need to be clarified at the outset. The London system is in essence a further example of the way in which specialisation can be used to everyone's advantage. It is not the only way. But it usually brings advantage to all participants. And it works. Or at least it has worked to the clear benefit of both the City and industry in the sixties and seventies.

The remaining question is whether the government (the third beneficiary of the money markets) has emerged with its monetary instrument as intact or as finely tuned as it was when the discount houses were playing their traditional role. This issue brings up wider ones, including the way in which the City generally helps or hinders government. In the next chapter I shall look at the City's historical relations with government, before assessing how the City's mechanism is used by government.

Chapter 9

The Government: Does the City Help?

Rulers and governments have been coming to the City for financial help for centuries. Two years after his success at Agincourt, Henry V sent this greeting to the Lord Mayor, merchants and citizens of the City:

> Trusty and welbeloved, we grete yow often tymes wel, doying yow to understande for your comfort that, by the grace of God, we ben savely arryved into oure lond of Normandy.

It was a progress report from a king to his financial backers. He had landed safely in Normandy and had just taken the castle of Touques (close to modern Deauville). It wasn't the first report of its kind; nor the last. But it was the first from a King of England in English. And on this occasion the money raised from the City had been vital: it had helped Henry to pay 10 knights, 190 men at arms and 400 archers for one quarter. Throughout his reign Henry had constantly turned to the City for loans for his expeditions and it is estimated that its total contribution came to some £32,000 during the ten years of his reign.[1]

The City had earlier been behind the Crusades, with interesting consequences for the present Port of London Authority and the Queen. Richard I granted the City, in a charter of 1197, 'the right and jurisdiction of the river', which had

[1] J. L. Kirby, *History Today*, April 1976.

hitherto been enjoyed by the keeper of the Tower. And three hundred years later the City was still claiming that the 'watercourse of the Thames' was 'wholly pertaining to the City'. In fact there is evidence that Richard and his successors had given the City the soil and bed under the river, as well as the river itself, as collateral for loans. But the evidence is later conflicting, sometimes deliberately so, with the Crown trying as hard as it could to undermine previous charters, often indeed still claiming rights to the river. Squabbles between Royal borrower and City lender often broke out about the lucrative weirs placed at points along the river, largely to catch fish. The last royal encroachment on City rights was attempted by Charles II but William and Mary eventually restored 'all former privileges' and the City's successors, particularly the present Port of London Authority, have continued to uphold them. The Crown had to content itself with owning the river bed opposite the banks where it owned (and still owns) land, such as opposite the House of Commons, Royal Arsenal (beyond Greenwich), part of Millbank and the Royal Manor of Richmond. All of which no doubt explains why the Chairman of the Port of London Authority so often escorts the Queen down river – from her property to his.

The pressures on the City to give financial help to the sovereign also had more weighty consequences, particularly for the City itself. Support for William III, for example, led to the establishment both of the Bank of England and of the London Stock Exchange:

> Under the rule of the Stuarts the rich merchants and land-owners had been bled by the monarchy in exchange for a number of specious promises. The kings had borrowed haphazardly and defaulted brazenly on their loans. When William III, a Dutchman, came to the throne he realised that a complete change of policy was required. And the first thing that he must establish, which is no different today, was *confidence* between the Government as a borrower and the merchants and other individuals as lenders. State credit was so shaky at this time that no members of the public would voluntarily lend their money to it. So the king

formed first of all a corporation under a special Charter to raise loans for the nation. This corporation was the Bank of England. At the same time he realised that there must be a market place where merchants, with funds available, could put this money to work in investing in state securities, and others holding such securities, could liquidate them easily and readily. The result was first the advent in the Royal Exchange of individuals who acted as go-betweens, arranging deals between borrowers and lenders, and finally the establishment of the London Stock Exchange itself.[1]

So what is new? Loans to the government (known as gilt-edged securities)[2] worth some £42 billion are now quoted on this same Stock Exchange. The principal and interest are the obligation of, or are guaranteed by, the British Government – a far cry from the gold collar studded with jewels left as collateral by Henry V with the Lord Mayor. The National Debt as we now know it has been increasing since the first issues of Exchequer stock were made, towards the end of the seventeenth century. Since then it has grown and grown – especially during the two world wars when the war effort was financed through public loans as well as taxation. Since the last war the nationalisation of coal, steel, electricity, gas and railways has added to the government debt and further stock has been issued in compensation.

Whereas the City of London originally lent its own money and that of its richer citizens to the King, the City now provides two separate kinds of help. It subscribes to the issues of government stock directly; it also provides a mechanism through which anyone else can be encouraged to invest in government stock. The efficiency and sophistication of this mechanism has enabled the government to finance huge 'borrowing requirements' in recent years with ease, but also with dire consequences for other competing borrowers, especially British industry. But more of this in a moment. Our

---

[1] J. Dundas Hamilton, Deputy Chairman, London Stock Exchange, November 1973
[2] The name covers all securities which are British Government and government-guaranteed stocks.

present purpose is to outline what form of help the City now provides for the government – apart from the huge slice of taxation which derives from the business and banking world.

The raising of capital needs two different markets: a primary market, where new money is provided to a borrower in exchange for securities, and a secondary market, where old securities can change hands. London had both by the end of the seventeenth century. Exchequer stock had been issued and the establishment of a market place where these existing securities could always be resold, thus providing the original subscribers with the assurance that they could always get their money back (or at least the current value of the securities), was the start of the essential secondary market that any fund raising through securities needs. London was also fortunate that, in the two centuries following the establishment of the Bank of England and the Stock Exchange, financial institutions were to grow up that would make a ready market not only in government securities but increasingly, after the introduction of the limited liability company, in industrial shares too. The merchant banks, overseas banks and private banks were in the forefront in the nineteenth century and were followed by the insurance companies, building societies, unit trusts, investment trusts and pension funds. Their successors are still with us and still form part of both the primary and secondary markets. Because of the varying investment needs of these institutions, there is a constant demand for government stock with varying redemption dates. The discount houses, for example, have an appetite for short-term bonds of from one to five years; the banks are interested in securities with a life expectancy of up to ten years; the building societies up to fifteen years; and the pension funds and insurance companies prefer securities with redemption dates at least ten years ahead.

This secondary market provides what is known as 'marketability' and helps encourage subscribers to put up new money when it is required. London's marketability has in fact become its greatest asset to the government. The fact that Britain has managed to win overseas wars and has never therefore defaulted on its loans has also helped considerably. As the City Capital Markets Committee once put it:

If, since 1945, the weakness of sterling has made foreigners reluctant to hold updated and longer-dated issues, their willingness to hold short-dated gilts has if anything increased in recent years by reason of the very feature of marketability. It is a well-known fact that the Middle Eastern owners of oil funds have been unable to find comparable outlets for these funds in the issues of German, French, Swiss or other West European Governments for the very simple reason that they do not enjoy comparable marketability. In crude terms it is impossible to buy £10 million worth of German Federal Republic bonds on a single day without moving the price: the same transaction can be carried out in British gilts within minutes without attracting attention. Similarly the German Federal Government is unable to float loans of DM 1,000 million [approximately £250 million] except at great issuing expense and at fairly long intervals. The British Government has been able to raise ten times this amount in as many weeks at no issuing expense and at rising prices. In both cases the determining factor is the breadth of the secondary [dealing] market.[1]

Let us turn to the primary market, where the new money is raised. When Britain's experience is compared with that of other Western nations the results are quite remarkable. In recent years, the government has succeeded in borrowing up to £8 billion annually by the issue of securities. As Mr Gordon Pepper[2] has stressed in an analysis of government issues in different countries, 'on average over the six years 1970 to 1975 the UK gilt-edged market provided 73 per cent of the Government's domestic borrowing, compared with 43 per cent for Switzerland, 39 per cent for the US and 37 per cent for Germany'. Thus the main feature of the London market is its capacity to raise long-term money for the government, giving the authorities the opportunity of timing their new issues and redemptions over an extended period rather than being forced to issue short-term stock on unhealthy markets. In technical

[1] City Capital Market Committee: Evidence to the Wilson Committee, 1977
[2] Gordon Pepper, W. Greenwell & Co's Monthly Letter, London, December 1976

terms, their 'roll-over' problems are eased. The British Government has 39 per cent of its entire debt maturing in not less than 15 years, compared with only 4 per cent in the case of the United States. At the other end of the maturity scale, 86 per cent of the American Government debt is due for repayment within five years, whereas only 44 per cent of the British Government debt will mature within the same period.

What are the reasons for all this? They lie mainly in the fact that the London mechanism was fashioned when London was acting not only as a source of funds for the British Government but also for governments round the world. It was in this period – mainly in the half-century before 1914 – that the City's facility to tap the country's savings and channel them to governments and industry alike was developed. Many refinements have been added since. They have their own peculiarities, as we shall see, some of which are difficult to transplant to other centres. But they work. On the Stock Exchange itself, the jobbing system gives the market depth and an absence of the kind of sharp price fluctuation seen in many other centres. Though it is coming under strain as the remaining jobbers (basically wholesalers in stocks and shares) grapple with taxation and have difficulty maintaining the capital needed to hold sufficient stock on their books, London is still largely protected from the shocks registered in the prices on other exchanges abroad, where buyers and sellers are in direct touch with each other without the intervening buffer of the jobbers. This buffer, however, is becoming thinner, not only because of the financial strain on the jobbers[1] but because of recent changes in the role of the Government Broker. This is another London innovation. Whereas in New York the Federal Reserve Bank (the equivalent of the Bank of England) deals direct with the govern-

[1] The jobbers are also helped by six firms of stockbrokers, recognised by the Bank of England as money brokers, whose role is to assist in financing the jobbing system – thus buttressing the buffer they provide – by the lending of stock or money as required for settlement. 'The jobber is able to borrow shares from the money broker, against cash security, so that he can fulfill his sold bargains, or borrow money against the security of stock to pay for shares he is holding awaiting a buyer. This facility is particularly relevant to dealings in government stock. . . . Without this facility the jobber would be unable to make a market in any worthwhile size' (Stock Exchange evidence to the Wilson Committee, Appendix A, 1977).

ment-bond dealers in Wall Street, in London the Government Broker acts as the link between the Bank of England and the jobbers. Until 1971, when the new regime of 'Competition and Credit Control' was introduced, the Government Broker acted almost as an extra wholesaler – sometimes making government stock available, sometimes absorbing stock from the market at certain prices. Since that date, however, the Government Broker has not always been available to 'support' the market and, as a result, prices have become a little more volatile than they used to be. Yet the London market still maintains one feature absent in New York and other centres and one which until recently has tended to favour the borrowing needs of the government. This is the system of the so-called 'tap'. Although the government issues an agreed amount of its stock on a certain date, some of the issue will be taken up by the authorities (usually the Bank of England) and will be available continuously from then on (that is to say 'on tap') to any individual or institution. In effect this means that the government can have different stocks always available to the investing community. Similarly, at the other end of the spectrum, the British Government begins to buy back government stock which is nearing its redemption (repayment) date. This too provides the authorities with a flexibility not usually available in other centres.

Consideration of these various means of controlling the flow of government debt to City institutions, and, through them, to the rest of the investing public, brings us to the role which the City's financial mechanism plays, or can play, in transmitting government monetary policy into the market place. Whether it should be used, how it should be used, and whether it has been used sensibly are questions that need not concern us here. That the City provides the British Government with an efficient method of putting its interest rate, money supply and fiscal policies into action is hardly in dispute. A strict monetary policy is based on the premise that not only can changes in the supply of money have an impact on economic activity, and prices, but that they should be controlled in certain specified ways and on a regular basis by the central bank. Economists still argue about which money supply figures should be used as the basis of such a policy. They talk of M1, M3 and DCE[1]. All are different ways of measuring changes in the supply of money in the economy. But, whatever the definition chosen and whatever money supply policy decided upon, do the authorities want to have an influence on interest rates and on the supply of money, and can they? At present the answer is 'yes' on both counts.

Both the Chancellor of the Exchequer and the Bank of England have announced annual money supply targets, and two of the closest analysts of the money supply have summed up this attempt at monetary control in the following way:

> Many commentators fail to understand the extent to which short-term fluctuations of the money supply are outside the control of the central bank. The correct interpretation is usually to assume that the money supply is outside the central bank's control over the short term and that the bank is reacting to it being off target. If the money supply is increasing above target, the mechanism by which the bank attempts to reduce the monetary growth is by raising interest rates. Conversely if the money supply is below target, the bank will induce a reduction in interest rates. The Bank of England at present appears to consider that the way in which the money supply should be influenced is through the price mechanism of interest rates influencing several of the components of the money supply, rather than by attempting to purchase or sell specific quantities of gilt-edged stock.[2]

What levers does the Bank of England have at its disposal to do so? This brings us to the heart of the money market and to the weekly Treasury bill tender. This is one of the key instruments since it is the weekly issue of short-term (i.e. three months) bills on behalf of the government. It enables the

[1] M1 is the total of notes and coins in circulation plus private sector current accounts. M3 is the same as M1 plus all deposits, whether denominated in sterling or in currency, held by UK residents in both the public and private sectors. DCE, Domestic Credit Expansion, measures the money supply before it has been increased or reduced by a country's overseas payments.

[2] Gordon Pepper and Geoffrey Wood, *Too Much Money . . .?* (Institute of Economic Affairs, 1976)

government, in addition to the normal issues of government stock and the 'tap' stock already mentioned, to raise large amounts of short-term money, especially in periods of financial stringency when tax payments are being made. The amounts raised weekly in this fashion have sometimes reached £600 million. While the discount houses accept as an informal obligation that they will cover the whole of the tender, that is to guarantee that all the Treasury bills on offer will be taken up by them, the Bank of England in turn provides the discount houses with an assurance that if, on any particular day, the banks recall enough 'call money' to leave the houses 'short' at the end of the day's business, the Bank will provide the difference – at a price. The Bank in effect is acting as 'lender of last resort'. One of the main instruments in influencing short-term interest rates is the terms on which this official help is given.

We are now in a position to summarise the different ways in which the Bank of England can use this special relationship to shape the future course of interest rates and of the money supply.

First, the Bank can call for 'special deposits' from the banks, which in certain circumstances will lead the banks to call in large amounts of 'call money' from the discount houses. Credit becomes tighter and the Bank can decide whether and in what way and on what terms to relieve the shortage. Such a daily shortage can occur, even without design, through the accidental flow of the vast sums between the banks, the government and industry.

If the resultant shortage is passed on to the discount houses by the withdrawal of 'call money' by the banks, the Bank may decide to provide help – 'direct' or 'indirect', depending on the technical means available – on current terms. This indicates that the Bank is not dissatisfied with current rates of interest.

Second, the Bank can decide not to relieve a shortage (whether artificially produced or not) and can thus force the discount houses to borrow at a penal rate – normally for seven days and at Minimum Lending Rate (the replacement of the old Bank rate). This is a strong indicator (working directly on the commercial operations of the houses) that interest rates are too low.

Third, the Bank can also influence the weekly Treasury bill tenders of the discount market both by the above actions and by other means – especially the weekly chat which the Governor has with the Chairman and Deputy Chairman of the London Discount Market Association. Since May 1978, Minimum Lending Rate, which is announced every Thursday, has also been decided by the Bank of England. This remains the key rate in the market.[1]

Money, like water, rapidly finds its own level, so that the cost of money (that is, the rate of interest) in one City market quickly affects that in another. The government and its agencies thus have at their service not only a mechanism that raises vast sums of money for their own use, with a larger proportion of it in medium and long-term securities than in other countries, but one which can be used to transmit government policy on interest rates and money supply to the array of markets in money and securities that exist in the City.

It might be thought that a system which, on recent evidence, has been capable of raising close on £8 billion annually on behalf of the government would be fairly free from criticism. Yet the whole system seems to have attracted more criticism, the more money it has raised for the government. The fact is that some parts of the mechanism have not worked as well as they should in recent years. The Government Broker, for example, has on occasion innocently raised hopes which have been dashed within days or weeks by contradictory actions by the authorities – sometimes the Treasury, sometimes the Bank of England. Whether the culprit was the pressure of outside events or simply a lack of adequate communication – down the line from Treasury to Bank of England to Government Broker to jobbers – is difficult to judge. But the resulting impact on

[1]Between 9 October 1972 and 25 May 1978, Minimum Lending Rate was directly related to the average rate in which Treasury bills were allotted at the weekly tender. This was then discarded.

dealers in the market-place, and on their profitability, has not helped. But the basic criticism has come from outside the City itself and was summed up in one particular phrase used earlier but repeated many times in the summer of 1978 and later. The City institutions, it was said, were again conducting an investment strike.

The phrase was damaging shorthand for the fact that the authorities occasionally found it difficult to sell sufficient government stock to finance the difference between their expenditure and revenue, but it also implied that the investing institutions were deliberately holding off the market and thereby interfering with official monetary policy. In some critical versions collusion was hinted at, though this has been difficult to substantiate. With so many institutions involved in the gilt-edged market, all with different needs, different assumptions and different purposes, collusion would be hard to organise and harder to justify. There are, for example, 20,000 multi-member pension funds (of which over 1,600 are members of the National Association of Pension Funds), over 600 insurance and assurance companies, over 300 banking institutions, over 300 building societies, 11 discount houses, 250 investment trusts and 400 unit trusts, quite apart from foreign governments and foreign institutions. Yet it is not hard to understand why, if one investment manager comes to the reasonable conclusion that a budget, for example, is inflationary and foreign investors are expressing similar views on the foreign exchange market, others might form similar views and act accordingly. Investment managers often do think and act alike. When they do, their actions naturally affect interest rates and monetary policy. When, in addition, their actions run counter to a government's borrowing requirements and expectations, it is not surprising that a lengthy analysis, both of the role of the City institutions in national policy and, at a more technical level, of the methods by which government stock is offered on the market, should ensue. Two particular questions have been asked. Should investment managers have the ability to pursue their private and perfectly legitimate investment policies when these are in conflict with national objectives as perceived by government ministers? Secondly, at a more detailed level, is the existing system of issuing so-called 'tap' stocks capable of coping with official selling needs running into billions of pounds?

Although the charge of collusion has not been substantiated, the feeling that a strike of some kind, whether deliberate or otherwise, has taken place has persisted both in the press and, occasionally, in Parliament. Here again the evidence of a deliberate withdrawal of funds by the City has been difficult to pin down. One sector of the City in particular never goes on strike in its role of providing the government with regular investment funds. The discount market, for example, is obliged to 'cover the tender', that is to promise to take up all the three-month Treasury bills on offer at the weekly tender, running into £600 million a week at the peak of the government's borrowing period. Moreover, a subsequent analysis of institutional gilt-edged purchases and sales in the early summer of 1978, following what the City institutions generally felt was an inflationary budget, has not revealed any concerted action. City institutions had already provided £3 billion to the government in the first half of 1978. Moreover, sales of gilts by the government in the second and third quarters of 1978 were actually higher than in the first quarter and the quarterly percentage provided by the pension funds was higher in these two quarters than the average of the previous three years.

On the other hand, there is no doubt that marked swings in the buying pattern of City investment institutions do take place. In periods when the government has to raise billions in a specified time, there are bound to be weeks or months when the various City institutions are unwilling to buy government stock at the price prevailing in the market-place. This is what a free market is all about. But could the market be improved by changes in the official system of issuing so-called 'tap' stocks? Doubts have been expressed whether the 'tap' system, which was explained earlier, is really in the best interests of the authorities, since the timing of gilt-edged sales, and thus the initiative, is left largely in the hands of the investing public rather than the government. The horse has to be persuaded to go to the trough. It has also been argued that the 'tap' method has a bad habit of distorting the money supply figures by reflecting the buying pattern of investors rather than the needs of the authorities.

Above all, in order to tempt institutional investors back into the market, following some investing indecision, the need for the authorities to sell stock to cover their financing needs has led to the recurrent spectacle of short-term interest rates being raised sharply only to be followed by a gradual decline in rates as gilt-edged buying has been resumed. When, in the spring of 1979, the institutions once again rushed to buy government stock in just such a situation (to such an extent that a scramble developed on the third floor of the Bank of England, where applications were being lodged), it was not long before critics were asking whether it was really necessary to force bank borrowers to pay more for their overdrafts in order to offer sufficient inducements in the form of capital gains to tempt City investors to take up government stock. It was only a small step from this to the proposal that perhaps the American 'tender' method of issue, similar to that used in issuing short-term Treasury bills, might have solid advantages. This method, which allows the authorities to choose the timing and amount of individual issues of stock, while leaving the price to market tender, gives some of the initiative back to the authorities.

There are several variations of an issue of stock through a tender. The method already introduced by the Bank of England has a minimum price and is underwritten. The simplest method is to issue stock at the prices tendered, without a minimum price. The latter achieves one objective, if repeated on a regular basis: it enables the authorities to meet their borrowing needs as and when they occur. It cannot, however, guarantee the price of issue and it might achieve its objective at the expense of the existing jobbing system, since members of the market do not automatically receive issues of stock in a tender system.

These are not the only innovations tried or considered by the authorities. Partly-paid stocks, under which the amounts raised are simply payable in instalments over a period of months, have been used in efforts to smooth out the issuing process; so have variable bonds, where the interest rate varies according to the average of the Treasury bill discount rate.

These have helped in some circumstances and not in others.

Yet, whatever method is chosen, the fundamental problem remains. Since the early 1970s the government has needed to borrow billions of pounds annually in order to finance part of its expenditure. A borrower on this scale is bound to find the market troublesome from time to time. The British Government has been no exception, even though it has stacked the cards in its favour by excluding its own securities from capital gains tax after one year, and, in contrast with industrial firms, has not been deterred from borrowing at high interest rates since taxpayers or other investors ultimately foot the bill. Institutional investors, on the other hand, are custodians for shareholders, policyholders and pensioners. The directors and managers running these funds are responsible for safeguarding savings and for investing them wisely. If they feel, whether rightly or wrongly, that to put money into government stocks at the wrong price is against the future interests of their policyholders and of present and future pensioners, should they be blamed for taking a decision which upsets a Government's monetary policy? Some critics say 'yes' or at least suggest that there is another solution, pointing to the need for some official direction of institutional funds. We discussed this in Chapter 7 in the context of the need for industrial investment. The additional argument here is that the power of the City's institutional funds should not be allowed to interfere with national policies. Whether the official direction of funds would resolve the difficulties better than the market-place is, however, highly questionable. The main objections have been admirably set out by a Labour Treasury Minister:[1]

> Some participants in the debate have suggested that the answer would be for the Government to take powers to direct the investment of funds. But I do not think that that is an acceptable solution. First, it would not necessarily secure the desired result of greater investment going into the areas to which the Government thought priority ought to be given. For example, if institutions were forced to put a

[1] Rt Hon. Joel Barnett, Chief Secretary to the Treasury, 22 January 1979

certain percentage of new funds into a specified form of investment, there would be a consequent adjustment in the prices and yields of such investment which would deter other investors who were outside the control, such as private individuals and trusts, from investing in that area, and indeed might induce them to switch out of it. It is therefore very doubtful whether there would be a net increase in investment in the desired area.

. . . On the other hand, as Chief Secretary I am very conscious that the direction of institutional funds could lead to a claim on the Exchequer which could prove hard to resist. If the investment managers of a significant proportion of funds found that they were unable to meet their liabilities, and could show that this was because the direction of funds had resulted in their earning less on their assets than they otherwise would, they would clearly turn round to the Government of the day to try to persuade them that the Government ought to underwrite the funds. I have to concede that there might be some case in equity for doing that, but such underwriting is a thing which no Treasury Minister could contemplate with equanimity.

In fact the insurance companies (mainly life offices) and pension funds have in recent years already shifted a large share of their money into government hands, quite voluntarily, as their contribution to the financing of the government's borrowing requirements. The life insurance companies, for example, invested some 30 per cent of their new funds in government securities in the period from 1970 to 1975; by 1976, 1977 and the first half of 1978 the proportion had risen to 72 per cent, 64 per cent and 68 per cent respectively. Pension funds, who invest a lower proportion of their funds in gilt-edged, because of the nature of their future obligations, raised their share from 20 per cent in 1970–5 to 40 per cent, 35 per cent and 37 per cent respectively in 1976, 1977 and the first half of 1978. In spite of occasional blemishes or hiccups, this is a massive shift of resources through the mechanism of the City's markets.

Chapter 10

Commodities: Who Are the Speculators?

The price of tea, bread or coffee is rarely far from the stock in trade of the active politician of any party. Ever since commodity markets boomed in the wake of the world boom of 1971–4, few Labour politicians have hesitated to put the blame for soaring food prices where they instinctively believe it to lie: at the door of the international speculator in general and the City's commodity market dealers in particular. When prices in some markets were reported to have risen (or slumped) by as much as 10 per cent in the course of a day's dealings; when Rowntree Mackintosh could notch up subsequent losses of £30 million on cocoa dealing; when a leading newspaper, the *Guardian*, spoke of commodity speculators on the London market 'playing a major role in worsening both the rate of inflation and the balance of payments deficit'; and when the cornering of coffee in Brazil was again hinted at darkly; it was certain that political action would soon follow.

The Labour Party made the most of it during the 1974 election campaigns and the government were soon under pressure to set up an official inquiry to establish, once and for all, how far speculators had been distorting the markets. Soon a Select Committee of the House of Lords was looking into the allegations, and much else too. Mr Harold Lever, a member of the Labour cabinet, was given special responsibility for commodity market affairs; and a Labour back-bencher was introducing a private members' Bill to prohibit speculation in both currencies and commodities.

The hunt was on, but the quarry proved more elusive than had been expected. In the first place, what exactly were they looking for? What was a speculator? When did an ordinary dealer become a speculator? 'If buying in anticipation of a price increase is "speculation" then all housewives have been guilty of it. If selling in anticipation of a price fall is "speculation" then all farmers, market gardeners, greengrocers, etc. likewise.' Thus said the City Capital Market Committee in its evidence to the Wilson Committee, putting its finger on one of the weak links in the political argument. It was not long before Mr Lever himself was nailing some of the wilder half-truths:

> It does not lie within Britain's power, acting on her own, to secure healthy commodity markets free from excessive speculation. . . . An attempt by the Government, or the Bank of England, to eliminate all speculation on the London commodity markets would be ineffective. The markets would move to a country which allowed the speculator to perform his function of insuring producers and consumers against adverse price fluctuation. The real loser would be our balance of payments to which the London commodity markets make a valuable contribution, amounting to around £100 millions directly in an average year.

The Bank of England later estimated them at over £200 million.

As commodity prices waned, the political pressure eased – until the next time. The very word 'speculator' leaves an uneasy feeling in most people's minds and we shall have more to say about it in a moment. The pity is that the role of the commodity markets rarely gets the sustained attention it deserves, yet they spring directly from London's original place on the Thames, her proximity to the sea and, above all, Britain's growing reliance on imports to feed herself and keep her industry going. It is not by chance that both the markets and several of the offices and warehouses serving them are so close to the river and the Pool of London. That was their original purpose: to bring in, value, and offer a market-place for the continuing inflow of food and raw materials. By the nineteenth century this activity had become an essential cog in Britain's world role, linking the commodity-producing countries of the Empire with Britain's industrial machine, using British ships, British insurance and British banks.

Moreover, from these markets near the river commodities were re-exported to other industrial nations. Through its commodity markets, Britain was not only providing itself with essential food and supplies, but also acting as a redistribution centre for other countries and making a useful income from her services. Many of these activities have continued but, while the physical movement of commodities has declined, and while re-exports are no longer so important, London has maintained her international supremacy by increasingly substituting paper for commodities in several markets (an entitlement to commodities instead of actual goods) and by deliberately fostering futures markets. I will now consider how this supremacy looks today.

It is not hard to locate the fish market in Billingsgate. Charles Dickens too, in *The Uncommercial Traveller,* found it easy to sniff out which churches were near which markets:

> In the churches about Mark Lane there was a dry whiff of wheat; and I accidentally struck an airy sample of barley out of an aged hassock in one of them. From Rood Lane to Tower Street, and thereabouts, there was often a subtle flavour of wine; sometimes tea. One church, near Mincing Lane, smelt like a druggist's drawer. Behind the Monument, the service had a flavour of damaged oranges, which, a little farther down towards the river, tempered into herrings, and gradually toned into a cosmopolitan blast of fish.

The smells are now less aggressive; but the markets in these and many other commodities are virtually where they were over a century ago. During the nineteenth century the Commercial Sale Rooms came to house most of the leading markets and were known generally simply as 'Mincing Lane'. When they were finally destroyed by enemy bombs in 1941, they moved (temporarily, it was thought) alongside the Rubber Exchange in Plantation House, also in Mincing Lane. By

1945, however, an amalgamation had taken place and a consolidated London Commodity Exchange had emerged, which
was to continue until the commodity futures markets decided
to find their own home in the autumn of 1973 in the Corn
Exchange building, a small block away in Mark Lane. Dickens
would have regarded it as the same parish. Still not far away
are the other commodity markets, the London Metal
Exchange in Whittington Avenue and the home, including
EEC, grain futures market in the Baltic Exchange.

These markets vary. Some sell standard commodities such as
sugar, cocoa, coffee and the non-ferrous metals without the
commodities appearing in the markets or on the exchange.
Some handle commodities, where quality is important or the
size of consignments small, by individual auctions. Some
markets where quality varies – such as in spices, herbs, gums,
nuts, fibres, etc. – conduct their dealings in sale-rooms. Some
use the outcry system, where the spectator is both deafened and
baffled by the competitive and incomprehensible bids. Some,
as we have said, take place in the 'shabby traditional' surround-
ings of Plantation House. Others in the eye-catching,
computerised, televised, over-colourful atmosphere of the new
Corn Exchange building. Yet all are providing what they have
always provided: a market-place where prices can move freely;
an international yardstick for commodities that may not even
touch Britain's shores; and, increasingly, futures markets to
enable manufacturers, and others, to eliminate some of the
trading risks of a free market.

The question is how they compare with commodity
markets elsewhere. The decline in re-exports, which accelerated
during the last war and in the early post-war years, as countries
were forced to obtain their food and raw materials direct from
the producing countries, naturally led to the growth of local
markets. It was not long, therefore, before these producer
markets had in some cases a higher turnover than London.
This is particularly true of the wool market in Sydney, the
rubber market in Singapore, the tin market in Penang and
the fur auctions in Leningrad, Copenhagen and New York.
Moreover, because of the huge needs of the American domestic
market and, in some cases, because of the large output in the

United States itself, turnover in some commodities in both Chicago and New York far outstrips that in London. There are also many more futures markets in the United States than in London, but most of them are dealing with domestic business and naturally reflect domestic conditions. In Europe too, the world's largest importing area, commodity rivals flourish in Hamburg, Rotterdam, Amsterdam, Paris and Le Havre.

Yet, in spite of this world-wide competition, London's markets have done more than survive. They can claim to be the dominant influence in more commodities internationally than any other centre. In the futures markets, London prices are now a major factor in transactions in copper, lead, cocoa and African-produced coffee, and are influential in both sugar and silver. On the spot markets London is also recognised as a leading influence in copper, lead, tin, zinc and silver, and is a key factor in world prices of sugar and cocoa. Outside London, the Liverpool cotton trade, the Dundee jute market and the Bradford wool market maintain international connections. Turnover in New York, Chicago and London can change dramatically from year to year, and from one commodity to another. But in the futures markets, London's pre-eminence seems assured in the world's main commodities. Turnover in futures can often be greater than the total of world production in any one year. Three years ago, the London futures market in cocoa had a turnover four times the world cocoa crop. Turnover in copper futures in London is often the equivalent of the total world output. Members of the London Metal Exchange estimate that between 70 and 75 per cent of their business is generated overseas. The potential threat from the variety of new futures instruments recently introduced on the Chicago market, I shall be examining in Chapter 16.

About half of London's futures business now comes from overseas. This is the main distinction between London, on one hand, and Chicago and New York, on the other. Moreover, London has two particular advantages over American markets. One is that New York and Chicago put a limit on daily price movements and, when they have been reached, freeze activity until the following day, whereas in London, apart from sugar, the daily fluctuations allowed are wider and the subsequent halt in dealings much shorter (usually half an hour). On the London Metal Exchange there are no fluctuation limits at all. Secondly, as in the foreign exchange market, London sits comfortably astride the world's time zones, managing to keep in touch with the Far Eastern market in the morning, and making contact with North and South America in the late afternoon and evening: essential links for those attempting to establish world prices.

All markets, of course, face the challenge of big producers, possible producer cartels, government purchasers and other structural changes in the commodity field. New ideas are being discussed within UNCTAD, the United Nations Conference on Trade and Development, and the so-called North–South dialogue for the stabilisation of commodity prices. Governments and government agencies are likely to intervene more rather than less in regulating commodity prices in future. Certainly the example of the oil producers in OPEC and the ambitions of the developing world are bound to encourage further experiments of the same kind. The only question is whether the free markets, whether in London or elsewhere, will have a part to play in establishing world prices. Apart from oil, recent experience strongly suggests that, even in cases where large producers and large consumers have by-passed the free markets, marginal supplies have often been used to establish world price levels and futures markets still have a significant role to play.

The importance of the futures markets in London can be gauged from recent official estimates of the foreign earnings (invisible earnings) of all London's commodity markets. The inquiry was undertaken by the Bank of England with the co-operation of the various markets. The results were impressive by any standards. For 1974/5 foreign earnings from physical (that is, spot) trade was estimated at over £90 millions. Futures transactions produced virtually the same figure, i.e. over £90 millions, making a total for the London markets as a whole of £190 millions. For 1975/6 the total earnings were 'rather larger, probably within the range of £200–£250 million'. The Bank of England points out that large fluctuations are to be expected from year to year, both in the totals and in the split between spot and futures business. But the size of futures business in these two years is a testimony to the international role now established by London's futures markets.

I have talked of futures in general terms so far, and have also discussed speculation. It is time to look more closely at both, for it is here that the heart of any political debate lies. As we have seen, the City seems to be one vast market-place or, to be more accurate, several different market-places in money, gold foreign exchange and commodities of all kinds. And the main feature of a free market is that some prices go up and some go down. These changes in price act as signals to different parts of a free enterprise economy, encouraging some industries to buy more (when prices have dropped) and some to buy less (when prices have risen). These reactions, of course, are not always so straightforward. Occasionally fears and expectations interfere, persuading businessmen to buy *more*, rather than less, when prices rise because they expect them to rise still further later. But, whatever their immediate impact, changes in prices – whether of money or commodities – can be troublesome and, above all, costly.

This is particularly true of industries where the time-lag between buying a basic commodity, having it shipped from overseas, and then converting it into a finished product is lengthy. In that crucial period, the price can soar or slump, leading to profits or losses, sometime before manufacture has even begun.

These risks are highest in commodities produced thousands of miles away overseas – such as cocoa, rubber, sugar and copper. The London markets in these commodities long ago produced the answer to the problem, with the introduction of 'forward' or 'futures' markets alongside the normal or 'spot' markets.

As a result spot and forward contracts have become familiar jargon in several City markets. We now need to define what is meant by them. A spot price is the price of rubber, wheat, copper, etc, for immediate delivery. It implies the immediate physical delivery of a commodity of an agreed quality or standard at an agreed price. It also implies the availability of supplies. Spot markets are also referred to as 'cash', 'physical' or even 'delivery' markets, thus putting the emphasis on the delivery of actual commodities. This is also true of certain forward markets where a forward price implies the delivery of a commodity on an agreed date in the future at a price agreed now. These transactions naturally refer to the delivery of actual commodities but, since this is not really necessary in order to provide traders with an insurance (or 'hedging', which I will explain in a moment) against future fluctuations in the spot price, the habit has grown up of trading in futures contracts which are simply *promises* to deliver goods in future and which can be mutually cancelled before actual delivery.

To see exactly how a manufacturer can benefit from a forward or futures market, we need to take a few concrete examples, such as a chocolate manufacturer 'hedging' his cocoa requirements, a tyre manufacturer 'hedging' his rubber needs or an electrical company 'hedging' its copper supplies. In each case the firm will have to buy, say, £100,000 worth of its main commodity and to assure itself first that supplies will be forthcoming and second that changes in commodity prices before the completion of its main products will not land it in unforeseen losses. The tyre manufacturer, therefore, *buys* £100,000 of rubber in the spot market at 66p a ton and, at the same time, *sells* the same *quantity* of rubber forward for delivery in three months' time also at, say 66p. The spot market assures the company's supplies; the futures market ensures that no matter what happens to the price of rubber in the three months, the company will be unaffected. If the spot price declines (thereby producing a paper loss, since the company will have bought its supplies at too high a price), the company will be able to buy at the lower price to fulfil its forward contract, making an identical futures profit to its spot loss. The same holds in reverse. If the price rises, the spot profit will then be offset by the corresponding futures loss. The company might then feel that it would have done better had it not entered the futures market at all. So it would. But it would have been involving itself in a quite different business – taking a view of a commodity (and therefore accepting an additional business risk) rather than confining itself to the risks of a manufacturing enterprise.

What happens when a manufacturer begins to take a view of the market and to act on it was graphically illustrated in *The Economist* in a report of Rowntree's cocoa losses in 1973:

> Rowntree has a cocoa buyer whose job it is to study the market for this important input while others do the chocolate making. As the price rose in 1973 (from £330 a tonne in December 1972, which was already high), he expected a turnaround to come – and gambled on it by selling forward cocoa that he hadn't yet bought. But the price took off with the world boom, and hit nearly £600 a tonne in mid-1973 (still only half the peak of a year later). Rowntree panicked and closed out its futures contract as quickly as it could, driving the price up against itself. Its next annual accounts revealed losses of £32m. simply on transactions in the cocoa terminal (or physical) markets.

Rowntree's were not alone in suffering commodity losses. William Baird lost £1½ million the same year. Dunlop lost nearly £5 million a year later. More recently Amalgamated Metal have announced losses on commodity trading of some £24 million. These upsets occurred in various markets, covering cocoa, rubber, sugar, coffee, lead and zinc. In some cases dealers judged the market wrongly; in others suppliers defaulted.

I have so far explained the uses of spot and futures markets. Before going further, however, we should pause for a moment to consider the relationship between spot and forward. At any one time there is a price for immediate delivery and prices indicate the market's expectations – about demand and supply, and about economic, financial and political influences affecting both. But there is also a fundamental connection between these prices – the cost to the trader of holding stocks for one, two or three months. Even if the spot price of rubber is expected to remain unchanged over the next three months, the three months forward price will be higher than the spot price, reflecting the cost of borrowing the money to acquire the rubber (the rate of interest), the cost of holding the rubber in a warehouse, as well as the cost of insuring it against theft, etc.

These costs, therefore, have to be taken into account in assessing a forward or futures price before any attempt is made to work out the market's expectations about the course of rubber prices over the next few months. If the forward price is lower than the spot price (known in the market as backwardation), this often reflects a shortage of immediate supplies; it may also indicate that the market expects the current demand to decline or the tightness of supplies to ease.

The reader may have noticed that so far I have used the words forward and 'futures' as though they were interchangeable. But, whereas a forward contract implies the delivery of a specific quantity of a commodity on a particular date, a futures contract is usually a promise to deliver in the future which might or might not be fulfilled depending on the agreement of the parties to the bargain. Thus a market in futures is far more flexible, and, not surprisingly, now forms the basis of most active commodity centres.[1] Successful futures markets depend on a high turnover in order to smooth out the prices at which transactions take place; and this high turnover can be helped by the attraction of traders who enter the market in the hope of making a profit from the movements in prices: in other words speculators.

That is an emotive word, so we need to be clear what we mean by a speculator and what role he plays in the commodity markets. The usual description is of a dealer whose sole purpose is to make money out of buying and selling. But the Concise Oxford Dictionary adds the other essential ingredient: one who 'engages in commercial operation that involves risk or loss'. In other words, a speculator hopes for a profit but runs a risk of losing his money. And it is in his role as an additional risk taker that the speculator makes his main contribution to the commodity markets. One of the best explanations of precisely this role was given by Mr Harold Lever in the speech already referred to:[2]

---

[1] The London Metal Exchange, however, does not trade in futures as defined here. It is a combined forward and delivery market and, in all LME contracts, delivery in warehouse is implicit.

[2] Conference on the Professional use of the Commodity Markets, London, 27 May 1976

To plan his business the producer needs an assurance of the price which he will get, and the consumer of the price which he will have to pay. This assurance can often be secured through forward trading in the commodity markets . . . The part of the insurer is played by the speculator very often. Contrary to a widely held misconception, the speculator can, and does, often lose money as well as make it. In most political arguments, the wicked speculator is always hypothesised as a guy who has managed to get away with enormous profits at the expense of a victim public, but the speculator's role is to take the risk both ways. When he loses, he takes on himself a loss which the producers or consumers would otherwise have had to shoulder by selling for less, or by having to pay more, than they had allowed for in their business calculations. The profit of the speculator is, in effect, the premium which the producers or consumers by agreement – by free agreement – pay to obtain the certainty on price. Provided that the speculator acts as an insurer in this broadly beneficial way, his function is healthy and we would be foolish to eliminate him.

In short, the speculator increases the turnover in the spot and futures markets and thereby smooths out price movements. But there are occasions when speculators, because of their strength and their conviction, can move the spot price or the futures price too far in one direction. This was also the view of the Lords Select Committee on Commodity Prices [1] which, having listened closely to views on both sides, came to this conclusion:

From their evidence it is impossible to say what the average effect of speculation may be. The nearest to a consensus which emerges from the evidence is that in normal times speculation is probably a stabilising factor. But if there are strong independent causes of major swings, speculation may add to rather than reduce their scale.

[1] House of Lords Select Committee on Commodity Prices (HMSO), vol i, pp. lxxi–lxxiii, 18 May 1977

The Select Committee also put its finger on a minor, though worrying, point. It reported that in the past two years more and more interest had been shown in these markets as a straight investment and hedge against inflation by investors not directly concerned with commodities, such as insurance companies, pension funds and even private investors. But the Bank of England expert before the Committee reported that the amount of money coming into the markets from this new source was not high enough 'to cause immediate concern'. The Committee rightly suggested that this new influence should be carefully watched (the Bank of England subsequently issued a clear warning against excessive speculation in zinc). But I believe that the dominant conclusion to emerge from this detailed inquiry was that, while speculators (especially ill informed ones) can push the market farther in one direction than it would otherwise have gone, these movements are temporary. Speculators, whatever the pressure from them, cannot add a *permanent* bias to prices, upwards or downwards, for at the point at which they decide to buy or sell (that is to make a profit or take a loss) their influence is immediately reversed. If they are right and make a profit, they act as stabilisers. If they are wrong and have to take a loss, they are certainly a bad influence on prices but are unlikely to remain in business, particularly as speculators.

Chapter 11

Ships and Planes:
The World's Charterer?

Ships have been coming up the Thames for at least two thousand years. London itself emerged from the first crossing over the river, and shipping still plays a large part in the City's activities. What is perhaps a little surprising is the involvement of the City in shipping that comes nowhere near the Thames, or even any other British port. For Britain's merchant fleet, many of whose offices lie around Leadenhall Street and St Mary Axe, is still the world's third largest (after Liberia and Japan) as well as the youngest, and both the Baltic Exchange and Lloyd's Register of Shipping provide essential services to shipping fleets everywhere. Britain's share in world trade may have declined; her involvement in the services that back up the world's ships has not.

These shipping offices are still surrounded by insurance companies and banks. The Baltic and the General Council of British Shipping are virtually side by side in St Mary Axe. Lloyd's is just across the other side of Leadenhall Street in Lime Street. The Commercial Union towers above the P & O offices. More important, all of them are in the midst of a foreign shipping community, for there are probably more overseas shipping companies represented here than anywhere else in the world. Greeks and Norwegians predominate. There are about 180 Greek shipping agencies alone. Even Liberian-registered companies (representing the largest merchant fleet in the world) are here, whatever their basic nationality, for they can get money and insurance and service their ships all within

walking distance of their offices. More than that, a short
walk takes them to the floor of the Baltic Exchange, of which
either they or their agents are members. Their predecessors
have been doing the same thing for well over a century and a
half.

The Baltic (short for the Baltic Mercantile and Shipping
Exchange) provides, like the Stock Exchange and Lloyd's, one
of the most active 'floors' in the City. Surrounded by marble
pillars, this vast echoing chamber is crowded twice a day with
ship brokers and agents – some seeking a ship for their cargo,
others a cargo for their ship, all intent on assessing the world's
shipping prospects for themselves or their clients. Shipping
exchanges exist in New York and Tokyo, but these are essentially
telephone markets where the bulk of the business concerns
American and Japanese shipping business, respectively, with
the rest of the world. The floor of the Baltic, however, not only
provides an alternative to the telephone and telex but is the
best clearing house for shipping intelligence in the world, and
as such attracts business in cross-trades that never touch Britain's
shores or use British ships. This floor is animated between ·12
and 1.30 and again between 4 and 4.30. But brokers and agents
are active between their offices well before this period and well
after the ship's bell sounds and the lights are lowered to mark
the end of official business on the Exchange at 4.30. Some
brokers will have been up since 5 a.m. dealing with Japanese
brokers from home and they may be grappling on the phone
with American brokers at midnight. An 18-hour day, with
strange bursts of telephone and telex business at odd hours, is
by no means unusual. As in commodities and foreign
exchange, shipbrokers in London have the advantage of
operating in the middle of the world's time zones; they also
have the personal problem of how to fit work in with a normal
home life.

This international flavour – if not the technological communications that now go with it – has been a feature of the
Baltic since it first moved out of the coffee-houses of the City
in the seventeenth century. Ships' captains and merchants were
in the habit of combining business with pleasure at such places
as the Jerusalem Coffee House and the Virginia and Baltic,

indicating the American colonies and the Baltic seaboard as the main sources of business. Even before the end of the Napoleonic wars, business had expanded to such an extent that it was being undertaken in one place – the Antwerp Tavern in Threadneedle Street, which was renamed simply 'The Baltic'. By 1823 a Baltic Club had been established with rules to regulate business; in 1851 a move was made to new premises in South Sea House; and in 1903 the Baltic merged with the recently established London Shipping Exchange (primarily concerned with the liner trade) and moved again – this time to its present premises in St Mary Axe.

Members of the Baltic have been undertaking much the same kind of business throughout these years. Whether under sail, steam or oil, ships have been put in touch with cargoes as quickly as possible in every port in the world, through a contact between broker and agent in London. British trade may once have dominated the Baltic as it did the world's sea routes a hundred years ago; now the Baltic has moved with the times and gone international. Chartering agents, representing merchants or other interests who charter ships to transport their cargo, are concerned with trade in all parts of of the globe. So are the brokers who represent the shipowners. Some broking firms represent both charterers and shipowners, again both at home and abroad. In all, there are about 700 corporate members and some 2,500 individual members. About 300 are foreign, including both Russian and Chinese.

The marrying of a cargo to a ship is simple to describe but complex to execute. Apart from the 'liner' trade, where ships are keeping to schedules, there are thousands of 'tramps' constantly searching for cargoes. The process could be both chancy and chaotic without a central point where the two – or at least their representatives – can meet. Even then, the details can be overwhelming. The charterer wants to know, ahead of time, which ships will be arriving and leaving which ports. The shipbroker, on behalf of the owner, will want to know whether it is worthwhile taking this cargo to Australia rather than that to the United States, and only when he has worked out return cargoes or onward cargoes to yet another port can he make any

assessment. Both sides need early information and full information – all the possible options open to them. The Baltic, by its very
nature, especially its provision of shipping intelligence on an
international scale, attempts to disentangle some of the difficulties. But the final decision lies between charterer and shipbroker. Here is the daily process seen through the eyes of a
former chairman of the Baltic Exchange:[1]

By constant contact with their fellow brokers members are
able to maintain a clear idea of what ships are being fixed,
what cargoes are offering and how the freight market is
fluctuating. Furthermore they learn quickly what ports are
congested, when ships are scarce, where strikes threatened or
taking place. When, therefore, a broker has to propose
business for a particular ship, he knows immediately what
places to beware of, where the most likely area of employment will be and which chartering agents to talk to about
suitable business.

Similarly a chartering agent, who wishes to find a ship
for his cargo, will quickly be able to find out what ships
are either in or trading to the right part of the world and
will know or can find out which brokers represent those
ships. The shipbroker, having discovered what business is
available will, by means of calculated estimates, decide
what voyage is most likely to show his principal the best
profit. With their encyclopedic knowledge of port charges,
costs of loading and discharging, as well as the likely time
involved in these operations, the cost of bunkers and the
running costs of ships, they have great expertise in making
these calculations.

Negotiations will then take place with the chartering
agent either on the floor of the Exchange or by telephone,
each side of course being in telephonic or telex communication with his principal. Firm offers may be made by either
side with a time limit for the reply. During this period the
side making the offer may not attempt to place the business
or to fix the ship elsewhere even if a better proposal is

[1] Mr M. T. Turnbull, Rio de Janeiro, June 1974

received. When verbal agreement is reached it is binding even though the confirmatory Charter Party may not be signed until much later.

The result of these deals is an agreed rate at which the freight will be carried. Hundreds of such deals emerge daily and weekly and make up the fluctuating freight rates in the various trades on the Baltic. As we have said, in most other centres at least one side of every deal is usually domestic. In London this is not necessarily so. The result is that Baltic members can claim to undertake the great majority of the world's freight fixtures. It does other things too, and again on an international scale. Probably half the world's transactions in sale and purchase are handled by Baltic brokers. And, considering what a dominant role commodities still play in world trade, it is not unexpected to find the London Grain Futures Market as part of the Exchange. Here again almost half of the members of the Grain and Feed Trade Association which runs it are from outside Britain and over forty different countries are represented on it. In addition, and this is another offshoot of the shipping side of the Baltic, more marine arbitrations take place in London than anywhere else, since charters concluded anywhere in the world usually specify English law and arbitration in London.

Finally, the Baltic has spawned a new market since the war, doing for aviation what it had already been doing for shipping for centuries. It was natural that people in the transport business should be aware of a quicker alternative and it is said that the first inquiries about the chartering of aircraft found their way onto the Baltic as early as 1925. What was probably the first 'air charter party' was signed in February 1928 to cover a return flight of cargo between Croydon and Cologne. It took another ten years, however, before the idea of forming an air section of the Baltic began to mature. Then the war intervened and not until 1948 was the idea revived and an advisory committee finally set up. The following February the present Airbrokers Association was formed and the Baltic Exchange air market was formally established.

Looking back, it is instructive to see the trials and errors of a new market, trying one thing, moving to another, sometimes hitting immediately on business that would survive a quarter of a century. I had the good fortune to see this particular market formed and to watch its first tentative steps. This is how I saw it nearly thirty years ago:[1]

> Air chartering is still in its infancy. Trade is generally spas-modic, but already a few definite markets have been established. Air brokers have come to expect early fruit to be flown in during the spring and summer. Last year there were apricots and grapes from Spain, cherries from Italy, and mandarines from Spain in the autumn. Strawberries picked in the South of France in the evening were in Covent Garden by four o'clock the following morning. Dakota aircraft brought berry fruits from Holland. The striking thing was that as soon as a large cargo arrived by sea, retail prices fell and flying ceased abruptly. Air freight rates were too high. . . . More urgent cargoes were replacement parts for ships. In 1947 a ship's propeller shaft was slung beneath a Halifax aircraft as an experiment and flown to a vessel in Singapore. The shipowner was saved a good deal of money in port dues and similar operations have developed con-siderably. Spare parts have been flown to Deauville, Sydney, Santos and, especially, the Far East. Oil drilling equipment has been carried to the Middle East.

Over the years the aircraft have changed and new business has developed but it is surprising how many of the original cargoes still persist. The Halifaxes have gone, the Dakotas (originally bought as war surplus for £5,000) have virtually disappeared and even Viscounts are not as numerous. As at the beginning, the pool of aircraft available for charter tends to depend on the replacement policy of the airlines. When the jumbos were introduced a few years back, many more Boeing 707s and Douglas DC8s became available for charter. But some aircraft nowadays are immediately available when new, especially the executive jets. Ships' spare parts (as well as ship's crews) are still flown round the world, but they have now been

[1] *Manchester Guardian*, 28 February 1949

joined by package-tour holidaymakers. The Baltic, however, is still at the heart of all these developments, with over 100 aircraft-operating companies represented from all parts of the globe. The Exchange believes that it is now undertaking at least three-quarters of the world's air freight fixtures.

In all these ways the Baltic has maintained its international flavour. So have other shipping service institutions nearby. Ship management and consultancy services are also available on a world-wide basis. The shipowner, it is said, has only to make three decisions in connection with a ship – when to buy, when to charter out and when to sell. But, over the period of twenty years that he possesses such an expensive piece of equipment, he can go bankrupt through a wrong decision at any time. The large groups should be able to look after themselves, but the small shipowners can lean on the advice and expertise of a 'ship management' company, of which there are several in the Square Mile, specialising in world-wide operations. Lloyd's Register of Shipping, the oldest and largest of the shipping classification societies, is also no more than a block away from the Baltic in Fenchurch Street. Its purpose is simple: to assess and classify the world's ships while under construction and throughout their working life. The phrase 'AI at Lloyd's' is a direct reflection of the high standards upheld by the society, which is both independent and non-commercial. It publishes a unique list of all ocean-going merchant fleets in the world. Not only does it have a large team of surveyors employed in London but it has more trained experts in all the ports of the world than all the other classification societies put together.

Again the emphasis is international, and, not surprisingly, the foreign earnings from these varied shipping activities in London has been impressive. The latest estimates of the foreign income of the Baltic, for example, show that the figure of £155 millions for 1977 was roughly three times the figure four years earlier and five times that nine years earlier. Lloyd's Register of Shipping, with a total foreign income of £23 millions in 1977, can claim to have nearly doubled it in two years and to have multiplied it by seven times in nine years.

It is clear, however, that these shipping earnings levelled off from about 1976 onwards. When can the expansion be resumed? I write in depressing times for ships and those who have dealings with them. The world's shipyards are a dismal sight; the laid-up shipping remains widespread. The world boom of the early 1970s reached unprecedented heights and so did the demand for shipping, leading to overoptimism, overordering and oversubsidisation. But doubts began to creep in throughout 1973, when the world economy was clearly entering a recession. The sharp rise in oil prices at the end of that year was the last straw, pushing the world's economy into depression and the shipping industry with it. The supply of ships was far greater than the demand for their services. The tanker market naturally received the worst of the subsequent buffeting.

In the ten years before the recent slump world sea-borne trade grew at an annual average rate of 8 per cent in volume and 11 per cent in ton miles. The difference was accounted for by the faster growth in crude-oil shipping and thus in the average length of voyages. In fact oil is now the dominant cargo, accounting for 40 per cent of the total tonnage and up to 55 per cent of ton-miles annually. Oil tankers account for half the world fleet. Moreover, recent oil discoveries in Alaska, the North Sea and Mexico – all quite close to major consuming areas – suggest that future demands on oil tankers will be lower than in the past, with the break-even point in the demand and supply of oil tanker tonnage being reached after that for dry cargo.

In these circumstances both the new and growing competition in shipping and the moves towards protectionism everywhere have sharpened considerably. Competition has arisen in three new areas: the large new oil-producing countries; the developing countries; and the Soviet bloc. Kuwait and Saudi Arabia, the richest of the oil states, were bound to consider ship owner-ship to carry their own oil, but Kuwait seems to be moving into dry cargo too. Others, like Iran, Nigeria and Algeria, are likely to follow. Some countries, such as Hong Kong, Singapore, Taiwan and Korea, have taken advantage of the troubled shipping companies of the West and bought cheaply. Other developing countries have moved into shipping for other reasons – because of their poverty and their dependence on the Western nations. They have also introduced discriminatory devices of all kinds, including cargo reservation and flag discrimination. Finally, Soviet Russia is now a major shipping power and is already firmly established in some regional trades, undercutting major liner trades by up to 30 per cent in some areas. The upshot is that both the pattern and size of the world's merchant fleet is changing. Both trends suggest the onset of further discrimination and restrictionism. Nor is it confined to the developing world. One of the worst offenders in shipping is the United States, which has been restricting cargoes to its own ships for years and, through the Department of Justice, seems bent on breaking up the liner conferences.

The City's involvement in shipping is bound to be affected by the underutilisation of capacity, which may well extend into the early 1980s, as well as the shifting forms of competition that are accompanying it. The shipping offices in St Mary Axe and along Leadenhall Street are geared both to Britain's and to the world's shipping prospects. If Britain's competitive position is undermined, the head offices of the leading British lines will immediately reflect it. If world shipping remains depressed, this will be reflected in the international services provided by the Baltic Exchange, Lloyd's Register of Shipping, and the hundreds of management companies represented in the City.

The real danger is that the current underutilisation of world shipping will bring in its wake trade protectionism, competitive depreciations of currencies and mercantilism of the worst kind – a climate that would hardly encourage the open competition in world shipping on which the fortunes of markets like the Baltic have been firmly based.

Chapter 12

Foreign Exchange: Where Are The Gnomes?

A market in which some of the world's leading banks can lose between £200 and £300 million and on which the fortunes of the world's leading currencies can be charted, hour by hour and minute by minute, is obviously one to watch. The City's foreign exchange market may complain at some of the political barbs aimed at it; it can hardly complain of any lack of attention from the press or television. At the height of every currency crisis, the television cameras have probed into the main dealing rooms on a daily basis. Buttons have been pushed; telephones clutched; lights have winked; and dealers have shouted unintelligibly round the world – all in the interest of instant news and comment. Yet is this feverish activity aimed solely at legitimate international trade – lubricating the efforts of honest traders round the world – or is it just the tip of a gigantic gambling casino, the home of gnomes and speculators whose only purpose is to undermine the pound one week, the lira or the dollar the next, and to line their own pockets in the process? When leading members of the Labour Party call for the strangling, if not the outright abolition, of a market which has a daily turnover of close on £25 billion,[1] it is time to disentangle myth from reality.

The foreign exchange market – where one currency is ex-

---

[1] See article in *Euromoney*, April 1979, which estimated London's daily turnover at $50 billion, New York's at $40 billion, Frankfurt's $10 billion and Tokyo's $2 billion.

changed for another at rates which fluctuate every minute – is not what it was. Just within living memory it was a market in which the clearing banks played hardly any part and which met on the steps of the Royal Exchange, opposite the Bank of England, only twice a week. Those who met in this way were the representatives of the larger merchant banks; their purpose was basically to buy and sell foreign bills of exchange and, at the same time, to consider rates of exchange and credit between the various monetary centres until they met again. It was a leisurely contrast to the technological market which now links Tokyo with New York, Singapore with Frankfurt, Paris with Hong Kong and London with them all and it came to an end in 1914. Thereafter, the incursion of the clearing banks into foreign trade financing, the growing need for a forward market amid the currency uncertainties of the interwar years, as well as the improvement in communications between the leading financial centres (primarily London, New York and Paris) – all led to the expansion of the foreign exchange market and the need for quite a different structure. This developed slowly during the 1920s and 1930s, but by the start of World War II over 140 banks and large firms in London were linked on a daily basis to thirty brokers acting as intermediaries.

Between 1939 and 1951 the London exchange market was virtually closed – banks obtaining their requirements through the Bank of England. This was a period of strict exchange control and little flexibility was allowed. Gradually, however, the banks were encouraged to do more business among themselves, a forward market was reintroduced and the margins between which rates could fluctuate were widened. Then, in December 1951, an embryo exchange market was once again allowed. Four broking firms restarted the old mechanism linking the authorised banks in a network of dealing reminiscent of pre-war days. I can well remember seeing one of the broking firms begin its operations, struggling to make a market in forward dollars, in a bare room above a hairdresser's shop in Bishopsgate. Since those early days of renewed dealings the structure has remained much the same, but the techniques, the equipment, the turnover, and above all the methods of communication have been transformed.

There are now nearly 270 banks in London authorised to deal in foreign exchange, linked to fifteen broking firms. Of the 250 authorised dealers, about 50 or 60 are very active.[1] Each has a remarkably well equipped dealing room, with dealers sitting at several desks, each specialising in particular currencies. Each desk will have its own switchboard with links to the brokers, the banks, the Bank of England (which has its own dealing room), and the leading financial centres abroad. Telex machines provide additional links with New York, Singapore, Tokyo and so on. One of the active dealing rooms of the main banks can clock up between 500 and 1,000 international telephone calls or telex messages every day. Its daily turnover could reach 700-800 million dollars. These dealers – whether in London, New York or Tokyo – are engaged in simple operations. They are trying to obtain the best exchange rate for their clients as quickly as possible.

Let us take two different views of the same scene, one from the outside, one from a dealer himself. First a television commentator, explaining the connection between a demand for foreign currency from tourists ('getaway people') and the hubbub of a dealer's room:[2]

The link between 'getaway people' and huddles of City gents, motioning and shouting at one another in a language as unintelligible as that of bookies and tick-tack men at Kempton, is not, really, all that obvious. But where there is muck, there is money. And where there is mayhem, there is foreign money. They look cuckoo, shouting prices at each other, and at others on the end of phones in faraway countries. They are called foreign exchange dealers. They deal in millions. Millions of pounds, dollars, kroner, francs, marks, yen, escudos.

[1] A few banks specialise in actual foreign bank-*notes*. They include the London Branch of the Trade Development Bank, Brown Shipley and National Westminster. They act as the City's main wholesalers in foreign bank-notes, supplying a list of some 150 different currencies from the afgani of Afghanistan to the kwachi of Zambia. Their main competitors are the Swiss Bank Corporation, said to be the world's largest dealer in foreign bank notes and Credit Suisse.

[2] John Swinfield, *The Money Programme*, BBC2, March 1976

Now listen to a dealer explaining what is in his mind as he puts through a call to a broker for a simple quote against the dollar for a certain sum in pounds. The broker cannot match the amount or the date but makes alternative offers:

What shall one do? Will one of the propositions fit the book? Many questions flit through the dealer's mind. Try another broker? But the first will already have scented blood and be out scouring the market for a chance to close up a deal. To put someone else in will accentuate the effect. Take him off? He might see the opportunity to deal and go elsewhere. Try Paris? They will read a change in the market and be nipping back on another line and clobber the market under one's nose. Try Germany? Might work against marks. Can the mark dealer help? Has he something on his books which will help the arbitrage price? Questions and answers are flitting through the dealer's brain and he alone must find the answer. Meanwhile he is probably dealing with a fractious importer who is demanding last night's closing price as shown in *The Times* for $27·53 drawn on Milwaukee, Wis.[1]

We have thus established three features of the market: it is extremely large; it is fast-moving; and it is highly complex. It also deals on two planes: it deals in transactions for immediate delivery of currency and it deals in transactions for the future delivery of currency. In short, there is a spot market and a forward market. The forward transactions provide a way of covering a trader's risks when he has to pay or receive payments in a certain currency three or six months ahead at a time when the rate at which his own currency will exchange into the other is moving daily. If an importer of American machinery knows that delivery will take place over the next six months and that he will have to make that payment at a fixed price in American dollars at the end of that period, he will be at the mercy of the spot exchange rate until he makes the payment. If the sterling/dollar exchange rate is affected by a steady depreciation of the pound, then he will

[1]Jack Higgins, *A Day in the Life of a Banker* (Institute of Bankers, London, 1963)

be faced at the end of the period with having to find a much larger sum in pounds to meet the same fixed price in dollars. If the pound appreciated over this period, he would, of course, have to find a smaller sum in pounds to meet his dollar obligation. But he is running an engineering company and is not in the business of taking exchange risks. He can therefore insure himself against this known risk by arranging to buy American dollars in advance for delivery in six months time on the forward market. In this way he is comforted by the knowledge that, whatever happens to the sterling/dollar exchange rate before his payments become due, his exchange risk has been 'covered'.

The forward market in all leading currencies is extremely active in London. As in the case of the spot market, the most active market is either between sterling and the American dollar or between dollars and deutschmarks. Some transactions can be undertaken up to five years ahead, but the bulk of the forward turnover covers periods of one month, three months and six months. Since the holding of currencies for these periods also raises the question of the rate of interest that can be earned by the holders, the exchange rates in the forward market naturally take into account the differences in rates of interest between one financial centre and another. And since London has not only some of the most highly developed sterling money markets in the world, but also markets in Eurocurrencies, it is not surprising that the forward markets which thrive on them should have expanded here too.

The spider's web of telecommunications spreading out from the dozen broking firms and well over two hundred banks in London to all points of the globe has dramatically altered the life of a foreign exchange dealer, not only from what it was in the Edwardian age of twice-weekly meetings at the Royal Exchange, but even from a decade or more ago. In the mid-sixties it was still normal for exchange dealers to operate an eight-hour day, with occasional dealings continuing from home with New York. The onset of floating exchange rates, and especially the growing importance of places like Singapore, San Francisco, Los Angeles, Hong Kong and Tokyo, at the extremities of London's working hours, have all extended the working life of the market in London. London sits comfortably astride the world's time zones – managing to catch Singapore operations in the morning and New York and Los Angeles at the other end of the day. Each bank organises its exchange dealers in its own way. But a combination of shift-working plus a system of being on call at home in the evening has succeeded in widening London's coverage of world exchange transactions. The start in London can now be between 7.30 and 8 a.m. As for the brokers, several have opened overseas offices and between them have close on eighty outposts round the world. The main targets so far have been New York, Hong Kong, Singapore and Zurich, and four of the London brokers can claim to have an office open somewhere in the world, whatever the time.

So far I have concentrated on the way in which the City helps to switch one currency into another. It also provides a market for switching currencies into and out of gold on the London bullion market. This too has been at the centre of the international monetary stage in the past decade, from the late 1960s, when General de Gaulle was trying to persuade the world to return to the gold standard, to the past three or four years when the dollar price of gold has dipped from over $180 an ounce to below $110 and back again to over $300. This London price, which emanates from a soft-carpeted, oak-panelled room at Rothschild's, twice a day, at so-called 'fixings', has become a guide to all world markets. London's bullion market is not the only gold market but, with Zurich, it handles, directly or indirectly, the bulk of the world's supplies.

The market itself, in contrast with the exchange market, is small and much calmer. There are five desks, one basically in a dominant position, the other four round the sides of the room, each with a telephone and a small Union Jack on a pedestal. An elongated table with a bowl of flowers runs down the middle of the room. The participants are representatives of N. M. Rothschild & Sons, who act as Chairman, and four other bullion dealers, Samuel Montagu, Sharps Pixley, Johnson Matthey and Mocatta & Goldsmid. Two are merchant banks, one is a subsidiary of a merchant bank, one a subsidiary of a British overseas bank and one is a bullion refiner. The market has its own peculiar way of 'fixing' the price of gold, though they mean an agreed price not a fixed one. A price is called at the outset, invariably at the lower end of the expected range, which is then adjusted in line with the demand and supply expressed by the participants who are in immediate touch with their offices by telephone, and they in turn are in direct touch with customers worldwide. The colourful Union Jacks are placed upright on a desk to indicate that a dealer is changing his position. The 'fixing' price which matches all the buying and selling positions is agreed when all the flags are down. For a time one 'fixing' a day was enough, but nowadays there are two, one at 10.30 in the morning and the other at 3 in the afternoon. The fixing, of course, is simply a guideline for London and other markets, for dealing takes place in London between the five houses outside these particular hours.

It has been a moot point since 1 April 1968 – when the London gold market was officially closed for a month following an unprecedented speculative demand for gold (up to $3 billion worth) and prior to the introduction of a two-tier new system under which the world's central banks agreed not to buy gold in the market – whether London or Zurich can claim the biggest turnover or the biggest influence. Until then London had dominated turnover because it handled the bulk of South African supplies and attracted most central bank business. Thereafter, the three leading Swiss banks succeeded in capturing the South African supplies from the London market, at least for a time. But in recent years London has fought back hard by providing a clearing house for orders from other centres outside London's time zones, especially Hong Kong.

For a time, Beirut and Dubai in the Middle East and Macao and Hong Kong in the Far East acted as the main centres outside Europe. Now Beirut, which has recovered some of its past trade, Dubai and Hong Kong have been joined by Jeddah, Kuwait, Tehran, Singapore and Tokyo. The new-found wealth of the oil states has shifted the source of demand. As Mr Timothy Green, consultant to Consolidated Gold Fields, has put it:

A decade ago Saudi Arabia was just a small client of the Beirut market; a handful of bullion dealers in Jeddah had little direct contact with the outside world and learned the gold price by cable twenty-four hours late. Nowadays telex links them directly to world markets, and their financial strength makes them potent speculators. In future we must anticipate increasing participation in gold trading in London, Zurich and New York both from the Middle East and from the Far East. The establishment of Hong Kong as the last link in a round-the-world, round-the-clock gold market has also brought into play the speculative energies of the Chinese communities in such diverse centres as Bangkok, Taipei and even Jakarta.

Hong Kong, therefore, which operates while London and Zurich are closed overnight, has become the fourth major link in the gold-chain (New York is the other link) and, because of London's historical and current connections (four of the London dealers have offices there and a fifth has a close relationship), has strengthened London's grip on Far Eastern trade. All five London dealers have either subsidiaries or interests in New York.

We must now try to answer one of the questions I raised at the outset. What role are these dealers and the individuals and companies who provide them with business – in both the foreign exchange and gold markets – actually playing in the world economy? Are they helping legitimate trade or speculating for profit? Let me take the gold market first. Demand for gold comes from the electronics, dentistry, jewellery and other decorative trades, as well as from central banks and private hoarders and speculators. Some of the demand is for coins or gold bars; some, and increasingly, for 'paper gold', that is for receipts for gold held in London or Zurich. Gold hoarding has traditionally arisen in France, India and parts of the Middle East and Far East, and some of this demand is being satisfied on domestic markets such as Paris and Bombay. It is estimated that well over a half of the existing stocks of gold are in private hands, the balance being in the hands of governments, central banks and other monetary authorities. The biggest private gold hoard is thought to be in

India, mainly in the form of jewellery, with 8,000 to 10,000 tons, with France coming second with 5,000 tons, largely in small bars and coins.

The private demand for gold is clearly stimulated by inflation, currency uncertainties and political doubts. Individuals, whether traders or not, would clearly prefer to hold gold in certain circumstances rather than their own currency. Governments too have to decide what proportion of their national reserves should be held in gold, and some of the same factors are involved. Thus the volatility of the gold market is a direct reflection of the instability of economic and political prospects. The question that primarily concerns us is whether the London gold market, in providing the facilities for the exchange of currencies into and out of gold, can act as a destabilising influence on the British economy. The answer, in my view, is a simple 'no'. British residents cannot hold gold bullion and can simply buy coins. The London market apart from trade demand, therefore, is in a sense a self-contained international market, centred in London, but separate from other domestic markets. It offers an international service, provides strong commercial help to gold producers and to individual customers, makes valuable foreign exchange through its operations, and does not pass on any international tremors to the British economy.

The assessment of the London foreign exchange market is not so simple, nor so clear-cut. The first question to be asked in this case is why people want to switch one currency into another on such a large scale. The scale applies not only to the individual deals (normally, it is said, between half a million pounds and two million pounds) but also to the turnover on a normal day. A glance at the annual size of international transactions provides part of the answer. Turnover of world trade alone has recently been running at close on £600 billion. Add in the movements of capital, both short- and long-term, and the total could easily be doubled. Finally, one has to allow, in crisis years, for deliberate delays in payments in terms of some currencies and accelerated payments in terms of others. These so-called 'leads and lags' in payments can add significantly to the demands on the exchange markets when doubts about individual currencies, especially leading currencies, arise. Who really influences exchange rates? Who are the people behind these huge movements? They are in truth a motley throng – traders buying and selling goods and services in world markets; governments making payments to their own citizens in other countries: one government giving or lending money to another; tourists buying currencies to spend on holiday; people buying services of all kinds – financial, professional, entertainment – from foreigners; multinational corporations making payments, borrowing money or lending money between one subsidiary and another in different countries; people buying villas abroad and industrial companies investing in new plants overseas; banks deliberately keeping their holding of currencies and debts in currencies as unbalanced as they are allowed; speculators borrowing one currency they have not got and switching into another which they believe will rise in value; and any of them accelerating or delaying the expected dates of any of their currency transactions.

The list is by no means exhaustive, but it will serve our purpose, which is to assess who influences exchange rates and, in particular, what moves them in moments of crisis. If a country is buying more goods and services than it is selling and this is not offset by other currency transactions, then the exchange value of its currency will fall. But, as we have seen in the United States in 1973 and subsequently in 1978 and in the United Kingdom in the spring and again in the second half of 1976, other factors begin to operate when the value of a currency is already in doubt. Then our questions become more pointed. How is the value of a currency undermined and by whom? A search for scapegoats starts and high on the list are speculators, gnomes, international bankers and multinational corporations. It is not so much a matter of how they manage it, monetary ingenuity being what it is, but whether they deliberately speculate against a country's interests and to their own benefit.[1]

[1]Sometimes big corporations operate *against* their own interests. See *The Economist* for 16 October 1976: 'Big deals can and do move prices. When Aramco found in December, 1974, that it had to make its end-year oil payment to Saudi Arabia entirely in dollars instead of 75% in dollars and 25% in sterling, it was forced to make large sales over a few days. The exchange rate moved sharply against Aramco.'

First the private speculator. Does he exist and how important is he now? It is worth listening for a moment to someone who perhaps ought to know – Paul Erdman, the author of the best-seller *The Billion Dollar Killing* and who, more to the point, was President of the United California Bank in Basle when it collapsed in 1970 and subsequently spent ten months in a Swiss jail.

Who are they, this small group of dealers who pit themselves against the treasuries of some of the most powerful governments on earth – and often win? One whom I know well – I have advised him in the area of currency speculation in years past – is Chinese and works out of Hong Kong, Manila, Vancouver, Costa Rica, London and, naturally, Zurich. He has four passports and a private jet. It is said that he made his first big money in the black market in the Pacific area after the war selling old bombers (and/or brassieres) to the surviving natives of the region. Since then he has settled down with his 25 odd million pounds in cash which he keeps on deposit with a large number of banks round the world. Most of the time he plays a waiting game. He sits back, collects interest and waits for the next big play to develop in the international exchange market. . . . Now that's the type of person everybody usually thinks of as the driving force behind the fall in the £, the crash of the lira and the demise of the franc. But, as usual, everybody is wrong. Such loners account for only 5 per cent of the real action for the simple reason that the entrance ticket to this biggest of games is at least £½ million in cash – and very few people have that. So aren't the Gnomes of Zurich the real culprits? Wrong again. Ten or fifteen years ago they were the superstars in this game, for the simple reason that nobody else was really playing it. So who are the real heavyweights in the game? Answer: the multinational corporations. They now account for well over half of the international currency speculation. . . . [1]

[1] *Daily Mail*, 24 March 1976

Private speculators will exist wherever free markets operate and where regulations do not impede their activities, but there seems little point in pinning the blame for major devaluations – whether of the pound or the dollar – on them when their resources are so marginal. In any case, they do not always make a profit. Like gamblers everywhere, they lose heavily too. The 'Gnomes of Zurich', however, are clearly in a different league, but the misunderstandings about their role are legion. In the first place they were not invented by Lord George Brown in the sterling crisis of 1964.[1] Seven years earlier Peter Thorneycroft as Chancellor of the Exchequer was already talking of 'imaginary hard-faced little men in Zurich' and in the same year Andrew Schonfield was reflecting, in his book *British Economic Policy Since the War*, how tough it was on the Swiss that William Tell should have been replaced 'by this new image of a gnome in a bank at the end of a telephone line'. Secondly, it is far from clear who these Swiss gnomes are and what they are meant to do. Some regard them as private speculators dealing with their own huge fortunes. Others think of them as the large Swiss banks operating both on their own account and on behalf of their rich industrial clients. Others again (British cabinet ministers included) seem to mix them up with the group of international central banks (including the Bank of England) who meet regularly at the Bank for International Settlements in Basle. The first two views are close to the mark, but the central banks, far from undermining the value of currencies, are determined to provide currency support whenever it is needed.

The Swiss gnomes, however, do not seem to have been quite so active lately, and the reasons for this will lead us towards our final bunch of suggested culprits – the international banks and the multinational corporations. Switzerland was in the forefront of international financial dealings in the first couple of decades after the war for special reasons. Zurich had become the centre of international money during the war because of Switzerland's neutral position and because of the closure of

---

[1] Henry Brandon mistakenly attributed them to George Brown in his book *In the Red. The Struggle for Sterling 1964–66* (Andre Deutsch, 1966).

London, New York, Paris, Berlin and Brussels. After the war this advantage continued, buttressed by a rising standard of living and a steady *cost* of living. Confidence in the Swiss franc blossomed further and this confidence, coupled with the freedom offered by the Swiss authorities as well as the numbered secret accounts made discreetly available by the leading banks, explains why Zurich began to attract the bulk of the Western world's short-term money. So far as sterling was concerned Zurich soon became the main centre for the market in what was known as 'transferable sterling'. These were pounds held by foreigners which were freely transferable from one foreign holder to another outside the dollar area. Much of it was deposited in Switzerland and it was not long before Swiss banks had established a free market in this particular brand of sterling – at a price. Thus, when holders of these various brands of sterling entertained doubts about the British economy in those early post-war years, they sold their pounds in or through Zurich and the obliging Swiss bankers were paid for their services and received most of the blame. 'Selling from Zurich' quickly became shorthand for the suggested machinations of the Swiss gnomes. In such easy ways are reputations made and lost.

Since then several developments have reduced the role of Zurich as a centre of international money, especially as the focal point of attacks on leading currencies. In the first place, the leading European currencies, plus the yen, joined the American and Canadian dollars in full convertibility on 29 December 1958. Thus a lot of switching business which previously could only be done outside the countries of individual currencies – primarily in Zurich – reverted to the other European centres. Secondly, with the onset of American investment in Europe and other parts of the world, and especially with the growing international operations of the multinationals, foreign exchange business which had previously been channelled through a handful of overseas financial centres, such as Zurich, was increasingly undertaken by special departments within these organisations and channelled through the new network of American and other banks in different centres.

Thus, although Zurich is no longer the focal point for international currency business that it once was, the same question applies to the new network of international banks and their clients, the multinational corporations as did to the Swiss gnomes. How far can they be blamed for the pressure on currencies at times of crisis? This is where we get to the heart of the problem and examine closely what we mean by speculation. Individuals and corporations buy and sell currencies for a variety of reasons – to buy foreign goods and services, to go on holiday, to invest abroad, to lend overseas or pay off foreign debts. The dates of those payments can also be accelerated or delayed. It is clearly speculation to sell currencies you haven't got in the expectation of future profit. Is it speculation to switch liquid funds from one currency to another in order to protect a corporation's liquid assets? Is it speculation to pay a bill ahead of time in one currency and to delay a similar bill in another because there is a risk of one currency appreciating and the other depreciating? Is it speculation to get holiday money ahead of time when your own domestic currency is likely to be devalued? Is it speculation to sell your pounds when you fear for their value? In other words, where does self-interest begin and end?

From the point of view of the individual, the potential tourist is simply protecting the cost of his holiday, whereas the buying of currencies you do not already hold nor even need in the expectation of future profit is pure speculation. The case of the large international corporation is less straightforward since the switching of funds from one country to another could be either 'money management' with a view to the maximisation of profits or a defensive move designed to protect the value of its overall assets. Either way, of course, it adds to the pressures on currencies. These were at their height against the world's two major currencies – the dollar and the pound – in the early months of 1973 and in 1976, respectively. The earlier pressure on the dollar reached its peak in February 1973, and led to the closure of most exchange markets in the world for seventeen days in March. When they reopened the previous currency alignments were abandoned, the leading currencies were allowed to float against each other and the *Wall Street*

Journal spoke of multinational corporations 'betting against the dollar'. But were they? As a detailed inquiry for the Senate's Foreign Relations Committee subsequently concluded, 'US multinational corporations did not use the forward market or the banking sector in order to hedge short term against the devaluation of the dollar in the first quarter of 1973'. They '*protected*' themselves, however, against the anticipated devaluation over a longer term 'by shifting the currency composition of liquid assets and debt and by delaying payments in currencies expected to be revalued, and by delaying payments in currencies expected to be devalued'. Not all corporations behaved the same way. But was their behaviour defensive (to protect themselves) or offensive (to make profits at someone else's expense)? The inquiry came to this conclusion: 'Although the line between protective and speculative activities cannot be drawn with any certainty, a *prima facie* case of speculation can be made against any firm or individual which, lacking any foreign exchange exposure, nonetheless operates on the foreign exchange market. But a sample of multinational corporations includes no such cases.' Thus 'leads and lags' and the switching of funds from one country to another for protective reasons were established: but no speculation.

Consider now a similar attack on the pound and a similar official analysis. In the late spring of 1976, Britain's exchange and gold reserves came under constant pressure and the pound lost its value against the dollar. It was later stated officially in the House of Commons (on 3 June 1976) that the exchange losses of the previous three months had amounted to some three billion dollars. Of this enormous loss one-seventh was caused by Britain's balance of payments deficit, one-quarter arose from sales of sterling balances held by foreigners and a further quarter was the result of 'leads and lags' in payments. Thus a half of the trouble was the result of sterling sales by existing holders and changes in payments by legitimate traders and industrialists. And nearly two-thirds could be accounted for legitimately even without allowing for the impact of legitimate long-term investments overseas.

Yes, you may say, but what about the international banks and especially those operating in the City of London, British or foreign? Are they to be blameless? In defensive terms, there can be no denying that they did, and no doubt will again, delay or accelerate payments on behalf of their world-wide clients. It is also no use denying that they, on the instructions of their foreign customers, did not renew short-term investments in sterling in certain periods of 1976. But it is not hard to understand why London banks, both British and foreign, were receiving such instructions in the spring and again in the late autumn of that year. Inflation was running at over 20 per cent and the payments gap was one of the widest in the world. Banks can, of course, take positions in currencies in the exchange market either deliberately or simply as the temporary result of carrying out an instruction on behalf of an industrial client. Since to some extent they are acting as wholesalers in currencies, they will naturally find it difficult to keep their assets and liabilities in the different currencies exactly matched. But, in periods of crisis, they would be foolish to maintain too many 'unmatched positions' and those that have – whether deliberately or through the dishonesty of their dealers – have paid heavily for their actions.[1]

How far, however, can *London* banks take positions against individual currencies, since this is the criticism which persistently rears its head at the onset of every sterling crisis? The answer is, not far. The Bank of England's controls on this are stricter than in any other leading financial centre. No bank can deal in foreign exchange without authorisation from the Bank and this is given only when it is satisfied with the bank's capital and the competence of its staff to undertake foreign exchange business. At present 250 banks have this authorisation. The twelve brokers also need the Bank's authority and are not allowed to act on their own behalf in the market or to take positions in foreign currency. In short they cannot deal or speculate for themselves and they simply earn a commission for acting as intermediaries. Each bank is given an individual limit within which it can take positions in each

[1] The banks losing money on foreign exchange transactions have included: Franklin National Bank; Bankhaus Herstatt; Lloyds Bank International; Banques de Bruxelles; Union Bank of Switzerland; Credit Suisse. None of the losses was sustained in London.

currency. These limits have to be achieved at the end of every dealing day, so that London-based banks simply do not have the ability to speculate against the pound, beyond the limits imposed by the Bank of England.

How, then, to sum up? Currency crises arise from a variety of causes: government action or inaction; political fears; economic disasters. They can be aggravated by decisions of central banks to defend their currencies at levels which, in the light of their own national economic and financial policies, are, in the long run, likely to be unsuccessful. Such actions simply put off the evil day of an exchange rate adjustment and inevitably encourage speculative movements. Crisis can also be aggravated by currency pressures resulting from the combined reactions of individuals, bankers, companies large and small. Some traders act defensively to avoid risks. Some speculate and take risks. The evidence of recent crises, however, strongly suggests that the speculators are in a small minority. It also suggests that to look for them in London is a waste of time.

Chapter 13

Sterling: How Important?

After close on a dozen crises, almost unending bouts of 'stop-go' policies, wage freezes and crisis interest rates, who can wonder that the market-place where all the disasters seem to be reported is going to share some of the blame for what has gone wrong. Take this excerpt from *The Politics of Power*,[1] the recent book by Mr Joe Haines, Sir Harold Wilson's Press Secretary. He is reporting about the pressure on the pound on Monday and Tuesday 30 June and 1 July 1975:

> We talked in the spacious area outside the Cabinet Room. The Prime Minister had received the first tranche of bad news from the City of London while he was still at Stoneleigh. He was severely shaken by it. Substantial sterling deposits were, apparently, being taken out of London. Kuwait had long made it known that it considered the floor for sterling was $2·20 and that they would reduce their holdings if the pound dropped below that level against the dollar. Saudi Arabia, an even bigger holder of sterling, has set their floor at $2.17 and that level had almost been reached . . . If the drain of withdrawals continued at that day's rate then the Treasury had warned there would be disastrous effects for the Economy.

Mr Haines's criticisms on this occasion were largely directed

---

[1] *The Politics of Power* (Coronet Books, 1977), p. 55.

at the Treasury, whom he suspected of exaggerating, or even conspiring to produce a crisis for its own policy ends. But the City of London and the Governor of the Bank of England too come in for criticism. And it is relevant to ask whether the City of London's monetary freedom, and its large foreign income, though curbed by Exchange Control, is bought at too high a price by the rest of the economy, when a sterling crisis can make us all tighten our belts once more, when no other crisis seems to be on the horizon. Why, for example, have there been more sterling crises than any other? Is the freedom which the Bank of England is said to accord to the City of London, and especially to the easy movement of foreign funds in and out of London, fully justified if it can bring on a sterling crisis overnight? How important is sterling to the City of London and is there no end to the pound's dominance of our affairs? Above all, why does the City put such a great emphasis on its international role, even to the extent, it is often said, of exporting capital that might otherwise be invested in British industry?

These questions deserve to be answered for I believe that they arise from a number of misunderstandings. First, the question of the frequency of sterling crises since the war. This relates to the importance of sterling in world trade and to the amount of sterling left in the hands of foreigners at the end of the last war. This is not the place for an exhaustive analysis of the sterling area and how and why it grew up in the 1930s, but a quick sketch of the main outlines will help to answer part of the question. In effect the whole world was the sterling area up to 1914, using the pound as a means of trade finance and as a basis for currency reserves. After the ill-fated attempt to return to the Gold Standard in 1925 (and to the golden Edwardian days it seemed to imply), Britain's monetary role in the world contracted sharply and, following sterling's break with gold again in 1931 and the accompanying world monetary crisis, a small group of countries decided to throw in their lot with Britain and to cut their own currency links with gold and formed what was clearly an embryo sterling area out of simple self-protection. Nearly all the Commonwealth countries joined this sterling grouping, as well as Egypt, Argentina and Japan, though over the next few years the countries moved in and out from time to time. It was in essence a grouping of countries with strong ties and with reserves held in sterling. Other defensive groupings were also formed in the early 1930s, mainly round the dollar and, to a lesser extent, round the French franc.

Then came the war and the first statutory regulations establishing the sterling area behind a rigid wall of British exchange controls. Sterling was allowed to move fairly freely within the area but was to be severely controlled in its use between each member country and the rest of the world. It paid members to pool their reserves in London, for they could still use them freely; and the arrangements helped Britain since it provided a larger support fund for sterling and Britain could use sterling in meeting debts within the area itself. But, as the war progressed, this became a double-edged weapon. It certainly enabled Britain to pay for part of the war effort, particularly when payments had to be made to members of the sterling area such as Egypt, India and West Africa. But it also led to the piling up by these and other countries of sterling balances which were virtually war debts to a degree which had not been expected and to a degree that was to dog Britain for the next three decades.

The sterling area continued in existence long after the war, though, as world trade expanded and trade financial barriers were gradually dismantled throughout the 1950s and 1960s, it became less and less cohesive. The original advantages – freedom within the area, the pooling of reserves and the ability to borrow on the London market – continued until the second major devaluation of the pound in 1967. At that point several sterling area countries decided not to devalue along with sterling and to move some of their reserves out of sterling and into other currencies. Some diversified their reserves for the first time. From these decisions it was not a large step to the contraction of the sterling area itself. And so it went on until, by the early 1970s and several sterling crises later, the sterling area had been reduced to Britain and the Channel Islands.

So much for the sterling area mechanism. But it was the heavy weight of sterling debt built up during the war years that virtually ensured that sterling would continue to be used as a reserve currency once the war was over. The one chance to escape from this role, in 1946–7, when the United States suggested that Britain's sterling debts should be funded or even wiped clean, was resisted by the British Government on the quite reasonable grounds that these balances would come in handy in a few years time when, as was then widely assumed, the expected post-war slump emerged and British factories would welcome the export orders arising from those countries holding such large sterling balances. The slump, however, did not materialise and Britain's balance of payments remained embarrassingly wide. The exchange rate came under pressure, partly because of fears that Britain would not be able to balance her overseas payments in a short period and partly because these fears led to sales of sterling by the large holders. Thus began the series of sterling crises, of government actions to take 'stern measures', of higher interest rates– in a word the cycle of 'stop-go' which was to become such a depressant on the British economy.

In short, the size of Britain's sterling balances produced an 'overhang' effect throughout the post-war period. Whenever something went wrong, or even was feared to be going wrong, with the British economy – sometimes the balance of payments, sometimes the rate of inflation, sometimes both – there was always a potential weight of sterling sales overhanging the market. It is not our concern here to analyse why the British economy has behaved the way it has over this period, but simply to point out that whenever it did run into difficulties the pressure on the pound was both greater and more immediate than that on other currencies in similar circumstances.

This is not to say that some balances held in London were not there because of the City's role as a leading financial centre. It is natural for a financial centre to attract deposits, and there is nothing new in this so far as London is concerned. Walter Bagehot was making the same point in his classic, *Lombard Street*, just over a hundred years ago:

London has become the sole great settling-house of exchange transactions in Europe, instead of being formerly one of two.[1] And this pre-eminence London will probably maintain, for it is a natural pre-eminence. The number of mercantile bills drawn upon London incalculably surpasses those drawn on any other European city; London is the place which receives more than any other place, and pays more than any other place, and therefore it is the natural 'clearing house'. The pre-eminence of Paris partly arose from a distribution of political power,which is already disturbed; but that of London depends on the regular course of commerce, which is singularly stable and hard to change. Now that London is the clearing house to foreign countries, London has a new liability to foreign countries. At whatever place many people have to make payments, at that place those people must keep money. A large deposit of foreign money in London is now necessary for the business of the world.

The question is: how large is 'large'? Between the wars, London managed to cope with its obligations as a financial centre with sterling balances of between £400 million and £500 million, which were comfortably close to the value of the country's gold and exchange reserves in the same period. But the size of Britain's sterling balances at the end of the war was far beyond the level that London, purely as a financial centre, needed for its international activities. This is even true now. Thus during the war the sterling balances rose nearly ten times and were around £4 billion in 1946, the bulk of them owed to India, Egypt and the Commonwealth countries of Africa and elsewhere. For the next twenty years, while several of these countries ran down their sterling reserves, others built up fresh ones, reflecting the imbalance of Britain's payments during the post-war years. As a result the total remained much the same and was still about the £4 billion mark in 1966.

The second major influence on their size came at the end of 1973 when the oil producers virtually quadrupled the oil price in a matter of months. This had an immediate impact on Britain's oil import bill and pushed her total payments deficit

[1] The other was Paris.

further into the red. For traditional reasons, the oil producers were paid in sterling and decided, throughout 1974 and part of 1975, to leave these payments in London. Accordingly, the sterling balances increased still further to over £7 billion at their peak in 1975. At that time no less than £4,600 million was officially held by central monetary authorities and the balance of around £2,500 millions by traders, corporations and private individuals. About half of the total of over £7 billion was held by official institutions or private corporations and individuals of the oil producing states.

We are now in a position to see what this meant for Britain and, more relevant for the purpose here, what it meant for the City. As we have seen, Britain's sterling balances since the war have been of two kinds – those held in London by overseas governments and official institutions and those held by private individuals and companies. The first represent the use of sterling as a *reserve* currency, the second as a *trading* currency.[1] The City is only indirectly concerned with the first insofar as City banks will be consulted by governments and official institutions overseas concerning investments in Treasury bills and British Government stock and may occasionally be asked to undertake the investments. The City, however, is intimately concerned with the use of sterling as a trading currency. This distinction is important because, in my view, it is the role of sterling as a *reserve* currency that has led, along with other economic factors, to the damaging series of 'stop-go' policies, since the official holdings of pounds overseas have not only been extremely large, but have proved to be far more volatile than those held on private account. Moreover, contrary to some widely held beliefs, it was the British Government that was acting as so-called banker to the sterling area in terms of these large official sums, not the banks in the City of London.

It is time to look more closely at the use of trading sterling by the City's banks and other institutions. Why one currency is used in trade rather than another can usually be put down to

---

[1] Although it is useful to make this distinction, the two roles overlap considerably. For one thing, central banks continually use their reserves to control the rate of exchange of trading currencies. Secondly, several governments readily employ their reserves on the trading markets of the world to obtain a useful return.

security and convenience. When the Irish banks were closed down for three months in the mid-1960s and again in 1970, it was remarkable how quickly their place was taken, virtually overnight, by local grocers and pubs. The reason was simple. Normal cheques could not be cashed through the banks, but cheques made out in the name of reputable traders were acceptable by publicans, in exchange for cash, and circulated in place of cash. The security was not as good as cash, but it was the best available, and it was certainly convenient with the banks closed. A similar phenomenon has been seen by holiday-makers in Italy in recent years where a shortage of certain notes has occasionally led to the use of local cheques. The same is true with international currencies. The use of sterling by traders throughout the British Empire in the nineteenth century was natural enough. British trade accounted for a large part of world trade; in addition many other countries found it convenient to use sterling, and the facilities that went with it in the City of London, in their own trade with third countries. The pound was also secure. With the rise of American economic influence, the use of the dollar has similarly expanded well beyond the immediate trading partners of the United States. And in both cases trading habits led to the deposits of spare money in the two centres linked to these two currencies – London and New York. In such an easy way are reserve currencies established. People, and governments, find it more convenient to keep their earnings in such major currencies, especially when they can earn a rate of interest on deposit, rather than switch them back into their own.

Habits, of course, change and so do economic influences. The United States is now the world's leading trading nation. So the roles of the pound and the dollar have slowly reversed. In world *reserves* the dollar had replaced the pound as the largest used national currency by the early 1960s. In *trade*, the use of the dollar in settling and invoicing world transactions grew continuously after the war and surpassed the use of sterling between 1960 and 1965. Just after the war half of the world's trade was still settled in sterling. This had dropped to 35 per cent by 1960 and to between 25 per cent and 30 per cent by 1965. It is now only 5 per cent, though even this percentage of total world trade amounts to close on £25 billion annually.

What have these changes meant for Britain and for the City? Rises and falls in the fortunes of empires, countries and financial centres are littered throughout recorded history. Moreover, the expansionary periods, when balances are being built up, bring advantages which are sadly lacking during the inevitable declines. Britain's problems came not only in the early post-war period when she had to cope with the overhang of the war-time balances, but especially after 1973 when they had been swollen still further by newly created oil debts. The City too, like any other financial centre during the declining phase in its currency's fortunes, suddenly found its domestic economy in difficulties, its currency under pressure, and the use of it overseas on the decline. It was – like the rest of Britain – living from crisis to crisis, in danger of losing its international business from the repercussions of the sterling crises.

Nevertheless the City's post-war experience has been unique in the history of financial centres. For the first time a major centre has survived the rapid decline in the fortunes of its domestic currency. Judged by its foreign income alone, it has gone from strength to strength, pushing its 'invisible income' from £50 million in 1946 to £205 million in 1965 and to over £1,700 million in 1977. These are net figures and account for no less than 35 per cent of the country's total net income from invisibles. Over this same period, as we shall explore in more detail in Chapter 16, the City more than maintained its international supremacy in banking, ship-brokerage, gold, insurance, commodities and financial services generally.

Why? There are a variety of answers but one factor is over-riding. It lies in the emergence of the Eurodollar market, which I shall be examining in greater detail in the next chapter, for this new multicurrency market, based on London, coincided with sterling's declining role. Thus for the first time a financial centre, faced with the decline in its domestic currency, was able to replace it with other people's currencies just at a time when a currency blood-transfusion was needed for survival. It was not the first time that the City had used other currencies in this way – both London and New York used the French franc in the 1920s – but this was the first time such a transformation had taken place on such a global scale. Major parts of the City of London had moved from a sterling standard to a Eurocurrency standard at a significant time. The move enabled City banks to offer credits, to provide longer-term capital and to keep in the forefront of international finance, drawing on the enormous pool of international currencies virtually at its elbow, which it had played a major part in creating, and without undermining Britain's central gold and exchange reserves. Moreover, because of the large variety of services available from London – from commodities to insurance and from securities to ship-brokerage – in contrast with most other financial centres, where the emphasis is often on money and capital markets, the declining role of sterling affected different parts of the City in different ways. Some had been used to invoicing in foreign currency and in operating through other centres and other currencies. Others had to learn to do so. The effort of readjustment was spread widely round the Square Mile.

Thus the City was able to help itself in a critical phase. But the creation of the Eurodollar market provided significant help to government and industry too. Britain's large corporations were provided with a large new source of credit, and those with income arising abroad did not hesitate to use it when it suited them. After being understandably reluctant to lend too much to British firms in 1974 and 1975, foreign investors in the Eurobond market found over $400 million for them in 1976 and nearly trebled it in 1977. The government's own use of this new international market, created on its doorstep, also reached new heights in the period of the Labour Government between 1974 and 1977, when the City's clearing banks led a special syndication to provide the British Government with a credit of $2,500 million, and local authorities and nationalised industries borrowed some $8,000 millions with government guarantees, in three years, on the Euromarkets. Thus the City not only provided the government with a domestic mechanism for covering its budget borrowing needs of up to £8 billion a year, as we outlined in Chapter 9, but also produced a new international market which the government could use as a flexible alternative to the International Monetary Fund.

Yet, in spite of this help, has the freedom of movement of funds provided by the government on currency transactions had other damaging side-effects on the economy generally? In a word, has lax exchange control led to the dangers of 'hot money' flows in and out of London, for the benefit of the City but against everyone else's interest? The plea 'don't play the international banker' has gone up on many occasions, with the implication that the authorities have acquiesced in providing too much freedom of movement not only for sterling funds but also for foreign currency deposits used in the Euromarkets, and that both have benefited the City at the expense of the British economy. The truth, however, is not so simple. In the first place it is necessary to distinguish between the freedom given to movements of sterling funds and that given to foreign currency funds. In the case of sterling, two points have to be realised at the outset. First, as we have already outlined in some detail, Britain (not the City) emerged from both the last war and from the recent oil price increase with enormous sterling debts. These are obligations which can be repudiated, frozen or paid off. Some were partially frozen[1] (or rather given only limited repayment facilities) in the early post-war years. No one presumably wishes to repudiate them and no one else is likely to pay them off. So holders have been given the facility to move them as and when they wish. Once again we are steered towards the country's obligations as the main cause for official action, not towards the machinations of the City. Moreover, and this is the second point, a major trading nation such as Britain must be more careful than most in imposing restrictions on the movement of its own currency, especially in the hands of foreigners. We have to import a higher proportion of our food and raw materials than most other nations. We have to export a large share of our total output to pay for these essential imports. Exports in 1975 amounted to 25 per cent of our gross domestic product compared with 14 per cent for Japan and only 8 per cent for the United States. Britain's overseas investments and the numbers of its multinationals with overseas links

[1] Creditor countries were often given two sterling accounts, one on which they could draw freely, the other on which they could draw only agreed amounts in limited periods.

are also second only to those of the US. To impose restrictions on the movement of sterling funds in the hands of foreigners would thus interfere with some of our essential interests. At the same time the Bank of England has, until recently, maintained one of the strictest controls over the movement of sterling in the hands of *British* nationals. Post-war experience also strongly suggests that, in spite of the freedom offered to foreigners, the main instability (the readiness to move funds rapidly out of London) has been shown by official holders rather than private holders of sterling. This was clearly the case in the crisis period of 1975–6 when official oil-producing holdings were run down dramatically, whereas private holdings remained relatively stable. Once again the role of the City (or the funds directly connected with its activities) was not the culprit it is too often made out to be.

The freedom of movement of foreign currency deposits is, of course, an essential feature of the vast Eurocurrency market. As we have seen, London-based banks attract deposits in non-sterling currencies and use them to finance projects and activities round the world. What is not so often appreciated is that these deposits have no direct connection with Britain's central gold and exchange reserves. When they are attracted to London, they do not increase Britain's reserves; when they leave London they do not deplete the reserves. They cannot, therefore, be blamed for the flows of hot money affecting Britain's reserves. Only at the point where these funds are borrowed by, and are to be used by, the British Government or by a British company, nationalised or private enterprise, are they switched into sterling and the underlying foreign currency moves into official hands in London; and only at this point do they increase Britain's central reserves. In effect, therefore, the banks in the City of London are normally acting in the Euro-dollar market as if they were in an offshore centre which is deliberately isolated from the British economy. Any attempt to equate these activities with 'hot money' flows pushing the British economy off course is simply misinformed.

One final point needs to be explored. It is the view that the City has neglected British industry at the expense of its foreign clients. We have already examined the charge about the neglect of British industry's needs in Chapters 3 and 7. This is usually allied with the feeling that, because of the City's involvement with international money, it has in some way allowed (even encouraged) credit and capital to flow abroad rather than encouraging it to stay in Britain. In the past few years, this attitude has been supported by statistics which are said to show the strong investment of British funds in overseas projects and the lamentable inadequacy of investment by British industry. It is time, therefore, to turn to the real meaning behind the overseas investment figures. When looked at closely they do not provide the construction often put upon them. Both the National Economic Development Council and the Treasury have provided the essential ingredients for an assessment. As NEDC pointed out in a discussion paper, early in 1976, UK net direct overseas investment in 1974 was estimated to have been £1,540 million. This excluded investment by the oil industry. Of the total over a half (£872 million) was provided by the unremitted profits of overseas subsidiaries and the remaining £688 million 'was mostly financed by foreign currency borrowing'. The Treasury came to this conclusion from its own analysis:

> The net additions to our overseas investments in recent years have been financed in such a way that the reserves have been fully protected, and the net effect on the balance of payments of *all* the identified items connected with international investment – past and present – has been both favourable and massive, averaging some £2¼ billion a year over the last three years. Such an outcome is virtually guaranteed by our exchange control rules.

Even in the case of portfolio investment the restrictions were as great and new investments had to be financed only by foreign currency borrowing or through the use of what was known as 'investment currency', a restricted pool which meant that one British investor could only obtain such funds from another one. In other words, neither British industry nor the City of London had channelled funds from Britain to these overseas territories at the expense of development here. The reason is not far to seek. Under exchange control rules direct investment overseas had to be financed in ways which largely avoided any direct export of capital. Even the charge that such investment (however it is financed) is at the expense of British industry is hard to sustain. A significant part of it is undertaken as an essential part of the British export drive in setting up sales, distribution and after-sales networks in overseas markets. In some cases it is the result of a decision by a British firm to manufacture in a territory to which it is finding it difficult to export. In others, especially in developing countries, the exporter may be given no alternative but to take on local manufacture or assembly. As the Confederation of British Industry concluded, after studying the NEDC evidence, overseas direct investment 'has a beneficial effect on exports from the UK' and 'does not reduce investment in the UK'. The City's main role in overseas direct investment is largely in an advisory capacity to British firms and, where necessary, in providing financial expertise and local funds overseas, apart from its own direct investment in setting up local branches of British banks, insurance companies, brokerage houses and the like (which, in 1974, accounted for some 15 per cent of the total).

We must now return briefly to the City's links with sterling, with which we started this chapter. The City provides markets in money, securities and foreign exchange where the fortunes of the domestic currency are reflected, though occasionally somewhat exaggerated. The causes of the recurrent sterling crises are to be found not in the City markets nor even among some of the City institutions who may operate there, but in the British economy, and, above all, in the vast sterling debts which this country has accumulated over the past four decades of both war and peace. Britain emerged from the war at the centre of a defensive grouping, the sterling area, which it helped to create and from which it benefited. But its obligations to keep payments free within this area and ultimately in a wider area owed more to the international climate of co-operation and free trade than to the special pleadings of the City of London. Britain, not the City, was acting as banker to the sterling area. Britain, as a major trading nation, as much as the City as an international centre, needed to keep restrictions on the movement of funds to a minimum. The City, in creating and developing the Eurodollar market, provided itself with an important adjunct to sterling and the government and industry with a large new source of foreign borrowing. Neither the City nor British industry can be seriously accused of investing abroad either to the detriment of British industrial development or at the expense of the British economy in general.

Chapter 14

Euromarkets: No Controls?

Over a half of the present output of the chemical multinationals, we are told, had not been invented ten years ago. Ask anyone in the City about its own innovations since the war, and some would point to the air charter market on the Baltic; others to the parallel sterling markets, others again to the coverage of nuclear risks or to the new ways of financing huge international projects; but virtually everyone would mention the Eurodollar market.

In 1956 the concept of a Eurodollar was unknown; now the market is worth over $700 billion. Its birthplace is disputed,[1] its place of development not. Nor, in spite of the rise of Nassau, the Cayman Islands, Bahrein and Singapore as rival invoicing centres, does anyone deny that London remains the centre of this vast new pool of international credit which it helped to develop and which, in turn, helped the City to survive the buffetings of so many sterling crises. Here is a market which has helped industry and governments to finance their activities on a world-wide basis; it is also a market that some say is out of control and a danger to the western world.

The term 'Eurodollar' is misleading. The currencies used in this particular market are confined neither to dollars nor to Europe, but both dollars and Europe were intimately con-

---

[1] Some say that the Russian bank in Paris, Banque Commerciale pour l'Europe du Nord, was the first to begin on-lending its surplus dollars in the late 1950s; others, that London banks were the first to deliberately seek out surplus dollars for such on-lending.

cerned with the way the market developed. It is now in reality a multi-currency market which supplies credit to borrowers world-wide. The currencies involved, however, have one characteristic in common. They are held by banks, corporations or individuals outside their country of origin. Thus Eurodollars will be held outside the United States, Euromarks outside Germany and Eurosterling outside Britain. This gives us a clue to the way in which the market developed in the first place. Immediately after the war only the American and Canadian dollars and the Swiss franc, of the leading world currencies, were freely convertible into other currencies or into gold; and even the Swiss resisted any use of their currency for outside purposes. But in 1958 the leading European currencies (including the pound sterling) and the Japanese yen also became convertible. This meant that exporters and business-men in general had more freedom with the currencies they earned. Some countries still imposed limits on the length of time their currencies could be held, but flexibility was creeping in. This move to convertibility also coincided with the first deficits in the American balance of payments. The rest of the world was earning more than it was spending in the United States. Thus surplus dollars became available just at the time when currencies could be more freely moved from one country to another. Moreover, most of the surplus dollars were ending up in European hands as European economic strength began to show itself for the first time since the end of the war. In addition, the profits of US companies in Europe and elsewhere tended to be held outside the US, for fiscal reasons, and after conversion into dollars they helped to swell the supply of funds of the new market. They still do.

The scene was set for a banking initiative. London's inter-national banks, already restricted in their use of sterling after the crisis of 1957, did not miss the opportunity, especially since internal American legislation had the effect of tying New York bankers' arms behind their back. This was the now famous Regulation Q, which controlled the rate of interest American banks operating in the US could offer to both resident and foreign holders of dollars. It meant quite simply that banks in London, faced with the knowledge of large and growing dollar deposits in European hands and knowing that American banks could offer only a fixed rate of interest for them, were able to provide a competitive rate of interest, secure the use of the dollars for agreed periods, and then, thanks to their world-wide contacts, use them in a variety of ways.

A simple beginning, but with a remarkable potential. The mechanism was not entirely new. Convertible currencies had been used in this way in the inter-war years as well as before 1914; sterling in the nineteenth century and French francs and occasionally dollars in the 1920s are examples.[1] But it was the scale of the operations that was new, and the reasons for this are to be found in the remarkable world-wide developments of the late 1950s and the whole of the 1960s, as I explained briefly in Chapter 2 and in the last chapter.

The West was poised for the biggest boom in prosperity the world has ever seen. The Common Market had been born at the end of 1958. Soon American firms were flocking to Europe, then extending their operations to the Far East and elsewhere. American banks were not far behind, setting up branch offices in the main money centres of the world. London became their main target. And they came because of their need to provide multinational clients with finance for world-wide operations. The American banks found they could do in London what they were unable to do in New York: that is to compete for surplus dollars held outside the United States. It was not long before American banks were as active as domestic London banks in this new and exciting source of international finance.

So much for the beginnings of the Eurodollar market. Its growth deserves the description phenomenal. In 1959 when the market was first measured, the amount outstanding was put at $1 billion. By 1967 it had reached $17·5 billion and by the end of 1970, $57 billion. The latest gross estimate puts it at no less than $789 billion. These figures, however, cloak a variety of developments that have accompanied the growth. At first it was mainly the London-based banks that dominated

[1] Paul Einzig even claimed to have found precedents in the medieval practice of drawing bills, some of them foreign, at quarterly fairs. See *The Euro-dollar System* (Macmillan & Co., 1964).

the dealings. British banks were encouraged to seek other means
of financing international trade because of restrictions on the
use of sterling outside the then sterling area. American banks
also soon found that they could procure dollars in London which
enabled them to finance the needs of their corporate clients and,
at the same time, avoid monetary restrictions at home. Thereafter other nationalities joined in. Each found a base in London
a necessary part of their growing international business and
within a decade the number of foreign banks with branches or
representative offices in the Square Mile had nearly doubled.
The numbers grew from just over 80 in the late 1950s (about
the number as in the 1930s) to over 300. Soon they were
joined by the establishment and growth of consortium banks
formed by banks eager to tap the new sources of international
money available in London but too small to do so on their own.
These banks also flocked to other prime centres, though not
in such large numbers as to London. New York, Frankfurt,
Paris, Zurich, Geneva, Tokyo, Singapore, Hong Kong – all in
their different ways became part of a new international
network.

While this cross-fertilisation of financial centres was taking
place throughout the 1960s, the new Eurocurrency markets
were developing. It was not, however, a steady growth. Nor, at
that time, was it expected to continue indefinitely. One leading
City merchant banker in the early 1960s devoted the greater
part of his annual statement to the theme that the Eurodollar
market was a passing phase and would not become an established
part of the financial scene. He rather hoped it would not. He
was listened to with respect, though the growth continued. But
there were others with greater insight and foresight. Sir George
Bolton, who had been put in charge of the new exchange
control department at the Bank of England in the 1930s and
had risen to be executive director of the Bank before taking
over as Chairman of the Bank of London and South America
in 1957, had this to say about the new market: 'Some critics
claim that the market is little more than a house of cards on a
shaky foundation of untested credit and doomed to auto-
destruction with the first breeze of adversity. These critics fail
to realise that the market is essentially the only practical

method, however imperfect, to fill the vacuum which has
developed in international finance since the last war.'[1] He
quickly put his confident views into practice and before long
BOLSA, as his bank was known, was one of the most active
participants in this new market. The participation of the foreign
banks, the consortium banks, the British overseas banks and the
merchant and clearing banks soon gave the Euromarkets a firm
base.

It is easier to describe the origins of the Eurocurrency market
than to keep pace with its instruments and its various developments. What was originally a short-term market, using surplus
currency deposits for between three and six months, was
gradually extended by various techniques – by the rolling over
(the renewal) of loans, by the introduction of floating rates of
interest and by various currency options (that is the ability
to switch from one specified currency to another). In the
early days, that is up to about a decade ago, loans were
generally extended up to two years, but eventually the demand
for larger and longer loans led to the medium-term syndicated
loans which now make up such a large slice of Euromarket
activity. The newly formed consortium banks played a significant role in these developments, but it was the introduction
of a flexible interest rate, adjusted on a six-month basis to the
current Eurocurrency interest rate, that enabled individual
banks to manage syndicated loans for longer periods. This
source of Euroloans, in contrast with the Eurobond market
which we shall be considering in a moment, is essentially a
market for banks, since borrowers receive their funds through
banking intermediaries and not direct from the market. The
banks in return receive deposits from a variety of sources,
from rich individuals, from large industrial corporations, from
central banks, but, above all, from other commercial banks.
The length of the deposit can be from virtually overnight to
five years. Longer periods are possible though unusual. The
normal period is a year. These so-called interbank deposits
attract current interest rates and the six-month rate is normally
taken as the basis for LIBOR, the London Interbank Offered

[1] *A Banker's World*, ed. Richard Fry (Hutchinsons, 1970)

Rate. Thus the interest rate charged on Euroloans to large corporations or governments is worked out on a margin, or spread, above LIBOR. This margin, which provides lending banks with their profit and can change and indeed narrow, has to cover a bank's administrative costs as well as its potential risk. The lending rate will vary over the period of the loan and will usually be adjustable on a six-monthly basis. The length of the loans can vary from, say, three years to seven years and beyond, rather depending on the state of the market and especially the severity of competition among lending banks. The more competition, the longer the period offered or the narrower the spread. An option can be given to switch into other currencies. The loans are managed by a leading inter-national bank, helped by one or two others, acting as co-managers, and with other banks joining the syndicate as participants.

Thus, although borrowers in the Euroloan market cannot be assured of a fixed rate of interest throughout the duration of the loan, they have the benefit of certain flexibilities: they can decide how much of the loan they wish to draw down; they have a choice of the monthly periods at which interest payments will be charged and rolled over; and they can some-times switch to other currencies to suit their own cash flows, should they wish.

The Eurobond market owes much to the development of the whole Eurocurrency market: the same factors stimulated both. But Eurobonds have their own historical roots too. They are the modern equivalent of the bonds issued by foreign governments and municipalities and sold in several European financial centres simultaneously in the nineteenth century. Their revival was the result of the extension of convertibility to the major European currencies and of the restrictions in-creasingly imposed on the leading capital market in New York in the early 1960s. While the New York bond market was open and other centres such as Frankfurt, Zurich and Amsterdam were available for long-term foreign loans, an alternative outlet was not given much encouragement. But the imposition of the US interest equalisation tax in 1963, which added to the interest cost of a foreign borrower, made it uneconomic for foreign corporations and governments to raise money in New York. This tax was followed by other American exchange control restrictions, the voluntary foreign credit restraint programme in 1965 and the foreign direct investment regulations in 1968, and combined to restrict New York for close on a decade, and, at the same time, gave ample encouragement to both London and Frankfurt to fill the gap. More important, it encouraged New York banks and investment banks to develop their fund-raising activities in Europe, rather than the United States. By 1965 the total of international bond issues had reached $1 billion. As I write, the annual total is nearer $14 billion, though activity varies considerably from year to year. Now, even though the restrictions in New York have been lifted and foreign borrowing has returned there, the Eurobond market is firmly established as a significant alternative source of international funds.

The main feature of a Eurobond is that it is for a stated period, usually between five and fifteen years, and carries a fixed rate of interest. The whole loan has to be drawn at once. Whereas an issue will be managed by one bank, and underwritten by anything up to a hundred banks, the bonds will be sold to a combination of individuals and investing institutions on a global basis. About two dozen international banks compete for the role of lead manager to the main issues, but well over three hundred international banks are also in the business as underwriters. The issues are usually quoted on two stock exchanges, often New York, Frankfurt or London and Luxembourg, and are mainly in US dollars, German marks, Swiss francs, or, more recently, Japanese yen. Other European currencies have been used on occasions. Sterling-related Eurobonds too have been issued, though their use has been strictly regulated by the Bank of England. In recent sterling-related issues, the UK residents wishing to subscribe would have been required to use investment currency while UK resident borrowers have been permitted to use the sterling proceeds only for investment in the United Kingdom.

The key to the successful management of a Eurobond issue is the ability to place the bonds with clients. It is estimated that over a half of outstanding Eurobonds are held by individuals and private corporations. They vary considerably, from South American residents keen to have their investments safely outside an unstable political area to rich oil sheiks in the Middle East. Some use their Swiss-based accounts. Beyond these are the large financial institutions, banks, pension funds and insurance companies and even international agencies.

There is also a secondary market in Eurobonds, now largely among the London-based banks and American investment houses in London, though other centres, such as Luxembourg and Brussels, are involved too in the telephonic transactions. As we outlined in Chapter 5, a secondary market where subscribers to new issues can resell their bonds is as essential as the prime issuing market itself. In the case of Eurobonds the annual amount being issued has recently reached close on $14 billion. Turnover on the secondary market is difficult to gauge since there is no central market-place, but an analysis of some of the recent clearing figures suggests that the *weekly* turnover might be about $1 billion. At the outset the main secondary market was made up of four dealers, two in London, one American firm in Zurich and a German bank. The introduction of two clearing systems and the eventual formation of the Association of International Bond Dealers brought some depth and stability to the market. Now there are 100 registered dealing firms. The market was recently described by Mr S. Yassukovich, the chairman of the association from 1976–9, as follows:

Geographic dispersal, which is an inherent characteristic of this market, the fact that the main participants are easily in touch with each other through telephone and telex, and importantly, the techniques utilised in the primary markets, have rendered the role of the stock exchange almost entirely redundant in terms of maintaining the liquidity of the international bond market.

There are belated signs of interest on the London and other stock exchanges in Eurobond activity, but the fact that the main participants have been banks and not brokers and that national exchanges are primarily concerned with regulating domestic issues may still prevent progress in that direction.

With so many of the same banks and financial institutions involved in both the Eurodollar and Eurobond markets as well as in the foreign exchange market, it sometimes becomes confusing to the outsider to know what the difference is between them. Eurodollar and foreign exchange deals can be done in the same dealing room. The Eurodollar market, like the foreign exchange market described in Chapter 12, is essentially a telephone market. By their nature the two markets overlap and, in some respects, are integrated with each other. The exchange market is, of course, concerned with the exchange of one currency for another, either today or on specified forward dates. The Eurocurrency market is concerned with the lending and borrowing of individual currency deposits over a period of time. This distinction can occasionally give rise to confusion since 'rates' in the foreign exchange market mean exchange rates, whereas 'rates' in the Eurodollar market usually imply interest rates. To add to the confusion, each market will be interested in both exchange rates and interest rates. The other main distinction is that, whereas the London foreign exchange market is made up of authorised dealers linked together by foreign exchange brokers, since the banks are not allowed to deal direct with each other, the banks making up the Eurodollar market deal both with international money brokers and with each other. Many more banks are active in the London Eurodollar market than in the foreign exchange market since the foreign banks and consortium banks tend to do little foreign exchange business and their prime purpose in being in London is to be able to participate in Eurodollar business.

These new markets are a significant remarkable addition to the domestic markets in credit and capital. Both now exist side by side and both vary in volume from year to year. Table 17 shows what these domestic and international markets have provided, in the way of new capital, in recent years. The question monetary authorities round the world have to face is whether these new flexibilities are being sought at too high a price – in potential risks to the world's monetary system.

Table 17   *International Market for Capital*

			($ billion)			
	1973	1974	1975	1976	1977	1978
Eurobonds	4·2	2·1	8·6	14·3	17·7	14·1
Foreign bonds on domestic markets	3·6	4·7	11·3	18·2	14·5	20·0
Total	7·8	6·8	19·9	32·5	31·0	34·1
Syndicated medium-term Eurocredits	21·9	29·3	21·0	29·0	42·0	70·0
Total	29·7	36·1	40·9	61·5	73·2	104·1

Source: Morgan Guaranty.

In the early days, the monetary authorities were extremely wary of this new market and the US Treasury sent a small team of experts to Europe to work out what exactly it meant for American interests. It did not take them long to discover that dollars which were being used in this way were not able to be presented for payment at the New York Federal Reserve and were thus helping to preserve America's central gold reserves at Fort Knox. Other Treasuries and central banks soon learned other ways of using the market to their benefit. The Italian central bank, faced with lira crises, found it advantageous to borrow dollars from the market and, occasionally, to on-lend them to the market. Belgium did the same. The countries running embarrassingly large payments surpluses, such as Japan, found it better to lend surplus dollars to the Euromarket than to allow the surplus to force a premature revaluation of the yen. Then came the oil crisis and soon individual governments, having to face huge deficits, were using the market as an alternative to borrowing either from the World Bank or the International Monetary Fund. (The first was becoming too expensive and the second, it was said, too restrictive.) Moreover, official finance from these sources was often too small in relation to the restrictive conditions often imposed. Italy once again was an early borrower; so too was Britain, both directly, by a large government borrowing, and indirectly, through the borrowings of public corporations and local authorities with government guarantees. They were not alone. Within a couple of years borrowings by the developing world and the Soviet bloc were dominating the Eurocurrency market.

It is tempting to join in the debate that has been going on about the risks being run by major banks from this vast borrowing by the developing world, but my immediate concern is somewhat narrower: to consider what impact this new market has had on the City and to assess its dangers. The City, like international business generally, shared in the prosperity of the sixties and early seventies. It benefited in several ways from this major new international money market on its doorstep. The impulse it gave to the development of the parallel money markets, which we outlined in Chapter 8, was beneficial to the clearing banks, merchant banks, discount houses and money brokers as well as to the domestic borrowers in these expanding markets. As we also saw in Chapter 9, the British Government was provided with an alternative – and highly flexible – source of foreign borrowing. Above all, the magnet of this new market brought to London an unbelievable variety of foreign banks, buttressing London's role as a leading international centre just when sterling (on which such a role had originally been based) was losing its appeal. This was naturally helpful to the main banks; it was also, indirectly, helpful to other international parts of the City (the commodity markets, insurance, shipping brokers and so on), providing them or their clients with an alternative means of finance. And it meant that the City's international markets in money, securities and commodities could contemplate the deliberate reduction in the use of sterling as a reserve currency and even as a trading currency with more equanimity than they would otherwise have done.

There is, of course, another side to the coin. The new Euro-currency markets have brought added competition to London, from other offshore centres, as well as added opportunities, and I shall be exploring these repercussions in Chapter 16. In addition, the City and the international community generally rely on the Eurocurrency markets to a degree that was unknown three decades ago. Thus the monetary authorities, in carrying out their traditional role of supervision, especially in protecting depositors' funds and in protecting the domestic banking system as a whole, have been faced with some novel problems by the increasingly intricate relationships of both the multinational corporations and the international banks. No longer is it enough to look after the interests of domestic depositors and domestic banks. When banks are lending huge sums to each other across frontiers, before on-lending to customers; when the industrial borrowers themselves have tentacles in different countries; and when such a large part of the lending is undertaken by foreign branches, foreign subsidiaries and newly formed international banking consortia; then the role of the national supervisor needs careful rethinking. The awareness of these new difficulties, combined with the occasional international monetary scare, has naturally led to growing demands for a close supervision of these new markets. Over the last few years there has been a considerable tightening of supervisory procedures at both the national and the international levels.

The fears have been of four basic kinds: that a vast volume of hot money, rising at 25 per cent a year, unless rigidly controlled, can upset exchange rates and lead to monetary chaos overnight; that the pyramiding of credit through the Eurodollar markets is a source of world-wide inflation as well as a potential source of credit risks; that a bank failure in one country might, through its Eurocurrency links, bring down the rest like a pack of cards; and that the size and quality of some of the new country risks being undertaken by individual banks could quickly become a threat to the whole system.

The first of these fears – that the amount of money involved in these new markets can upset exchange rates as well as domestic monetary and fiscal policies – has been expressed largely by the monetary authorities themselves. Germany's attempts to fight inflation, for example, have often been undermined by the inflow of foreign funds on a huge scale. Each currency crisis has brought demands for stricter controls. Yet the demands have occasionally been refuted from other authoritative quarters. In 1971, for example, after the US dollar had been forced to relinquish its link with gold and been devalued for the first time since the end of the war, the

Bank for International Settlements (the bank to which all leading central banks belong) quashed any suggestion that the Eurodollar had played any part in the monetary disorders: 'The quarterly statistics do not lend much support to assertions that the Eurocurrency market played a leading role in the exchange turmoils of 1971.' In any case – it was argued by other central banks, especially the Bank of England – rigid controls operated through the main centres such as London, New York, Zurich or Frankfurt would simply ensure that Eurocurrency dealings were switched to other less regulated centres in other parts of the world. Supervision would become that much harder.

The other general fear – of the excessive pyramiding of credit – is heard on fewer occasions than it used to be, though it has recently begun to fascinate the writers of best-selling novels, such as *The Crash of '79*.[1] The rapid expansion of the market has naturally led to the fear that it could quickly spiral out of control, and there is no denying that the market has become an alternative to the gold discoveries of the last century in the manner in which it has oiled the wheels of international trade. But the pyramiding of credit on credit, it is now increasingly being realised, still depends on the cash and liquidity ratios imposed by individual monetary authorities. These monetary controls are as vulnerable as the central banks operating them choose them to be. In fact, recent discussions on the best way to control the Euromarkets have concentrated more on the home countries of the international banks operating in these markets, than in the markets themselves. In the words of the Governor of the Bank of England, 'the international banking markets are primarily a transmission mechanism – a very efficient mechanism indeed – and not an important source of independent credit creation.'

Yet a weak link in this new chain of credit remains a weak link. And it is this fear – the third we mentioned at the outset – that has been the prime concern of the leading central banks since the shock of the Herstatt failure reverberated through the Euromarkets in the early summer of 1974, even though the

[1] Paul Erdman, *The Crash of '79* (Secker & Warburg, 1977).

collapse was not the result of Eurodollar market transactions. The markets were already in a sensitive state, following the shock of the oil price increase in 1973, the repercussions of Watergate, the changing governments in Britain and France and the continuing currency doubts throughout 1973 and 1974. But the collapse of the Herstatt bank in Cologne, coupled with the way in which the Bundesbank allowed it to close its doors while dealings with it were still going on in New York, for example, provided the Eurodollar market with its first major crisis. Confidence was severely shaken and the expansion of the market was halted, and then reversed, for virtually the first time. It was not the only shock. Lloyds Bank International, Banque de Bruxelles, Union Bank of Switzerland, Westdeutsche Landesbank, Girocentrale – all had to reveal large losses on their foreign exchange dealings, though not, it should be noted, on their borrowing and lending in Eurodollars. But it was a smaller collapse, the Israel-British Bank in Tel Aviv, that really alerted the main central banks to one of the new dangers. The bank's parent operated in Israel but was controlled by a group whose major business interests were in the United Kingdom. The group took advantage of the difference in regulatory regimes between Israel and the United Kingdom.

This episode was the start of central bank regulatory co-operation. The Bank of England learnt the lesson and was soon persuading other central banks to sort out the tangle of divided responsibilities. The first decision was taken later that year when the governors of the leading central banks agreed to provide 'lender of last resort' facilities to their own national banks to support their Eurocurrency operations. This meant that banks were expected to stand behind the activities of their branches, subsidiaries and partly owned operations in overseas countries. At the same time the central banks set up a joint supervisory agency, the Committee on Banking Regulations and Supervisory Practices, with a secretariat provided by the Bank for International Settlements in Basle. Early warning systems of possible banking troubles were soon set up; then came tentative agreements about the supervision of foreign bank branches and subsidiaries and of the new international consortia. Their aim is to ensure that no bank or offshoot of a bank escapes supervision by someone. This does not mean that banks won't go bust. It should mean that, if and when they do, the repercussions should be minimised, as happened in 1976 with the collapse of the Banque pour l'Amérique du Sud, when four countries co-operated for the first time in containing the dangerous ripples.

The final fear I outlined earlier – that the appearance of large country borrowings might undermine the whole basis of the market – is being tackled in a different way. This question began to emerge between 1974 and 1976, when Italy and Britain borrowed large sums directly from the market which were accompanied by huge individual borrowings by several developing countries.[1] These transactions raised two separate problems. In the first place banks were being asked to assess the creditworthiness of sovereign countries. Secondly, the size of the loans was introducing an element of lumpiness into a market that had existed on its ability to spread risks widely. Banks could no longer put their eggs in several baskets, or rather they were putting more of their new-laid eggs in a more limited number of baskets. As one critic put it 'They have inevitably got to decide whether they want, or not, to be "long in Britain" or "short in Italy", for instance'. In 1890 Baring's decided to 'go long in Argentina' and the well-known crisis[2] followed. Other examples of the same kind can be provided, the most famous being the Creditanstalt.[3] Unless the price of oil declines suddenly, it can be expected that borrowings from the developing countries at least will continue for some time. At the same time it need not be assumed that all these countries are courting disaster. But a strengthening of the resources of the

[1] The bank debts of the non-oil developing countries rose from $46 billion to $102 billion between December 1974 and the spring of 1978.

[2] Baring's loans to Argentina (and Uruguay) increased throughout the 1880s on a tide of euphoria until, in November 1890, general doubts about the Argentine land boom, the outflow of gold from the Bank of England and, eventually, pressures on Baring's liquid assets led to a major City crisis. A City banking consortium, including the Bank of England, was needed to resolve it.

[3] The collapse of the Austrian private bank on 11 May 1931 was a major turning point in the events leading up to Britain's suspension of the gold standard on 20 September 1931.

International Monetary Fund, coupled with the development of what is called 'parallel financing', under which private banks provide Eurofinance contingent upon the borrowing country's meeting credit conditions laid down by the IMF, would do much to restore confidence.

All these fears have been based on specific dangers. The moves now being taken to buttress the market's defences whether or not they include reserve requirements on Eurodollar deposits should help not only to ward off future speculative dangers, but to keep at bay some of the more rigid controls once being urged upon it that could only result in the strangulation of the market as we know it or at least its transfer to the most unregulated offshore centres of the Caribbean or the Pacific. But it should not be overlooked that the defensive moves have primarily stemmed from the leading industrialised countries and that the monetary authorities of the developing world – especially in the world of offshore centres – have not so far shown a similar determination.

Chapter 15

Who Controls the City?

The City is often accused of having power without responsibility. Sometimes it is seen as the power that comes from a combination of money and inside information; sometimes it is the financial power to manipulate people, corporations or even countries; sometimes it is the power to frustrate a government's economic, or even foreign, policy. Whatever the reason, controls are called for and often imposed. My concern in this chapter, therefore, is to assess how far the City is under control, what the controls are intended to do, what effect they have had on the day-to-day workings of the City's markets, and whether anything further now needs to be done.

Controls are hardly a new feature of City life, but the size and extent of the controls both used and available to the authorities, as well as the additional ones being urged on them, are greater than ever before. They have accumulated rapidly since the war. Some have been inherited from wartime experience; some are the result of crisis measures introduced to cope with avoidable currency pressures; others again have been introduced out of ideological conviction; and over a space of well over a century there has grown up a code of professional conduct, backed by legal sanctions where necessary, to protect the public whether as consumer, investor or shareholder.

It is as well, however, to try to make a distinction between the controls that are intended to create orderly markets and those designed to protect the public or to promote government policy. The City has developed a sound tradition of mutual trust over a long period. Almost more important than *what* is said in its main markets is *who* says it. These habits have grown

up because of the narrow world in which these markets operate,
stemming from the closeness of one market to another and
from the way in which so many markets are integrated.
Familiarity has followed, encouraged by the village-like
atmosphere of the City streets and the frequency of personal
encounters. The tradition of clinching deals by word of mouth
was a natural development.

Deals on the gilt-edged market, all done by word of mouth,
can range between half a million and a million pounds each.
In the foreign exchange market telephone deals can vary
between one and two million pounds. Individual contracts of
up to £20 millions have been reported. The discount house
representatives will be borrowing individual amounts of £10
million on no more than the strength of their name. These oral
deals are based on trust between one dealer and another. It
was, and still is, essential for any transgression against this code
to be punished by an immediate expulsion from the inner
circle. The relationships which still exist within the discount
market, within the accepting houses, between brokers and
jobbers on the Stock Exchange and between brokers and underwriters at Lloyd's have all been based on this slow development
of market behaviour. It has also been backed up by the framework of company law, by the codes of conduct introduced by
professional bodies such as the Law Society and the Institute
of Chartered Accountants, and by the market rules introduced
by the Stock Exchange.

Yet what was appropriate for City men dealing with each
other and with a narrow sector of society which could seek
and get professional advice is no longer adequate for a City
that has deliberately and successfully widened its horizons at
home and abroad. A code appropriate for the main clearing
banks, the discount houses and the inner members of the
Accepting Houses Committee – where a nod and a wink over
tea at the Bank of England was often enough to assure action – is
unlikely to be as effective with the growing numbers of hire-
purchase and fringe banks that have mushroomed over the
past quarter of a century. What is adequate in London looks
different in the markets of Djakarta, Manila and Hong Kong.
What might be enough to protect the large investing institu-

tions is unlikely to be adequate in the world of the smaller investor. The spate of take-over deals from the late 1950s onwards, the property developers, the asset-strippers, the international mutual funds, the go-go investors – all have brought threats, sometimes losses, to depositors or shareholders. It is not the job of the City or government to protect the investor from his own follies: it is their job to see that the dice are not loaded against him by operators with inside knowledge, prior knowledge, or sharp or dishonest practices of any kind.

Protection needs grow with a boom and the world-wide boom throughout the sixties and early seventies (not always in the stock market) brought with it new opportunities, new developments and new dangers, especially when it was followed by the sharpest recession since 1931. Throughout this period the London Stock Exchange, the Take-over Panel, the Department of Trade, and the British Insurance Association continually tightened their rules to protect the public. Borrowing from the public was carefully monitored; behaviour in the stock market, especially before and during take-over battles, was watched carefully; the Take-over Panel established new rules and a method of enforcing them; directors' obligations were underlined. Yet, at the same time, there were examples of insurance companies failing, of fringe banks being wound up, of depositors' money being lost, of chairmen using company funds for unauthorised purposes, of bribery charges against multinationals, of directors receiving huge loans from their own companies, and of inside knowledge being used for personal gain. Some involved the City; some did not. But it was only a short step from the disquiet that followed to persistent demands for additional controls, preferably from government or from a new-style government-appointed SEC[1] along American lines.

The City debate has rarely been about the need to strengthen existing methods of control (that has been assumed), but rather about the best way of doing so – by tightening self-regulation or by imposing a new form of statutory surveillance from outside. The SEC kind of proposals, involving a new

---

[1] The Securities Exchange Commission in New York, set up in 1934, following the Securities Act of 1933 and the Securities Exchange Act of 1934, has broad supervisory powers over US stock exchanges.

government agency to supervise City markets, are understandable but they have left one nagging thought: would they
protect the public at the expense of strangling the various City
markets they are intended to supervise? London is different
from New York. It has a freedom and a trust that are worth
preserving for they give the swiftness of decision making on
which so much of London's reputation is still based. For the
past quarter of a century and longer the Bank of England in its
own area of supervision has deliberately controlled the City in
full knowledge of how each market worked: it has a full operating unit in the foreign exchange market and has its own
broker in both the discount market and the gilt-edged market.
It has had the advantage of day-to-day contact with market
people. It has therefore been able to operate the highly
complex exchange control regulations with both firmness and
understanding. Britain has probably the tightest controls on
outward investment in the Western world; yet, thanks to the
Bank of England, it has administered them with due regard to
their impact on day-to-day management. In contrast, the
SEC-style supervision is far more akin to New York practice,
with its reliance on legal back-up to money negotiations. It
can also be extremely costly. The City's Take-Over panel has
cost about £300,000 a year while the United States Congress
has had to authorise $65 million (about £35 million) for the
SECs operations.

In the twin efforts to ensure orderly markets and to protect
the public, the present system of City controls is a combination
of self-regulation, Bank of England guidance and statutory
instruments. It is thus a blend of statutory and non-statutory
regulations. While the law imposes rigid rules on everyone
and is slow to adapt to changing market conditions, self-
regulation, even when backed up by statutory powers, can
allow for the spirit, as well as the letter, of the law. The
Bank of England's role is central to all City markets, but it
varies from one to another. Its role as a central bank gives it
full responsibility for the banks and the money markets,
though its surveillance of individual banks is still shared with
the Department of Trade. On the other hand, the Bank is more
concerned with the general surveillance of the securities

market and the commodity market than with outright control. It is less directly concerned with insurance and shipping. Its role as referee, however, is still acknowledged by all.

In assessing future supervision, attention has naturally focused on the control of the banks and the stock market. Future banking controls will essentially reflect the lessons learnt from the lifeboat operations of the Bank of England in rescuing fringe banks from 1974 onwards, together with the shape of recent Common Market legislation. What has come to be called the 'Secondary Banking Crisis' of 1974–5 was in essence the biggest run on domestic banks for several decades. It can be argued that the authorities were as much to blame for the crisis as anyone and that, without a combination of fiscal and monetary stimuli, the ambiguity in the status and control of certain fringe banks, and the blurring in the City's new wholesale money markets between a real bank and a near-bank, the crisis might have been avoided. It can also be argued, with equal force, that private individuals and institutions locked up short-term money in illiquid assets, primarily property, to a dangerous degree. Whatever the cause of the crisis, however, I believe that the Bank of England was right to launch its lifeboat when it did.

The episode has a direct relevance to the kind of banking supervision now needed. It is clear, with hindsight, that the division of overall supervision of banks between the Bank of England and the Department of Trade, prior to the secondary banking crisis, was unsatisfactory. It is also clear that the bewildering number of categories both of 'banks' and the forms of supervision appropriate to them did not help. Since then the Bank of England has separated, and enlarged, its own supervisory division. Its staff seek quarterly returns from banks as well as regular interviews to assess the nature of their business. For the future, new legislation, which will owe a great deal to the need to toe the Common Market line (especially its Second Banking Directive), will confirm the Bank of England as the main supervisory authority, will establish a two-tier system of banks and deposit-taking institutions, will limit the future use of the name 'bank', and will set up a new deposit-protection fund to help small depositors in institutions which run into trouble.

In the area of the money and foreign exchange markets, the Bank of England already has a remarkable variety of informal arrangements. It has the ability to check on the quality of the acceptances traded in the discount market; it calls for regular details of foreign exchange and Eurocurrency positions from authorised banks. It has informal arrangements with all the appropriate banking, money market and broking associations to keep a constant check on both the standing of members and the quality of the instruments in which the markets trade. The merchant banks, for example, have stated that they are now obliged to submit something like three hundred returns to the Bank of England each year. The cost of this exercise to the seventeen members of the Accepting Houses Committee is estimated at (including computer time) at least £50,000 a year to each of the major banks. A list of the main returns is shown in Table 18. The Bank of England has also encouraged the main banking and broking associations to draw up and supervise codes of practice for each market. But these informal codes are likely to come under increasing pressure from the legal bias of the Common Market. The difficulty is that Article 85 of the Treaty of Rome prohibits 'all agreements between undertakings . . . which may affect trade between member states'. Since Sarabex, a money-broking firm with Middle East connections, complained to the European Commission that the Foreign Exchange and Currency Deposit Brokers Association was denying entry, all these informal arrangements have been at risk. The result is that the Bank of England has been forced to accept responsibility for licensing money brokers. Similar arrangements may ultimately be necessary in other City markets.

The same fears have surrounded the recent efforts to tighten up and extend the supervision of the stock markets, which we touched on briefly in Chapter 5. What soon became clear was that, if the heavy hand of Government (and especially of detailed legislation) was to be avoided in the interest of maintaining market flexibility, then the City had to

Table 18   *Regular Returns Made by Merchant Banks to Bank of England*

	Number of Returns per annum
Annual valuation	1
Annual valuation of British Government stocks for overseas residents	1
Appropriation return	1
Balance sheet	16
Sterling certificates of deposit	12
Foreign securities and investment currencies – residents	12
Transactions in gold bullion	4
Overseas direct investment (outward)	2
Overseas direct investment (inward)	2
Transactions on behalf of overseas clients	12
Transactions in sterling securities in overseas markets	12
Sector details	4
Transactions in capital investments, etc.	4
Analysis of advances and acceptances	4
Lending for exports	4
Interest paid and received	4
Maturity analysis of sterling liabilities and assets	4
Analysis of shareholders' funds	4
UK claims on overseas residents in sterling	16
UK liabilities to overseas residents in sterling	16
Claims in currencies other than sterling	16
Liabilities in currencies other than sterling	16
Foreign currency positions	52
Forward sales and purchases of foreign currency	4
Maturity analysis of non-sterling liabilities and assets	4
Weekly balance sheet	36
Maturity analysis of external sterling claims	1
Maturity analysis of external claims other than sterling	1
Disclosure letter	1

Source: Evidence of Accepting Houses Committee to Wilson Committee

produce its own supervisory body made up of the main institutions concerned. This was the position in 1976 when the Labour Government finally decided to encourage the City to provide its own regulatory body in close collaboration with the Department of Trade. The Secretary of State for Trade told the House of Commons,[1] following a review of the supervision of the security markets: 'The review has shown that our present combination of statutory and self-regulatory control, although, perhaps a good deal more effective than its critics admit, could with advantage be improved in a number of respects.' It was a clear indication that even the Labour Government would prefer to avoid the over-detailed, and costly supervision of an American-style SEC in Britain. By the spring of 1978, such a voluntary body had been set up, known as the Council for the Securities Industry. It had the blessing of, and some control by, the Bank of England, since the Governor would appoint both chairman and deputy chairman. It was built around the existing machinery of the Quotations Department of the Stock Exchange, the City Panel on Take-overs and Mergers and the other professional bodies.

Its task is to improve the effective supervision of the securities market, to maintain ethical standards, to investigate alleged cases of misconduct, to initiate new policies and, where necessary, to resolve differences among the various bodies it represents. A tall order, it might seem, especially from a voluntary body and one lacking legal sanctions. While the advantages of such an arrangement are not hard to recognise – the City's markets would remain free from the pressure of legal restrictions which so bedevil New York markets and clog up their flexibility – the question is whether the new Council will have enough sanctions to make its regulations bite. The TUC, for example, has suggested that the Council should be armed with extra legal powers to curb the actions of individuals and companies – to halt trading and to ban certain traders – and should, eventually, extend its surveillance to banking, foreign exchange and commodities. The Council's sanctions at present simply depend on the voluntary recognition of the member bodies that the Council's recommendations cannot be ignored. This in turn depends on the codes of conduct of the professional bodies which make up the Council being brought into closer alignment with each other, if the pressures of the Take-over Panel on merchant banks, for example, are not to

[1] 21 October, 1976

remain much stricter than those of other bodies or other market operators.[1] There are also the natural doubts whether a self-regulatory system can not only be fair, without the legal backing of a government agency, but be seen to be fair. This need not imply that representatives of trade unions or consumer interests should be on the Council itself, but it should mean that self-regulatory bodies, like the Council and other parts of the City, need to be particularly open in their regulatory role and that sanctions against members should be undertaken in the public gaze. Having been given the chance to keep its own house in order, the onus is now on the City to show that it can work in the interests of everyone.

There remains the background role of government legislation in relation to the stock markets, particularly in company law and fraud. Both have been tightened up considerably over the past quarter of a century and there is a temptation to tackle each fresh scandal by a further turn of the screw. The temptation is greatest in the area of 'inside information'. It is clearly wrong for one person to operate on the stock market with inside knowledge about a company denied to the rest of us. This is why the Stock Exchange monitors over a thousand price movements a year and sets up committees to inquire into any that are not readily explicable; this is also why they and the Take-over Panel have introduced certain regulations about company information and why most leading City banks and institutions have their own strict rules about when their directors and employees can and cannot deal in their own shares. Beyond this the Stock Exchange Council and the Confederation of British Industries have issued what they call a 'model code' for share dealings by company directors. Among other things, it suggests that directors should not deal in their own companies' shares when they possess information that will move the share price. This obviously covers the period when a

---

[1] In evidence to the Wilson Committee, the Take-Over Panel has stressed that as a result of its hearings directors have resigned from boards, insider dealers have been made to pay improper gains to charity, where an obligation to bid following share-buying has not been fulfilled the buyer has been stopped from voting his shares or has been forced to cut his holding, and companies and individuals have been publicly censured.

company's annual accounts are being prepared and have not yet been published, as well as occasions when take-over bids have been made or big contracts gained. The 'code' is even more specific. It suggests that company directors should not deal in their company's shares in the two months leading up to the publication of interim or preliminary profit figures. Even when a director can deal, he should first inform his chairman. It should perhaps be added that many City institutions have voluntarily introduced restrictions on share dealings by their directors that are far stricter than this 'model code'. In fact, it is now questionable whether some of these self-imposed disciplines are not in danger of going too far and imposing unfair restrictions on directors. One City company, of which I am a director, has voluntary rules which, in practice, allow directors to deal in the company's shares on only 60 days out of a full year.

In addition to these voluntary curbs a new Companies Act will eventually emerge. The aim will be to make insider dealing a criminal offence. City institutions have been in favour of such a move, but their main anxiety has centred on the definitions used. The City has been naturally concerned that any Act should be drawn narrow enough to restrict the illegitimate use of confidential information but wide enough to allow institutional investors to seek, and obtain, detailed information from companies and to encourage the continued holding of shares by directors. The key question is whether legislation will prevent an investment manager or stockbroker obtaining information from a company which, although not yet published in detail, is freely available to anyone on request. Beyond this is the anxiety that, whatever the legal framework, the investigation of cases under such clauses should be conducted speedily and should not undermine the legitimate business or those undertaking it.

The question of commercial bribery is also difficult to legislate against. This is a problem that has to be faced by anyone handling large sums in many parts of the world. What is acceptable business practice and what should not be tolerated? As *The Banker*[1] put it:

---

[1] *The Banker*, London, June 1977

What constitutes a bribe plainly depends as much on custom as on morality. The largest bribe on record involved the payment of £30 millions to the then Sultan of Abu Dhabi by a Saudi official in connection with oil concessions, yet it is public knowledge and immortalised in the *Guinness Book of Records*. Is it corrupt to pay £50 to speed up the chairman's visa or £15,000–£20,000 (the going rate according to *The. Times*) to have the company's name removed from the Arab boycott list? There is a twilight zone where the fringe bribe rules.

Moreover, what is the difference between a bribe and a dealer's legitimate commission; between a bribe and a donation to an Italian political party; or between a bribe and 'a commission' in the Middle East, where usury is frowned upon? How should small payments, essential to obtain contracts in some countries, be separated from normal expense accounts – or should they? How should the accounting profession deal with them? How should payments for major concessions, whether to people or political parties, be dealt with in an era of increasing disclosures? How indeed can countries like the United States and the United Kingdom, with democratic pressures and strict company laws, allow their international businesses to compete in a world not of their making?

There are no easy solutions and legislation is unlikely to help. The spotlight which was focused on leaders of American multinationals, foreign royalty and even on some large British firms[1] by Congressional inquiries in the United States raised issues which anyone undertaking business overseas, including the City's financial institutions, is bound to meet from time to time. The dilemma is a real one. As Sir Frederick Catherwood, when Chairman of the British Overseas Trade Board, put it:

[1] 'In the course of inquiries carried out by staff of *The Money Programme*, twenty of Britain's top exporting companies with large developing-world interests were asked about their own financial practices abroad. Ten of these companies admitted, in confidence, to having special payments built into foreign contracts. Four of that ten admitted to paying bribes. Whatever the moral issues, British companies are involved on a large scale in commissions and pay-offs' (*The Listener*, 29 September 1977).

In about one third of the markets in which we operate, there are extortionate demands, and in those markets, if you don't pay some kind of money, you don't get the business. Politicians can get up in the House of Commons and say this must not happen. But they do not live with the consequences of its not happening. The businessman is faced with the position where he has 2,000 people in a factory. The factory requires a job in a Third World country, and the people in that country are absolutely demanding a payment. So what does he do?

The other question is : what can governments do? Some, alas, are directly involved with the whole chain of payments. In the United States a new bill threatens to impose stiff penalties for those convicted of bribery – up to five years in prison for individuals, and fines of up to £1 million for companies. Yet the only effect may be to push such activities further under cover. More promising, outside the legal framework, are the efforts of international business to draw up its own code, through the International Chamber of Commerce, with the aim of strengthening the hand of companies resisting extortion.

We must now turn to the second of our initial two kinds of control. I made a distinction at the outset between those controls intended to protect the public and those intended to promote government policy. Here it is not just a matter of the furtherance of government policy through taxation, monetary policy and the like, but also the issue of whether the City can in some way frustrate, whether deliberately or otherwise, the wishes of a democratically elected government. It is usually this connotation that is intended in discussions about who controls the City. It is worth dealing with this first before looking more broadly at the controls now in the hands of governments. We do not have to seek far for examples. The selling of sterling, pressures on the gilt-edged market, so-called investment 'strikes' and gloom in the stock market – all have figured prominently in recent years whenever suspicion has been directed towards the City. Conspiracy theories abound, but most of them involve the City, in a corporate sense, moving as a body to undermine government policy in whatever market is under attack. The

City of course is convenient shorthand for over a dozen markets and industries, so each market needs to be considered separately.

We have looked at the foreign exchange market in some detail in Chapter 12 and at the broad use of sterling in Chapter 13. Pressures on the pound can undermine and have undermined government policy and intentions. Banks and foreign-exchange dealers can, and have, taken gloomy views about prospects for the pound, but rarely are they operating on their own account, whether to make money or frustrate the government or both, since British dealers are given specific daily limits for their operations. When they are selling sterling in large amounts, therefore they can only be undertaking it on behalf of clients with specific trading obligations in mind. But there can be no denying the dilemma they face, and have faced, so many times since the war. Their clients can be British or foreign. In either case the question before them is simple: if for good economic reasons they believe that their clients should sell sterling to protect their legitimate trading interests, what should they do, recommend the opposite and run the risk of losing a client (and thus future income for the country) or sell sterling on their behalf, and be accused of being unpatriotic at best and a deliberate saboteur at worst?

The stock market has seen the same phenomenon, though here the problem is of a different order. Large sales of gilt-edged stock, if accompanied by no corresponding private purposes can undermine the government's monetary policy at crucial times for the Chancellor of the Exchequer. While the Stock Exchange can rightly say that it simply provides a market-place on which buyers and sellers are brought together to produce a varying movement in the prices of stocks and shares, the leading City investment institutions cannot give such a neutral answer. In some cases, for example, sales of government stock will be made by merchant banks or stock-brokers on behalf of foreign holders. Once again, the same dilemma emerges as with the foreign-exchange dealer and his advice to the foreign client. But what if the sale is made by an insurance company, a pension fund or a unit trust on purely domestic grounds? The dilemma here is of a different order, but just as acute. The insurance company may be concerned with the future income of policyholders, the pension fund with the future pensions of its members, and the unit trust with the income of its unit-holders. There are occasions when it would be right to sell gilt-edged and to buy either equities or foreign stocks or even remain liquid (keep the funds in cash). There are also occasions when, as I argued in Chapter 7, it would be wrong to buy government stock on behalf of policyholders or pensioners, whatever the impact on the government's monetary policy. The investment managers must judge when these turning points are likely to emerge. When they do, should they put the interests of their policyholders, pensioners or unit-holders first or should they refrain on national grounds?

In an open society and a relatively free economy, there can be no doubt that investment decisions must be left to, and made by, each institution on behalf of its own clients or other interests and that *national* decisions, whether on currency or monetary policy, must be left to governments. A ground swell of investment decisions in one direction may *appear* to be inspired by political motives. The evidence of such intentions, however, has still to be produced.

It is not conspiracy that provides the main danger, in my view, but market psychology. There are strong grounds for believing that gloom can feed on gloom in a narrow investment community. Euphoria too can get out of hand. But events usually bring back sanity in the end, for if the market moves too far one way, against all the trends, those taking a saner view stand to make a profit out of the situation. This is the conclusion from stock market experience of the past thirty or forty years. But there have been exceptions, mercifully small in number, when a ground swell of investment decisions in one direction – upwards as well as downwards – has begun to feed on itself and lead, psychologically, to such a depressed (or elated) stock market that the economy itself has been in danger.

These exceptions are worth looking at for they have arisen especially in falling markets, not from conspiracy but from a total lack of confidence in immediate prospects. The outstanding example, of course, is the 1929–31 period on Wall Street. On Thursday 24 October 1929 Winston Churchill looked down from the visitor's gallery of the New York Stock Exchange on a remarkable scene: it was the morning of the first major break in stock market prices, when nearly 13 million shares changed hands; there was hardly a buyer in sight and, amid confusion and not a little panic, the visitors gallery was closed at 12.30. Reports of organised support for the market followed. A rally took place on the strength of a meeting of bankers at J. P. Morgan and Company, and the market steadied. But it did not last. Soon a further avalanche of sales followed. The rest is history. On 29 October the New York Stock Exchange had its worst day ever. 'Few men ever lost position so rapidly as did the New York bankers in the five days from 24 October to 29 October.'[1] Professor Galbraith has a point, but the psychology behind the New York market had a far wider ancestry. A nation-wide boom mentality had quickly given place to doubts, then to anxiety, and finally to fear. In such circumstances the bankers were unable to stem either the fears or the subsequent selling, as they had done once before in 1907.

Two more recent examples had happier outcomes. In Tokyo in 1966, at a time when the Japanese economy was heavily dependent on the United States, in spite of its own new-found strength, the stock market was suddenly undermined at a psychological moment by a sharp fall in Wall Street. Once again a boom mentality – in which Tokyo taxi-drivers and messenger boys had happily joined in – switched to anxiety overnight. The Tokyo market, without the cushion of a jobbing system, quickly lost ground and a rapid, almost uncontrolled, slide began and was not halted until the government moved decisively by forming two special companies to buy stock to support the market. One of the three leading security houses went bankrupt, but the market was eventually stabilised and the danger was averted.

Nearer home a similar slide seemed to be developing at the end of 1974. Once again the boom mentality of the late sixties and early seventies had been shattered by the onset of the deepest recession since 1931 and the sudden fourfold increase in oil prices in the second half of 1973. The stock market had reached a peak in 1972, and, at first, only a mild recession was expected. But

---

[1] J. K. Galbraith, *The Great Crash, 1929* (Penguin Books, 1961)

the evidence of something quite different quickly emerged throughout 1974. Fringe banks started to get into trouble; depositors money was at risk; and some banks were even allowed to go bankrupt. The property boom collapsed. Major international banks ran into difficulties in Cologne, New York, California, Lugano. The Eurodollar market contracted for the first time in a decade. Inflation and interest rates soared. So did unemployment. Governments too were having difficulties: the aftermath of Watergate in Washington; communist threats in Rome and Lisbon; the defeat of a Tory Government by the miners and the uncertainty of a minority Labour Government in London. By the end of 1974 the London stock market was showing marked signs of deep anxiety. The index had dropped from a peak of 543 in May 1972 to well below 200 in the autumn of 1974. Allowing for inflation the drop was already far greater than it had been in London between 1929 and 1932. Between Christmas and New Year, when the market was about to be faced by a further major blow, the collapse of Burmah, stock market morale was in disarray. The index touched a low of 146 on 6 January 1975. It was clearly time for concerted action. Little has been said publicly about what was then agreed, but it is now clear that a meeting of institutional investors over lunch at the Prudential Assurance Company was influential in providing support for the equity market. The results were soon seen. Burmah was rescued by the Bank of England and buying in the stock market brought some resilience to prices. The turn-round in the next few weeks and months was astonishing. Industrial share prices rose 75 per cent in seven weeks, some shares doubling and trebling before the summer; and the government managed to sell £1,500 million of its own securities in five weeks. Two and a half years later the index was back over the 500 mark.

The moral of these three examples is that the biggest threat to government policy from the stock market (and other markets too) is not from any deliberate conspiracy but from the onset of fears and expectations, often induced by government and market dealers alike, which on the rare occasions that it occurs needs concerted action to reverse it. It also needs accurate timing, for even large-scale support from big institutions can be swallowed up by private share sales if the wrong psychological moment is chosen. King Canute could have been advised to await high tide before attempting to rule the sea. The other lesson perhaps is that self-regulatory controls over excessive margin dealings (large loans for short-term purchases), whether in stocks and shares or commodities, is the best way to damp down earlier excessive rises and to prevent the onset of the psychological disease in the first place.

I have been concerned so far mainly with the effects of preventive controls, protecting the public or protecting government policy. It is time to turn to the positive side, and to consider how the government controls the City and its activities in its efforts to implement its own economic policy. This covers taxation, exchange control, and monetary policy generally. As we saw in Chapter 13, controls over the movement of sterling and foreign funds were introduced during the 1930s and consolidated during the war. A succession of sterling crises ensured their maintenance until recently. But they were not confined to Britain. Virtually every country, apart from Germany and Switzerland, relied on them heavily for currency protection. Britain's controls were administered flexibly by the Bank of England, but they still impeded legitimate City business. Exchange control, until its recent partial demise, had already led to the decline of certain major City markets in foreign (especially South African and American) securities; it had frustrated investment trusts and insurance companies in their efforts to switch out of some overseas securities and move into others and, in some cases, had forced institutions to cut out some of their foreign security analysts; and it had allowed major City institutions to lose significant amounts of traditional sterling financing business in Commonwealth and other markets.

In the case of taxation, too, every aspect of City life has been involved. This is not the place to argue the case for or against recent taxation levels. Both main parties have found it difficult to reduce the growing weight of government expenditure. But the City has suffered the resulting impact of high marginal tax rates since, like all service industries, it is primarily dependent on highly paid professional expertise for the efficient workings of its markets. The City has suffered in several ways. Earnings after tax for top executives, following the various phases of incomes policy which have deliberately squeezed differentials, are still well below those in North America or Western Europe and it is still difficult to attract and retain key personnel, when they always have the option of going to other centres abroad. The foreigners in the City's midst, particularly the American bankers, Greek shipowners and foreign insurance companies, also have this option. It was touch and go in 1975 and 1976 whether leading American banks and Greek shipowners left the City for other centres. Significant business would have gone with them.

Finally, monetary policy is at the heart of the main City markets – the stock market, the discount market and the foreign exchange market. Each can be influenced by the various levers at the disposal of the authorities which we outlined in Chapter 9. Monetary policy has often involved sharp shifts in government attitudes and thus correspondingly sharp changes in City markets. In a mixed economy, the encroachment of government is to be expected. The City may have had more than its share because of the succession of sterling crises directly affecting its markets. But, as North Sea oil revenues grow and lead to the expected balance of payments surpluses, the City lives in hope that taxation may be lowered, exchange control be fully dismantled and monetary policy becomes less volatile.

It is time to return to the issue I raised at the beginning of this chapter. There are growing demands – some practical, some idealogical – for more controls over the City's manifold activities. This has arisen from the evidence of a secondary banking crisis, from a general feeling shared by many City people that more might still be done to protect the investing public, and from a politico-economic tide which has put increasing power and control in government hands. The question to be faced is whether such safeguards should be provided by self regulation or by a further turn of the statutory screw. The number and variety of controls already in operation are both large and widespread. The cost in time and energy to City institutions is already burdensome. When a single merchant bank estimates that its regular returns to the Bank of England alone costs £50,000 a year, that can only erode its competitive position. Statutory controls are, by their nature, over-precise and do not cover the spirit of the law as do self-regulatory arrangements; nor can they be changed in a flexible manner to fit corresponding changes in the market environment. On the other hand, those City markets imposing self-regulation will increasingly have to justify their actions publicly on four major points. Can they show that there is an adequate forum of appeal if and when people or companies who are not members feel that they do not have an adequate right of access to a market? Do they have adequate powers of investigation to consider public complaints? Do they have sufficient sanctions against wrongdoers? Will they deal with transgressors, among them their own members, squarely and openly? With the establishment of the Council for the Securities Industry in a major City market, on a voluntary basis and with a Labour government's earlier backing, the City has been given the chance to show that self-regulation is in everyone's interest. But the CSI, Lloyd's, the commodity associations and the money and foreign exchange markets will all in future have to give a fuller account of their actions, both to the public and to their members, if the legal strait jacket they all deplore is to be avoided.

Chapter 16

Survival: Challenge from New York?

Species, races, even nations struggle to survive and financial centres are no exception. Some survive; some do not. Some decline slowly, imperceptibly; some vanish overnight in gunfire. The pages of economic history, as well as yesterday's newspapers, are littered with the proof. Florence, Bruges, Antwerp, Vienna – all, in their time, were the centre of European activity. Now they are financial backwaters with Vienna, in the eyes of one City observer, no more than 'long echoing corridors and a modest little list of provincial Austrian securities'. Berlin and Beirut, thirty years apart, were destroyed by war. Tangiers strode the post-war stage as the centre of black-market currency deals and promptly disappeared. Newcomers have developed rapidly in Frankfurt, Tokyo, Hong Kong and San Francisco. Some have mushroomed in most unexpected places – Singapore, the Cayman Islands, Jersey, Kuwait and Bahrain. Some, like Amsterdam and Paris, once leading centres, still survive. And throughout it all the main centres have continued to battle it out: first London, Berlin and Paris in the nineteenth century; then London, New York and Paris in the inter-war period; finally, London, New York and Zurich over the last quarter of a century.

This immediately raises the question of what one means by a financial centre and what a leading international centre should offer to remain in business at the top. This is a matter of judgement. In an earlier booklet,[1] I described a financial

[1] W. M. Clarke, *Money Markets of the World: What the Future May Bring.* (Laurie Milbank and Co., London, 1971)

centre as 'a place where both domestic and international money can flow freely both in and out, where money can be found for trade, and capital can be found for industry and where foreign merchants, traders and industrialists can find wider commercial facilities'. This conveniently divides the sheep from the goats. It leaves aside the newer offshore centres. It even throws doubt on the pretensions of some well established places. Another definition, equally useful and to the point, used before the war by Paul Einzig, has the same narrowing effect. He spoke of a number of essential factors of which the most important were: (1) ample capital resources available for lending abroad, (2) an adequate banking organisation, (3) freedom of the financial market, (4) an investing public willing to acquire and keep foreign securities, (5) a stable currency, (6) a good money market, and (7) a good foreign exchange market. He might have added political stability.

Immediately after the Second World War both New York and Zurich would have come out of these tests with reasonably full marks. Not so London. She had no capital resources for lending abroad (except to the sterling area); an investing public which was unable to acquire foreign securities on any significant scale; inactive markets; a currency that was hardly stable; massive sterling debts; and a Labour Government which instinctively embraced the existing wartime controls over the economy and was determined to nationalise the Bank of England. Zurich, on the other hand, though she has never had a money market with short-term domestic paper, emerged with a thriving economy, the advantages of neutrality, banking secrecy and a strong currency – all the attributes of a secure financial centre. New York too dominated the richest country in the world and had at its fingertips the strongest international currency for its manifold activities.

Yet, as chapter after chapter has shown, London had re-emerged in a dominant position within a decade and a half of the end of the war and has continued to survive even in a period when financial centres have blossomed as never before. With ingenuity, contacts, a large slice of luck, some inept decisions by the US monetary authorities and the development of the Eurocurrency markets, London managed to fill the gaps in her armoury. While New York found its business on its doorstep, London had to scour the world for it and, fortunately, with its network of bank branches, its merchant banking contacts, its insurance tentacles and its shipping interests, it found what it was looking for – overseas. By the late 1960s, when British politicians were exhorting British industry and the British economy generally to embrace what they called export-led growth, the City had been practising it again for nearly a decade. In the nineteenth century London had the contacts, the expertise and the money. Now it no longer had the money but, as we have seen, it learnt how to use other people's and to its own advantage. The Eurodollar market set the seal on London's come-back after 1958 and the rush of foreign banks to London in the wake of this new monetary discovery brought a permanency to the further parallel money markets which soon developed there.

London had discovered a method of exploiting its natural advantages. Most international bankers speak English and the Eurocurrency markets are conducted predominantly in English. London's communications, both transport and tele-communications, compare well with rival centres. It lies comfortably astride the world's main time zones, enabling it to communicate by telephone with all other leading centres some time during its extended working hours. In the banking area, the Bank of England welcomes foreign banks and does not insist on reciprocity, while the large clearing banks offer their unrivalled clearing facilities to newcomers. Above all, as our American friends insist, it happens to be a pleasant place to live. As a result, London's lead in international business has been maintained; so has the spread of its international services. In insurance it has the biggest international turnover. Its banks have many more foreign branches than any other country's. In gold transactions it still battles it out for first place with Zurich. In the Eurocurrency market it claims the biggest individual share, in spite of the rise of new invoicing centres in Nassau, Singapore and Bahrain. There are more foreign banks in the City than anywhere else, and double the number of New York. In foreign exchange its turnover is bigger than New York. The Baltic Exchange claims to undertake well over a half of the world's shipping freights. Several of London's commodity markets have the biggest world turnover in spot transactions and even more in future deals. The London Stock Exchange has the largest listing of foreign securities and its turnover is bigger than the other European exchanges put together. The result of all this can be seen in Table 19, where the rise in the City's foreign income is set out in detail. The expansion speaks for itself. The City's invisible earnings have increased four times in the past decade alone, and now account for over a third of the country's net invisible income. But it is the contribution of the non-banking sectors of the City that remains impressive and contrasts so sharply with many other centres – especially New York, Zurich, Frankfurt and Tokyo – where money, securities and capital market activities still dominate.

All this is encouraging. Yet none of it can be taken for granted. It would be idle to assume that London, having survived will continue to do so. It should not be overlooked that four-fifths of the Eurobusiness done in London is conducted by foreign banks, not British ones; that no British bank is among the top ten banks in the world; that one of Britain's biggest industrial firms, ICI, got a German bank to organise one of its latest Eurobond borrowings; that only three British banks are in the top ten in the Eurobond market; and only one is in the top ten in the Eurosyndication loan market. Some of these trends are hardly surprising, but they are a useful antidote to euphoria, and a helpful reminder of current realities, before I attempt to assess London's competitive position with other leading money centres and her complex relationships with the newer centres.

The demands of international business and the ready response to them of international banks, insurance brokers and underwriters, shipping brokers and companies, commodity exchanges, stock exchanges and money markets of all kinds have transformed the kind of financial centres one knew a quarter of a century ago. By the early 1960s big firms were demanding services on a world-wide basis to help them with their world-wide subsidiaries and their world-wide trade. To provide these services, banks opened branches both in existing centres and in new ones. The newer centres were often places

Table 19 *What the City of London Earns Abroad*

	1956[1]	1963[1]	1965[2]	£ millions					
				1968	1973	1974	1975	1976	1977
Insurance Total	70	85	81	198	356	388	442	795	909
Companies				90	157	148	138	307	345
Lloyd's				74	139	164	200	334	379
Brokers				34	60	76	104	154	185
Banking (net)	25–30	45–50	82½	67	123	46	215	416	254
Commodity trading									
Total				57	165	220	299	309	229
Commodities				40	110	140	209	201	109
Merchanting	25–30	20–25	80–90	17	55	80	90	108	120
Brokerage total	15–20	20–25	30–35	55	99	160	207	215	235
Baltic Exchange				33	53	103	146	147	155
Stock Exchange				9	18	19	18	16	20
Lloyd's Register of Shipping				3	7	10	14	17	23
Other				10	21	28	29	35	37
Investment trusts				35	33	40	41	47	51
Pension funds				5	9	10	16	14	17
Unit trusts				2	6	8	9	11	12
Solicitors					13	15	19	29	40
TOTAL	135–150	170–185	250–290	419	804	887	1,248	1,836	1,747

[1] Unofficial estimates by William M. Clarke published in *The City in The World Economy* (Penguin, London, 1967)
[2] From *Britain's Invisible Earnings* (report of the Committee on Invisible Exports, London 1968)
Source: Balance of Payments 'Pink Book' (Central Statistical Office)

with low tax or tax-free facilities. Businesses also began to use the flexible Eurocurrencies that initially became centred on London.

As a result of these new facilities, London became the first financial centre to survive the decline in its own currency. It was also the first to link itself to the important network of new centres which had also been made possible by the spread of the Euromarkets. This is how I described this phenomenon soon after it had become clear for the first time:[1]

> Now, with the post-war swing of economic power back to Europe and with a major new development (the establishment of new international markets incorporating and spanning several centres at once) a 'network' seems to have grown up to replace the previous prime centre. What we are witnessing, therefore, is a new international layer being spread over the old pattern of individual domestic centres, a linking of financial centres by an international currency (this time the Eurodollar, next time a European trading currency?) rather than the dominance of one centre by the use of its domestic currency as an international vehicle, as sterling was in the last century.

This had important implications for London. It meant that she could tap a new source of money and capital; it meant that, given the right contacts and the right efficiency, she could play a major role in international monetary affairs without imposing a strain on Britain's depleted gold and exchange reserves; and it meant that financial centres had entered a new era of both competition and co-operation. While individual banks – American, British, French, Japanese, German, Swiss – would compete fiercely, as always, for new business, the financial centres in which they were based would probably be co-operating in new issues and Eurosyndicated loans and Eurobond issues would be issued in several centres simultaneously. In short, London had provided itself with a way back into the business it knew a little about; it had also ushered in a new era in international finance.

[1] Clarke, op. cit.

Thus a variety of financial centres, old and new, became linked together partly through bank branches, partly through the use of new Eurocurrency techniques. Leading banks flocked to the main money centres such as London, New York, Zurich, Paris, Tokyo and Frankfurt. They opened up in the regional centres, such as Hong Kong, Singapore, Caracas, Rio/Sao Paulo, and Beirut. And they were attracted by the specialist services provided in Nassau, Bermuda, Panama, Bahrain, Jersey and Luxembourg.

Some of the newer centres have no financial expertise, but simply the convenience of low taxation or specialised company laws. All offer something essential to the international business and financial community. Panama attracts the registration of international shipping. Luxembourg is used for the listing of Eurobonds and as a Eurocurrency base for German banks. Bermuda is a useful low-tax registration centre, especially for captive insurance companies, set up by multinational groups for their own purposes. Jersey offers low-tax investment facilities for offshore funds, that is money earned by expatriates outside their country of origin. Singapore is the centre of the Asian dollar market – simply another name for the use of dollars or other currencies available in that part of the world. Hong Kong provides fierce local competition in arranging Eurocurrency deals in that part of the world. Nassau and the Cayman Islands are convenient invoicing centres for Eurocurrency deals initiated in New York. And Bahrain, lacking the volume of oil of its neighbours and having an entrenched historical stake as a regional trading centre, offers offshore banking facilities and has outpaced many other centres (apart from London, Nassau, Luxembourg, and Singapore) as a convenient invoicing point for Eurodeals started elsewhere.[1]

The proliferation of financial centres has made it increasingly difficult to judge what role each plays in a network that grows more complex almost daily, but it is worth trying to unravel their relationships, for London's apparent lead, especially in

[1] An invoicing or booking centre is a place that has tax and exchange-control advantages which can be used by the big international banks in allocating their Eurodollar business, even though the administrative, legal, even dealing, operations may be done in a large centre like London or New York.

Eurodollar transactions, could be undermined from a score of different places. In some respects, of course, the Eurocurrency business now passing through Luxembourg, Nassau, Singapore, the Cayman Islands, Hong Kong, the new Hebrides, Panama and Bahrain, as well as New York, Zurich, Paris, Tokyo and Frankfurt, has already led to a steady decline in the percentage of world turnover moving through London. There are several ways of calculating the world Eurocurrency market. All start with the figures published by the Bank for International Settlements in Basle, though these account for only part of the world picture. I have therefore taken the latest calculations of Mr David Ashby, the chief economist of Grindlays Bank in London, who has been regularly adding his own estimates to those of the BIS. They are set out in Table 20 and show the changes in different centres over recent years. Table 21 works out the shares of various centres on a percentage basis. The two tables show that, while London's share has dropped from 40 per cent to about 33 per cent since 1973, Nassau and the Cayman Islands have risen to about 12 per cent. One of the main reasons is that the Caribbean branches of American banks now hold more dollar assets than their London branches.

In trying to analyse what lies behind these trends, we need to know what each centre does, can do or will be allowed to do. In the complex process of attracting world-wide deposits and on-lending them through the banking network, different centres take on different roles. It is easy to oversimplify and to be out-dated by new developments, but for our purpose three or four different actions take place. First comes the attraction of the surplus currency deposits. This can take place in regional centres, like Singapore, Nassau, Luxembourg or Bahrain, or in the main centres like London and Paris. It is significant that the regional centres in turn will make deposits in London, which tends to act as a wholesale clearing centre. There are, for example, some $8 billion in Bahamian deposits and $2 billion in Singaporean deposits in London.

The next stage is the business of lending the deposits. It is here that several processes are involved. Banks have to arrange loans, to switch currencies, to discuss terms with borrowers and finally to book them through one or more centres, usually for

Table 20   *Size of the World Eurodollar Market*

(US$ billions, end of period)

		1973	1974	1975	1976	1977	1978[1]
I							
A	**EUROPE-BASED MARKET**						
	Gross	251	294	348	407	512	633
	Austria	n.a.	n.a.	n.a.	n.a.	10	13
	Belgium	} 29	} 38	18	22	27	37
	Luxembourg			30	38	52	65
	Denmark	n.a.	n.a.	n.a.	n.a.	2	3
	France	33	40	51	60	78	92
	Germany	8	10	11	15	20	25
	Ireland	n.a.	n.a.	n.a.	n.a.	2	2
	Italy	28	16	19	18	26	23
	Netherlands	11	15	19	25	31	43
	Sweden	2	2	3	3	4	4
	Switzerland	11	15	19	22	27	33
	United Kingdom	128	158	178	202	231	242
B	*Net*	132	177	205	247	300	376
2							
C	**NON-EUROPEAN MARKET**						
	Gross	69	92	115	158	192	240
	Bahamas and Caymans	26	35	50	74	88	102
	Bahrain	—	—	2	6	16	23
	Canada	12	14	14	17	18	21
	Hong Kong	4	7	9	13	17	21
	Japan	17	21	20	22	22	33
	Netherlands Antilles	—	—	—	—	1	1
	Panama	2	5	6	8	10	12
	Singapore	6	10	13	17	21	27
D	*Net*	30	40	50	69	81	101
3							
	TOTAL WORLD EURODOLLAR MARKET						
E	*Gross* (A+C)	319	386	462	565	704	873
F	*Net* (B+D)	162	217	255	316	381	477

Totals may not add, due to rounding.

[1]Provisional

Source: David Ashby (Grindlays Bank), based partly on BIS statistics

Table 21 *Shares in the World Eurodollar Market*

(Percentages, end of period)

	1973	1974	1975	1976	1977	1978[1]
EUROPE-BASED MARKET	78.5	76.2	75.3	72.0	72.7	72.5
Austria	n.a.	n.a.	n.a.	n.a.	1.4	1.5
Belgium	} 9.1	} 9.8	3.9	3.9	3.8	4.2
Luxembourg			6.5	6.7	7.4	7.4
Denmark	n.a.	n.a.	n.a.	n.a.	0.3	0.3
France	10.3	10.3	11.0	10.6	11.1	10.5
Germany	2.5	2.6	2.4	2.7	2.8	2.9
Ireland	n.a.	n.a.	n.a.	n.a.	0.3	0.2
Italy	8.8	4.2	3.9	3.4	4.0	3.2
Netherlands	3.4	3.9	4.1	4.4	4.4	4.9
Sweden	0.6	0.5	0.6	0.5	0.6	0.5
Switzerland	3.4	3.8	4.1	3.9	3.8	3.8
United Kingdom	40.1	41.1	38.5	35.8	32.8	33.0
NON-EUROPEAN MARKET	21.5	23.8	24.9	28.0	27.3	27.5
Bahamas and Caymans	8.3	9.1	10.8	13.1	12.5	11.7
Bahrain	—	—	0.4	1.1	2.3	2.6
Canada	3.9	3.6	3.0	3.0	2.3	2.4
Hong Kong	1.3	1.8	1.9	2.3	2.6	2.4
Japan	5.4	5.4	4.3	3.9	3.1	3.8
Netherlands Antilles	—	—	—	—	0.1	0.1
Panama	0.7	1.3	1.3	1.4	1.4	1.4
Singapore	2.0	2.6	2.8	3.0	3.0	3.1

Totals may not add, due to rounding.

[1]Provisional

Source: David Ashby (Grindlays Bank), based partly on BIS statistics

tax purposes. The arranging centres are tending to become more regional, partly because project finance, the provision of money for large international projects, has become increasingly reliant on the Euromarkets as the size of projects has increased and because the location of the project requires regional knowledge and contacts, partly because borrowers at present are tending to wait for banks to appear on their doorstep rather than the other way round (the next world boom could quickly reverse that), and partly because international banks are increasingly working on a regional basis themselves. Thus the arranging of large loans for projects in Indonesia or the Philippines, based on equipment supplied from Europe and with the involvement of American banks, could be arranged partly in New York, partly in London and partly in Hong Kong. But Hong Kong will play an increasingly important part in the arranging process. Yet, when the putting together of the loans begins, it is quite possible that the seeking of the deposits, above all the switching of deposits from one currency to another, may be done in a prime centre, such as London, which has at its core a vast interbank market and an equally vast foreign exchange market. The booking of the final loan by the participating banks is something else again. Here taxation is the basic consideration, for centres such as Nassau, the Cayman Islands, the New Hebrides and Jersey are either tax-free or low-tax areas.

We are now in a position to assess how these processes have affected the main centres. While London remains a key centre for the accumulation and the switching of the basic deposits, other centres such as Singapore, Nassau and Bahrain are playing similar roles, though they have no comparable facilities to the London interbank and foreign exchange markets. As arranging centres, New York and London still lead, though Hong Kong is increasingly important in the Far East. In fact Hong Kong's competitive role with Singapore is extremely difficult to unravel. Singapore has been the centre of the so-called Asian dollar market since it was established, with a Bank of America initiative, following uncooperative noises from Hong Kong. This means that Singapore is the deposit-receiving centre of the region, though part of this activity is the result of the subsidiaries of Hong Kong banks in Singapore. As an arranging centre Hong Kong clearly leads, though the extent of the lead is often hidden by the number of Hong Kong-arranged deals which are booked through the New Hebrides for tax purposes. The same thing happens from London and New York, with Nassau and Bahrain acting as booking centres.

What is also becoming clear is that the leading international banks are deliberately spreading the arranging of their loans on a geographical time-zone basis. This has been encouraged by the size and location of the international projects now being financed through the Euromarkets. For example, Citibank, the biggest New York bank, uses four basic centres overseas as booking centres for dollar loans to non-US borrowers: Nassau, London, Bahrain and Hong Kong/Singapore, each in a different time zone. London was the first to feel the effect of this spreading of bookings round the world, as Nassau and the Cayman Islands attracted bookings nearly a decade ago. Now the share of new bookings in the Bahamas is declining as Bahrain and Hong Kong/Singapore attract more bookings.

Thus London's role in the complex Euromarket mechanism has been changing as other centres have emerged and as international banks, in their efforts to provide a world-wide service to their business clients, have used the new centres as adjuncts to the main centres. London's strength still lies in the depth of its interbank market, based on the 300 or so foreign banks represented there, and the size of its foreign exchange market. It also lies in its ability to muster foreign bank representatives to arrange loans on a world-wide basis, and London tends to dominate loans to Europe, the Middle East and Africa, while sharing arrangements in other parts of the world. As for booking loans, it has to be remembered that, although other centres offer tax-free or low-tax advantages, London's tax rates of 52 per cent can be offset against taxes in New York and similar centres, where additional state and city taxes often push them above the basic London rates.

While London has little to worry about in relation to the normal offshore centres, which lack the financial infrastructure available in London (especially the legal and accounting firms), any change in New York, Paris or Zurich would be another matter. Hence the close analysis now being made in the Square Mile of the proposals to turn New York into an offshore centre for some purposes. These ideas are not new, but they now have the clear backing of the New York State authorities, who see in them a possibility of absorbing up to 50,000 unemployed in Lower Manhattan. The plan, as outlined by the New York Clearing House Association and backed by New York's leading international banks, is to establish a kind of monetary free-trade zone or international banking facility limited to foreign transactions in New York. These banking units would be free of the Federal Reserve's reserve requirements, of the deposit interest-rate restrictions, and of New York state and city income taxes. 'There is every reason to believe', a leading New York banker has claimed, 'that this foreign banking window would make New York once again the world's foremost financial centre by bringing home much of the dollar-based business.' And he calculated that, whereas ten years ago London and New York employed roughly the same number in their financial sectors, some 290,000 people, London has since added a further 150,000 jobs, a 55 per cent increase compared with the modest rise of only 14 per cent in New York City.

As I write, the decision still lies with the United States Federal Reserve Board, which continues to ask itself a number of pertinent questions. Can it trust the American banks not to abuse the new facilities? Can it be sure that the provision of a foreign currency concession would not undermine its control over the reserve requirements of member banks and would not affect its monitoring of the American money supply? Above all, is it really possible to have two different dollars in New York, one domestic and one offshore? It might also imply that the Federal Reserve was taking full responsibility for the effective regulation of the dollar section of the Eurodollar market. If the answers are eventually settled to the satisfaction of the Federal Reserve authorities, what kind of a threat will these moves be to London?

There is little doubt that Eurodollar loans booked outside the United States would, increasingly, be repatriated, if only for convenience, especially by American Banks. The centres that would suffer directly from such switching would be Nassau, the Cayman Islands and Panama, all of which are in, or close to, the same time zone as New York. Bahrain, Singapore and Hong Kong would be protected to some extent by the time difference. London would be too, but there is little doubt that, given time, New York could begin to match London in the size and depth of its money and exchange markets.

This analysis strongly suggests that, in spite of the growth of scores of new centres, London's prime competition will continue to be felt from the existing well established money centres. London banks, brokers, and insurance and shipping men will have to keep abreast of the services offered by the new centres and have them available for their own clients, even if that means opening up branches or representative offices in out-of-the-way places. London banks are already in Nassau, Singapore, Bahrain, Jersey and many other offshore centres and if, say, Athens decided to offer tax-free facilities to banks, insurance and shipping companies, in an attempt to rival London as a major shipping centre, no doubt British bankers would be the first to join the three British banks already there.

Competition with the larger centres is another matter. Tokyo in the past decade has attracted growing numbers of foreign bank branches, as Japanese banks in their turn have spread themselves round the world. Yet, in spite of the strength of the yen, the Japanese authorities have still to encourage true international business through Tokyo, the Bank of Japan has found it difficult to embrace a policy of reciprocity, and official controls hamper the development of Tokyo as a major centre. Frankfurt too has not achieved what it once seemed poised to do, and the British Bankers Association reckons it to be 'the weakest of the four' main European centres (the others being Brussels, Zurich and Paris). Again, official controls over the Eurocurrency business of the German banks have hampered its development and, incidentally, led to the development of Luxembourg as an alternative outlet for the German banks.

This leaves Paris and Zurich in Europe and New York in North America as London's main rivals. Paris still has the banking infrastructure and has recently attracted both Middle East money and Middle Eastern banking consortia. British bankers regard it as the most important financial centre in Europe, after London, in terms both of the number of foreign banks operating there and of its outstanding Eurocurrency business. Recent finance ministers have even paid lip-service to the physical establishment of a 'Cité de Paris', closely modelled on the City of London, near the Opéra. Yet, when the testing time has come, the banking authorities have continued to operate their controls in a restrictive way, both in Eurocurrency business and in the activities of foreign banks in France. As for Zurich, her international banking business has, like Frankfurt, suffered rather than gained from the strength of her currency and from the reluctance of her monetary authorities to see the Swiss franc used as an international currency. Hence the strict division between domestic and international business. Zurich's basic strength derives not from the activities of a foreign financial community in its midst, like London, but rather from its attraction as a safe haven for investment funds, legitimate and illegitimate. These funds are estimated at no less than $150 billion. Zurich can also boast of a gold market capable of rivalling London, of the world's largest reinsurance company, the Swiss Re, and of three of the most active international banks in the world. But it cannot be said to be a natural centre for the world's financial community to do its world-wide business.

That mantle is still being fought over between London and New York. New York's post-war strength was never in doubt. Nor is it now, as foreign banks are showing by their continuing decisions to open up there. Yet, unaccountably, New York did not play the role in the post-war world that London had done when sterling was dominant. There were, as we have seen, several reasons for this. It did not act as the major source of the economy's surplus dollars; that role was shared with government agencies and international agencies. New York was not in the diplomatic business and, in a world of cold wars and big-power rivalries, her capital market was not allowed to oil the wheels of international trade and industry in a neutral-market fashion as London once did. The Marshall Plan for Europe, the more general American aid programme, and also American contributions to the World Bank and the International

Monetary Fund, all tended to bypass New York's financial markets. Nor was this all. It was a political decision to keep interest rates low in New York, known as Regulation Q, that at the right moment for London (and the wrong one in New York) encouraged the Eurocurrency market to take root in London. Then in 1964, in efforts to protect the dollar, the US Treasury introduced a new interest equalisation tax, as well as other exchange controls on the movement of capital from the United States. Their effect was to strangle New York's foreign capital market for almost a decade and to give a remarkable boost to the embryo Eurobond market which was just beginning to blossom in London and other European centres. It had another, more permanent, effect, which was not to be fully realised until the restrictions were finally removed. In this period New York naturally turned its attention to its own economy's domestic needs and developed new sophisticated techniques for assessing and promoting domestic issues. Ten years later, when the New York market was finally reopened to foreign borrowers, it was found that these new domestic techniques (which were largely based on huge turnover) were not automatically appropriate for the smaller number of foreign borrowers, and by this time the Eurobond market had taken root, helped as much as anything by the activities of leading New York investment houses. New York too had become an essential part of the new Eurobond market network, stretching from Tokyo to Frankfurt, from Zurich to London and from New York to Paris.

North American competition – from both New York and Chicago – has not been confined to banking. The New York authorities are actively encouraging insurance developments and Chicago, along with New York, is pressing London hard in the fields of commodity futures and traded options. In the case of insurance a distinction has to be made between Britain's interests in the 'London market' and her interests, through British brokers and companies, in foreign markets such as New York. One British broking firm, for example, Willis Faber, has already indicated its intention to set up a joint company (with Johnson and Higgins, the second largest US broking firm) to introduce underwriting members to the New

York Insurance Exchange and to manage syndicates there. British composite companies have been contemplating the same kind of involvement in New York. Thus British firms will be sharing in the New York insurance developments. At the same time it will clearly take time for New York to rival the London market, which already offers, internationally, three important features: capacity, flexibility and individual expertise. All hang together, and it may be at least a decade before the strength of New York's challenge can be seriously assessed.

In commodity futures, however, Chicago is already providing major and growing competition to London. This is hardly surprising, given the size and depth of the American commodity markets. The Chicago Board of Trade and the Chicago Mercantile Exchange, between them, already had highly prosperous markets in wheat, pork-bellies, corn, oats, soy beans, frozen broilers, and so on. In recent years they have also developed futures markets to a significant degree[1], not only as backing for these basic markets but also as innovations in the monetary area, offering futures in interest rates and gold. General National Mortgage Association certificates, which are interest-rate futures known colloquially as Ginnie Maes, were offered for the first time in 1975 and similar interest-rate futures on US Treasury bonds and a 90-day commercial paper were introduced in 1977. Further monetary innovations, seeking government approval, will cover Treasury notes and even three-month Eurodollar certificates. The New York Stock Exchange has announced similar intentions.

The expansion in these monetary futures in Chicago – which basically offer a way of protecting an investor against changes in future interest rates – has outpaced similar facilities in London. They have had a somewhat chequered career. As one local dealer recalls, 'when the first Ginnie Maes were traded in October 1975, the financial community could not decide whether we were a gambling saloon or a load of corn dealers with funny ideas – but either way they did not like us'.

---

[1] The volume of futures contracts traded by the Chicago Board of Trade rose from nearly 8 million in 1970 to over 24 million in 1978 and that by the Chicago Mercantile Exchange from over 3 million to nearly 11 million.

The *Financial Times* later concluded: 'The federal monetary and banking authorities viewed the novelty with a distinct lack of enthusiasm, which lingers on.'

The prospects for these monetary futures markets and their successful introduction into London depend on the use made of them. Will they simply attract speculators and introduce an element of short-term instability into the monetary markets? Or will they be used by legitimate investors as a new weapon to eliminate future risks? Both are possible. In London the International Commodities Clearing House, whose basic job is to clear and guarantee contracts on London's soft commodity markets, is studying the possibility of introducing interest-rates futures trading. Much will eventually depend on the reaction of the financial community and of the Bank of England. But the problems remain, as in Chicago: how to obtain a big enough turnover, without incurring speculative swings in activity, and thus possibly undermining (in the case of government issues) official monetary policy.

Let me sum up. In New York's (and Chicago's) favour are the size and resiliance of the vast American economy and the size and number of the commercial and financial institutions servicing it. American commercial banks dominate the world scene, particularly Citibank (earning 82 per cent of its profits overseas), Bank of America (with its headquarters in San Francisco), Chase Manhattan and Morgan Guaranty. So do her investment banking groups, which dominate the Eurobond market. Yet a financial centre is not to be judged by the size of its domestic units. It should be assessed on the ease with which foreign banks and brokers can operate there and the ease with which they can conclude international business. It is on these grounds that New York still lags behind London. The Federal Reserve still hampers foreign banks, even domestic banks from outside New York State, wanting to set up branches there. Countries such as Canada, which do not offer full reciprocity, are restricted in their operations. Moreover, if under the promised new legislation foreign banks will simply be allowed to set up branches in only one state of the Union, will they choose New York and debar themselves from lucrative business in California or elsewhere? In contrast, the Bank of

England's open-door policy to foreign banks and the attitude of the British clearing banks to foreign competition have been the basis of the City's post-war renaissance. The American banks themselves had this to say about London's welcome in their own evidence to the Wilson Committee:

The attitude of the clearing banks to competition and to the introduction of strangers into the London market is very positive. They co-operate fully in providing access for foreign banks to clearing, money transmission and other related services which they alone can offer. They compete strongly and use their natural strength fully but fairly without attempting to inhibit competition or stifle new techniques. Their power, at least in sterling, was such that there is no doubt that they could have stunted the competitive thrust of foreign banks ten years ago had they chosen. They did not do so but rather reacted to the spur of competition and counter attacked to the benefit of their customers and competitors alike. The contrast with their European equivalents is wholly favourable to the clearing banks in this area, as the variety of facilities open to British industry demonstrates.

This open-handed approach has clearly helped to re-establish London as one of the world's financial centres, even in competition with such powerful rivals as New York.

Chapter 17

The City in the 1980s: What Lies Ahead?

In this chapter I shall try to take a broader view of the City and what lies ahead of it in the 1980s and beyond. Throughout the book I have attempted to combine an outline of the way the City works with a reasonably neutral analysis of the issues already bubbling to the surface. In some cases I have revealed my own views; in others not. But in charting the way ahead analysis is not enough. Policy prescriptions are needed too. This is what I want to concentrate on in this final chapter.

The City will have to contend with three separate, though overlapping areas of influence throughout the 1980s: the world economic climate; the domestic political environment and governmental controls at home and abroad; and, finally, competition from developed and developing countries alike. I want to tackle them separately.

The City of London is providing commercial and financial services to the British economy and, at the same time, offering similar services to customers overseas. The same banks and insurance offices which provide services to people in this country often form part of a wider world market. Some City firms still concentrate on the home market; yet their international involvement remains large. Others do most business abroad. They are in effect practising export-led growth, using a wider market to maintain their total turnover.

This delicate balancing act between home and domestic business has been based on several fundamental features of City business:

- The City's compactness, coupled with its commercial habits of word-of-mouth contracts and widespread self-regulation, has enabled decisions to be swift and often unhampered by legal details.
- The City's international links, with larger foreign commercial communities than other centres and with equally larger networks of overseas branches and correspondents, have given it a marked advantage when world trade barriers have been declining.
- The variety of services available in the Square Mile has contrasted with the narrower range of services in most other leading financial centres, such as New York, Zurich, Paris or Frankfurt.

As the world economy blossomed and flourished as never before between the end of the 1950s and the first half of the 1970s, the City not only survived but introduced some remarkable innovations. Its foreign earnings rose dramatically. It actively developed the Eurocurrency markets. It attracted literally hundreds of foreign banks to London. It developed a vast new parallel money market, linking British and foreign borrowers to the world markets in money. It maintained its lead as a world price barometer for gold and several other commodities. It developed and dominated a new air-charter market on a world scale. It introduced new banking techniques at home and abroad, offering half of its domestic loans on medium term and using project finance (based on earnings rather than assets) round the globe. It introduced new insurance cover for multi-million industrial complexes and coped with nuclear risks.

In a word, the City responded to, and benefited from, a world economy which was not only expanding but encouraging innovations on a global basis. Can it be expected to go on doing the same when the world political and economic picture seems to have clouded over and when the urge to control financial and commercial activities is once again growing at home and abroad? For half a decade now the world economy has been grappling with the aftermath of the oil crisis of 1974 (when oil prices were quadrupled in a matter of months), with the inflationary excesses of the world boom of the late 1960s and early 1970s, with a virtually non-existent world financial system, and with the political fall-out in Africa, the Middle East and the Far East from American defeat in Vietnam. Trade barriers are threatening once again; currency instability is not yet contained; and world political summits prescribe for, but have not yet cured, the ills of the global economy. At home the urge to prevent future secondary banking crises and to impose more legal restrictions on the City's financial markets is accompanied by fears of the growing power of the investing institutions.

The City, therefore, faces three basic questions. Will the current economic and political doubts persist well into the 1980s? Will the urge to raise commercial barriers and to impose domestic controls act as a damper on City innovation and enterprise? Will competition from other centres, especially in the newly emerging world, add to that already being generated in New York, Chicago, Zurich, Paris and Frankfurt?

The City of London is part of a world invisible market worth between $250 and $300 billion annually. This is the size of world trade in services and in the return on overseas investments, as opposed to the world trade in goods. Since these figures also include shipping, tourism, civil aviation and especially the large return from, say, multinational manufacturing businesses, the market which primarily interests the City is around $50 billion, of which Britain accounts for some 10 per cent. Is this market likely to show the same kind of expansion we saw in the 1960s and early 1970s and is Britain's (and therefore London's) share likely to be maintained or even enlarged? I doubt the first and am still not sure about the second.

World trade plainly reached some kind of a watershed in 1974–5 and, along with world economic activity, has been desperately searching for the same kind of buoyancy ever since. The longest sustained expansion in the American economy since the 1930s, extending from 1975 to nearly the end of the decade, has failed to lift either world activity or world trade to their former annual rates of expansion; nor has it managed to make deep inroads into the growing pool of world unemployment, especially in the industrialised countries of the West.

It is true that the Middle East, with its newly found oil wealth, has sustained many City institutions in a period of general world stagnation, though some markets in Iran and some of the Gulf states have proved treacherous to the uninitiated. It is also true that the Common Market has proved more lucrative to invisible exporters, from the City and elsewhere, than to visible exporters and that the City still looks forward to a truly European market in banking and insurance by the late 1980s and early 1990s as the Freedom of Services begins to be a reality. But until governments throughout the world can use fiscal expansionary policies freely, without a fearful glance at the likely impact on inflation rates, former rates of expansion seem to me to be a remote possibility. This at least is the immediate prospect in the early 1980s.

Against this background and until inflation rates in different countries converge more closely, thus ensuring some semblance of currency stability, I cannot foresee a buoyant world market for the City's services, though I do not rule out marked recoveries on a cyclical basis in some areas (such as insurance) alongside continuing depression in others (such as shipping).

I am, however, becoming more sanguine about the threat to world trade from growing barriers and from currency instability. It is remarkable how deep the world recession has gone without the kind of self-protection which became such an instinct throughout the 1930s both in trade and currencies. International co-operation has remained firm, under enormous political strain. Moreover, the City's markets have coped well with a regime of so-called floating exchange rates, in which government interference has hindered rather than helped commercial transactions. As I write the American authorities are taking action to support the dollar and Britain's Common Market partners (in varying degrees) have been introducing the first phase of a European Monetary System. Both moves are intended to bring stability; both will need a more stable world economy; and both are prerequisites to the kind of climate the City will thrive in. Having coped with the worst currency instability for three decades, the City's financial markets should readily survive the many false dawns that still lie ahead.

It is tempting to lay down an exchange rate formula which

would ensure the City's success in world markets. British manufacturing industry has often been quoted as wanting a stable financial system with a modestly depreciating pound, enabling it to maintain its competitive edge in world markets. No such simple formula would suit the City. Some City markets are, of course, geared to the use of sterling and invoice in sterling, along traditional lines. But others do not and automatically receive payments in foreign currency terms. It is thus not easy to produce an exchange rate formula that suits all parts of the City's activities. Yet all have suffered from a too rapid depreciation of the pound – either in pushing up domestic costs or in eroding their sterling capital base – and from the uncertainties of an unstable financial system. Thus currency stability, rather than any particular exchange rate, would suit the City's operations best.

At the same time there has long been a need for some early dismantling of the web of exchange controls which successive sterling crises have added to and successive sterling recoveries have left intact. The Conservative Government promised to undertake such moves and has made a start by lifting some restrictions on the financing of third country trade in sterling, imposed in the 1976 sterling crisis which have already distorted the traditional activities of British export houses and British overseas banks, at a direct cost to their foreign earnings. In addition the Government has also lifted the strict control over the use of foreign currencies for direct investment in foreign countries, a restriction that is hampering both banks and insurance companies in their efforts to set up or support foreign branches or subsidiaries. In due course, the remaining restrictions on portfolio investment abroad and the use of the dollar premium should also be removed. They have not only diverted several markets in foreign securities from London to Continental centres but are inhibiting the foreign activities and the flexibility of several City investing institutions.

It may be argued that such relaxations will lean heavily on the central gold and exchange reserves. I do not believe so. There should be a once and for all impact, at a time when North Sea oil should be protecting Britain's overseas payments, and even that impact might easily be offset to some extent by the accompanying increase in foreign confidence and the consequent support given to foreign investment, both short- and medium-term, in Britain. At all events, I believe that the added flexibility given to City institutions, enabling them to add to their foreign earnings, will produce a better return than the same amount invested short-term on government account in New York. North Sea oil, whatever its other results, has at last provided an opportunity to peel off layers of restrictions which have accumulated like barnacles at every previous sterling crisis.

Let me turn to the second of my initial questions. Will the urge to introduce domestic controls act as a damper on City innovations and enterprise? The pressures have arisen from a variety of motives: from the doubts and anxieties of the secondary banking crisis in 1973–5; from the feeling, as a few made money from financial manipulations, that wealth creation could not be part of it; from convictions that, as domestic markets have grown and financial intermediaries multiplied, the old-style self-regulation of traditional markets should be exchanged for statutory controls; and from the fear that, unless controls were imposed, the growing strength of the investing institutions, especially of the pension funds, might quickly get out of hand.

There is much to be genuinely concerned about. Only now is it possible to realise how close to disaster Britain's banking system was in 1973 and 1974. Only now can it be estimated that, in saving the structure, the Bank of England and the clearing banks between them may have had to find some £2 billion. And only recently have the main actors in the drama begun to talk about it.[1] What is already clear is that a combination of officially induced competition in the banking area, a deliberate monetary stimulus, an over-optimistic economic and financial climate and a plainly divided banking control – between the Bank of England and the Department

---

[1] See especially the Governor of the Bank of England's comments in evidence to the House of Commons Select Committee on Nationalised Industries, January 1978; Bank of England evidence to the Wilson Committee, 'The Secondary Banking Crisis and the Bank of England's Support Operations', *Bank of England Quarterly Bulletin*, June 1978; and Margaret Reid, *The Banker*, December 1978.

of Trade – led to a situation where, once the storm signals were raised, waves of rumours swept through the City indicating, in the words of the Governor of the Bank of England, 'that various members of the true banking system, the accepting houses and even a clearing bank, were in danger and would be unable to meet their commitments without help from us'. And he added: 'There is no doubt that without the boost to confidence which the lifeboat operation gave, some of those rumours would have tended to become self-fulfilling and would have been translated into fact. If we had had a major established bank which had defaulted – however unlikely that was – I do not know where we would have stopped the course of collapse.'

How can such a situation be prevented from arising again, or, rather, how can such a situation be coped with if or when it does arise? My change of emphasis underlines the dilemma faced by anyone imposing controls on a flexible financial system. For it is not difficult to impose rigid controls over a banking system, as the Russians have already demonstrated. What is less easy is to impose controls which allow innovation and enterprise on the one hand and which adequately protect the public and ensure orderly markets on the other hand. This is the challenge faced by the authorities in considering how best to police not only the banks but also the City's various markets, especially the security and insurance markets, where the public's involvement is greatest.

In the case of the banks, the Bank of England's overall supervision has already been tightened both domestically and internationally. The regularity of bank reporting to the Bank of England has increased both in detail and, in some cases, in frequency. The recent Banking Act has established a new category of registered banks which will be more exclusive than in the past, as well as licensed institutions which may undertake some kind of banking business but will not be able to call themselves banks. The intention is to ensure that banks do not slip between two supervisors, as well as to curb the activities of the so-called fringe banks. In the stock market, which a Council member was still defending as a 'gentlemen's club' not many years ago, the newly established Council for the Securities Industry is, with government support, being given the chance to show that self-regulation not only works but can protect the public and punish its own kind. The insurance world has gone further not only in helping to shape background legislation, but in providing self-regulatory roles for the insurance companies and the insurance brokers. The Corporation of Lloyd's has set up a special working party to explore and recommend changes in its self-regulatory machinery. And the Department of Trade has also recognised that some of its own sanctions, under the Companies Act, especially Section 54, which concerns itself with share dealings, are derisory.

Virtually all City markets (though not all industries) are facing interference with their efforts towards self-regulation from two particular directions – from the Office of Fair Trading in London and from the legal interpretation of the Treaty of Rome in Brussels. So far the stock market has felt the main impact of the first and the foreign exchange market that of the second. They will plainly not be the last.

The Office of Fair Trading has already got the Stock Exchange to register its existing rules, largely summarised in its Rule Book, and has decided to refer them to the Restrictive Practices Court. This in turn may eventually decide that the Stock Exchange should dismantle its existing fixed Commission System, the separation of jobbers and brokers and the Rule Book in general, with all the disturbing consequences which were outlined in Chapter 5. It would be a destructive action, since neither the Office of Fair Trading nor the Restrictive Practices Court have any mandate to consider what, if anything, should be put in their place. As the Chairman of the London Stock Exchange has reminded us, the Stock Exchange's Rule Book is the result of a hundred years of evolution and its aim is to regulate the stock market and protect the investor. 'To regulate the market,' he rightly said, 'you have to have voluntary agreements and voluntary agreements are by their very nature restrictive practices.'

. A similar danger lurks in Brussels, as was seen in the case brought by Sarabex, a money-broking firm with Middle East connections, against the Foreign Exchange and Currency Deposit Brokers Association on the grounds that the latter was denying them entry, contrary to the spirit of Article 85 of the Treaty of Rome. Again, as we saw in Chapter 15, the result was to undermine self-regulatory arrangements by traders and to stress the need for authoritative contrŏ⌣ (in this case by the Bank of England). And again the lesson should not be lost on other City markets.

Thus the City still has a battle on its hands in its efforts to maintain as much self-regulation, and hence flexibility, as it can. It already has more hindering legislation to cope with than it would like. At the same time City markets have so far been given more opportunities for self-regulation than their critics would wish. Efforts to stiffen the effective auditing of accounts and to support a tougher role for non-executive directors should be part of any City response. The City may also live in hope of reducing the legal undergrowth; it must also make sure that the bodies undertaking self-regulation do so in a way that protects the public and, at the same time, punishes transgressors in its midst both adequately and publicly. The establishment of the Council for the Securities Industry was seen by some people as a recognition that the City could regulate itself in the public interest. It, and other City representative bodies, must now prove the point in a rigorous and open-handed way.

The spectre of £20 billion flowing annually by the mid-1980s through the insurance companies and pension funds for investment on the stock market and elsewhere, without adequate safeguards, has already produced a variety of reactions, from the fear that the stock market would be overwhelmed or, in Sir Harold Wilson's classic phrase, 'reduced to little more than an electric scoreboard at a cricket match', to the determination to see that a significant share will be invested in predetermined ways. I have already analysed the main changes and likely changes in Chapter 8. What I want to consider now is this: is the dominance of the institutions really inevitable?

The estimate that the institutions will have £20 billion at their disposal annually by the mid-1980s is a dramatic way of stressing the City's future financial power. *The Economist* has added its own sense of drama to the extrapolation game. 'If the [Post Office] pension fund continues to grow at the rate it grew in the five years to March, 1978,' it has calculated, 'it will match the total equity capitalisation of today's stock market (£60,000 million at mid-May, 1978) by the year 1989.' In a later issue *The Economist* estimated that the Post Office pension fund is already so large that 'it could take over the conglomerate Peninsular and Orient Steam Navigation, Vickers and Pearl Assurance, with a single year's cash flow were all three for sale at their present stock-market price'.

We know that the institutions have large funds at their disposal now, but are they bound to get bigger in the way now being estimated? The calculations need careful scrutiny. In the first place, they are based on statistical assumptions that may not be fulfilled. The estimate of an annual investment flow of £20 billion by 1985, for example, is based on a continuation of domestic inflation of 10 per cent a year throughout the period and on a continuation of a 3 per cent growth in the gross national product. There is also an underlying assumption that most pension funds will continue to be operated on a funding basis (that is that future pension commitments will be paid out of earlier regular savings) and that French-style 'pay as you go' arrangements will be rejected. Above all, it is apparently assumed that the economic and political climate – including current high marginal tax rates, which have led to the slow demise of the private investor, coupled with the tax advantages of corporate pension schemes – cannot be changed. In any case, there are reasons for believing that the growth of the past five years has been affected by special factors, such as the heavy company contributions arising from a combination of an inflation of salaries and poor returns on equity investments, some sharp improvements in company pension schemes requiring some 'topping up' of funds, and the large funding of the nationalised industry pension schemes.

To sum up my views about the investing institutions, I do not expect the rate of growth of their annually investible funds will reach £20 billion by 1985 unless inflation gets wildly out of hand. I have no strong views about the suggested switch of the nationalised pension funds from a funding basis to a 'pay as you go' basis,. though it might help to lower the political pressure for the direction of funds. I would be against the introduction of any minimum percentages for compulsory investment in government securities. There is no need for such a limit on grounds of prudence (that is, to protect the public) and such a move could bring other distortions with it, particularly in the pattern of savings. And I see no merit in the setting up of a national fund to invest institutional funds in industry on special terms. But I do see advantages in City institutions getting closer to industry, up to the point at which management must still manage. Pension funds should voluntarily move towards more public accountability along the lines they themselves have already outlined. I also feel that the Stock Exchange is right to press for a 'code of conduct' and to consider the possibility of including some such accountability phrase in future listing agreements.

I am convinced, however, that these moves are simply tinkering with a problem without searching out the fundamentals. I am depressed by the widespread assumption that it is already too late to reverse the tide. The move away from the private investor towards the big institutions was initiated and encouraged by high personal taxation, high inflation, the officially encouraged spread of occupational pension funds, high stock-market dealing costs and the provision of tax incentives towards certain kinds of institutional savings. As the Stock Exchange has stressed, 'the most effective way to arrest the trend towards the domination of the stock market by the savings institutions is to encourage the direct investment of personal savings . . . this can only be achieved by a combination of reducing the rate of inflation, and adopting a policy of fiscal neutrality towards all savings, or at least removing the tax disadvantages of *direct* investment in industry and trade'. The French, to their credit, have already shown the way. They have deliberately provided tax incentives to encourage private investors to invest either directly in individual shares or by way of unit trusts. Further relief is given to older people wanting to save, again through the stock market, for retirement. Why not a similar tax incentive for specified amounts saved in specified ways in Britain too? An encouragement to the private individual to save again and, where necessary, to support the enterprising firms could not only protect us from the proliferation of centrally controlled efforts to find money for small businesses; it would help to curb, even in a small way at the outset, the excessive growth of institutional investments and lead to a more balanced and healthy capital market. It would not, of course, resolve the dilemma, which continues to haunt the City's large investing institutions, of the need to decide how far they should go in getting closer to industry. (My answer is 'much closer, but not too close'. They are trained to advise on financial investment, not management.) But at least the introduction of such fiscal measures might begin to tilt the pressures back from interventionist policies (whether undertaken by Whitehall, the City or the usual triumvirate of unions, management and government) towards a wider use of the capital market and with it the role of the smaller shareholder.

I turn to the last of my original three questions. What sort of competition can the City expect over the next decade and what may it imply? During two decades of world prosperity, the City benefited from the expansion of overseas markets and from a domestic market based on full employment, but had to contend with widening competition at home, as various institutions encroached on each other (like the building societies and the American banks on the domestic clearing banks), and with new competitors abroad, as emerging nations created their own embryo financial centres and as foreign bankers, insurance companies and brokers followed their customers into the international field. The oil crisis, with its quadrupling of oil income, brought with it an immediate transfer of wealth into new hands and again brought new opportunities as well as potential competitors.

At home competition will depend partly on the fiscal and political climate provided by government, partly on the economic climate. It is quite clear that not only bank customers and insurance policyholders, and the companies themselves, but also the unions see no merit in the nationalisation proposals of the Labour Party. But amended proposals or even the alternative idea of a public sector banking unit made up of the National Giro and the Post Office Savings banks could quickly insert a new element into the domestic financial market. Even without such a disruptive initiative, competition among the various savings media – including the banks – would benefit from a levelling up of the various tax advantages offered to some and not others. This at least would put the building societies and the banks on a competitive footing. The clearing banks are also right, in my view, to seek some alleviation of the rule which forces them to keep non-interest-bearing reserves at the Bank of England and which at present applies to them but not to other banks, especially foreign banks. On the other hand, I hope that the clearing banks in turn will allow merchant banks and overseas banks to maintain their independence and flexibility, rather than be absorbed into ever larger banking units. The City's financial markets have always benefited from the competition provided by variety and recent efforts to buy rather than develop merchant-banking techniques have not always been successful.

On the broader international canvas both London itself and the British units forming part of it will, I assume, be facing a less expansionary market in the early 1980s, though some fundamental trends may still be moving in its favour, such as the continuing expansion of tertiary, that is service and know-how, industries. After all, as Professor Stonier has reminded us,[1] 'the principal wealth producer in post-industrial societies is neither land nor manufacture. But knowledge'. And the City of London, like Britain's service industries generally, has had a head start in this particular race, which still goes on on a worldwide basis.

Competition, of course, will be rising too, not only from New York (in banking, Eurodollar developments and in-surance), Chicago (in traded options and both commodity and financial futures), Zurich and Paris, but also from such recently established international places as Singapore, Hong Kong, Nassau and Bahrain, and from more indigenous financial centres such as Tokyo, Caracas, Kuwait, Dubai, Mexico City, Manila, Rio, Sao Paulo and Buenos Aires. There are, it seems to me, two ways of meeting such developments. One is

[1] Professor Tom Stonier, University of Bradford, *The Business Location File*, June/July, 1978.

to ensure that London maintains its world lead as a whole-sale and innovative centre. It still seems capable of doing so in banking, money market developments, insurance and brokerage of all kinds. Secondly, it must concentrate on developing the right relationships with the newer centres, partly because a new network of centres has been established over the past two decades, in which centres have complementary roles as well as competitive ones; partly to feed business back to London's wholesale markets; and partly to keep abreast of innovations wherever they occur. This implies that a British presence – sometimes in representative offices or branches on the ground, sometimes through regular contacts by air travel – will be needed whenever and wherever a new financial centre is beginning to emerge. It also implies that the domestic base must be politically and economically secure, and that City markets must continue to operate in an appropriately competitive, vigorous climate.

Glossary

City Jargon: What Does It Mean?

People *outside* the City have a simple notion that everyone *inside* the City talks the same language, uses the same jargon and, above all, can readily understand one another. It was an assumption I quickly discarded after only a few months of moving from one City market to another. The foreign exchange dealer uses one kind of shorthand, the stockbroker quite a different one. I once helped an overseas bank to compile a list of City jargon for the use of its industrial customers. Some jargon they understood. 'Bridging finance' was familiar, but what exactly was a Eurodollar'? It was clearly no help to be told that it need not be either a dollar or in Europe. Even within the bank itself, jargon understood in one section was a mystery in another.

The same is true of the City as a whole, both sector by sector and even over time. From Dickens onwards ('things that go up and down in the City'), jargon has been changing year by year. New phrases have emerged; others have died away. Go to New York and another world opens up. Move from a bank towards the Stock Exchange and you are immediately among 'stale bulls' and 'bear covering', though 'bucket shops' are harder to detect these days. Go up Lombard Street and you become familiar with 'maturity dates', 'short calls' and 'liquidity ratios'. Further along Leadenhall Street and Mincing Lane and you will meet 'bills of lading', 'charter parties' and 'red clauses'.

The list seems endless. But for the purposes of this book and the convenience of readers, I have set out the main items of City jargon used in the book in alphabetical order.

Acceptance facilities short-term fixed interest loans, normally related to a company's trading activity; based upon bills of exchange, drawn on a bank, the bills being discounted at market rates

Arbitrage dealings in foreign exchange or securities, with the aim of making profits out of the differences in exchange rates or security prices existing in different financial centres, or at different times. In the case of commodities the term implies the simultaneous purchase of futures in one exchange against the sale of the same commodity futures in another to take advantage of price differentials between the two markets.

Asian dollar market the Eurodollar or Eurocurrency market in the Far East, at present based on Singapore

Bank and trade bills See *Commercial bills*.

Bear market A 'bear' is an investor who sells shares (often those he does not possess) in the hope that prices will fall, thereby enabling him to buy them more cheaply later. A bear market is a period of falling share prices. Statisticians and chartists have technical formulae for recognising a 'bear' market.

Big Four shorthand for the four large English clearing banks: Midland Bank, Lloyds Bank, Barclays Bank and National Westminster Bank

Bill-broker originally a middle man who helped others to buy and sell bills of exchange for a commission. Nowadays used in a broader context to include both individuals and firms making a market in bills of exchange, Treasury bills and other money market instruments.

Bill of exchange essentially an order, signed by the person giving it, to a second person requiring him to pay a certain sum on demand or on a given date, normally short-term. It is in effect a form of post-dated cheque. It is defined by the Bills of Exchange Act, 1882. These bills, when 'accepted', can be sold for cash to discount houses.

Bill on London a bill of exchange issued in any part of the world and accepted in London. The 'bill on London' was the traditional method of sterling finance throughout the nineteenth-century. (See *Bill of exchange*.)

Broking houses firms of brokers, generally acting as middle men, linking sellers and buyers for a commission, in commodities, money, foreign exchange, securities, shipping freights, gold, etc. Nowadays they often buy and sell as principals on their own account, depending on the habits and regulations within their particular trade.

Building societies Basically they are savings banks which specialise in loans for house purchase. The societies borrow short-term money, by the issue of shares or the creation of deposits, and lend long-term on house mortgages. They are supervised by the Chief Registrar of Friendly Societies.

Bull market A 'bull' is an investor who buys shares now in the hope that prices will rise possibly within the Stock Exchange Account so that he can take a profit without paying for them. A bull market is a period of rising share prices. Statisticians and chartists have technical formulae for recognising a 'bull' market.

Call money deposits placed by banks with discount houses which can be withdrawn on demand

Capital base basically the capital employed in a business: derived from capital reserves, certain types of loans and other sources

Capital issues the issue of securities with a view to raising capital for a company

Capital market a general term covering the place where existing forms of securities, such as bonds, stocks, shares, etc., are traded and where new securities can be issued (and thus capital raised). It is sometimes used as shorthand for the investing institutions which provide new money, in exchange for securities.

Certificates of deposit, or CDs certificates given to a lender of funds by a bank, which the lender may then trade in the market, if he wishes, to realise his assets. This enables the bank to hold the funds for a guaranteed period of time, while the lender is free to trade the CDs whenever he wishes.

Clearing banks normally used to describe banks which are members of the Committee of London Clearing Bankers. The six members of the Committee (Barclays, Coutts & Co., Lloyds, Midland, National Westminster and Williams & Glyn's) jointly own and control the Bankers' Clearing House which administers and runs the clearing of payments within the British banking system.

Clearing house normally used in banking where cheques are cleared and credited to the appropriate accounts. By extension the term describes a centre like London that is convenient for many financial transactions. The term also applies to certain commodity futures markets. The International Commodities Clearing House Limited fulfils this function for the soft commodities on the London Commodity Exchange.

Closing price the value or price of any currency or stock market security at the end of the day, when the markets close

Commercial bills bills of exchange issued by commercial companies which can be accepted or endorsed by banks (referred to as 'bank bills'), or are not so accepted by banks (referred to as 'trade bills')

Commodity markets blanket term covering the activity involved in buying and selling commodities such as tea, coffee, cocoa, sugar, non-ferrous metals, grain, etc.

Consortium banks banks jointly owned by a number of other banks. This has been a way for small foreign banks and others to engage in large Eurocurrency business in London and elsewhere.

Convertible currencies currencies whose monetary authorities allow the holders to switch freely into other currencies or gold

Debenture a document issued under a trust deed which creates or acknowledges a debt. It usually relates to a secure transaction, is repayable within a specified period, carries a fixed interest rate, and is secured against the general assets of a company.

Discount houses companies which specialise in discounting bills of exchange, Treasury bills, etc., and in dealing in short-dated government bonds. The 'discounting' of a bill implies the offer of cash for it below its face value. This discount is a reflection of the current rate of interest, the quality of the bill and its maturity date. (See *Bill of exchange*.)

The Dollar Pool a limited pool of foreign currency in London available for investment by UK residents in foreign shares, and other foreign assets (see *Investment currency*)

Eligible liabilities funds received by banks on deposit, or in other forms, according to a formula laid down by the Bank of England for purposes of monetary policy and credit control

Endowment policies a combination of life assurance and investment whereby the sum assured is payable on a predetermined date or on prior death

Equity stake Equities are another name for ordinary shares, which provide that the ultimate ownership of companies should carry votes at all general meetings of companies and thus control overall policy. An equity stake represents the ownership of the company, carrying with it the right to a share in profits and the risk of bearing any losses.

Eurobond issues bonds or notes with a final maturity and either a fixed or floating interest rate, issued in a Eurocurrency. The buyer of the bond or note usually holds the bond or note outside the country of origin of the currency in which it is denominated.

Eurobond market covers both the primary market of new issues of Eurobonds and the secondary market on which they are traded

Eurocurrencies the name given to any currency held by banks, corporations or individuals outside its country of origin, e.g. Eurodollar, Eurosterling, Euroyen, Euromark, etc. The 'Euro' appellation derives from the place where the first market in such external currencies (primarily dollars) actually arose.

Eurocurrency loan loan in a Eurocurrency, usually lent by a bank or syndicate of banks, mostly medium-term

Eurocurrency markets an all-embracing term covering dealings in Eurocurrencies. The market covers the issuing and trading of Eurobonds, the raising of Eurocurrency loans and the accepting of Eurocurrency deposits.

Eurodollar market a term often used for the Eurocurrency market, since dollars held in Europe were the original basis of the market

Eurosyndicated loans fixed maturity loans in a Eurocurrency put together by a syndicate of banks. Syndicates are necessary when the banks managing the loan are too small to raise the funds alone, or when the loans are particularly large.

Factoring This service, provided by a third party, generally offers sales accounting, debt-collection services and protection against bad debts. Customers also receive immediate payments of a high percentage of debts owed to them.

Floating rates rates of interest calculated as a fixed margin above the variable London, Singapore or other Inter-Bank-offered Rate. Usually the rate of interest used in syndicated Eurocurrency loans and Eurobonds known as floating-rate notes.

Foreign bond issues bonds issued on a domestic market in the name of a foreign government or corporation

Foreign issues securities issued on a domestic market on behalf of foreign borrowers

Forward market a market in forward contracts of a commodity, or currency, which are agreements to sell or purchase a certain amount of a commodity or currency at a future date

Full convertibility refers to the state of individual currencies, whose monetary authorities allow foreign holders to switch freely into other currencies and gold (see *Convertible currencies*)

Futures market a market in futures contracts which basically require the delivery of a commodity in a specified future month, if not liquidated before that date

Gilt-edged stock fixed interest securities, issued and guaranteed by the British Government. The term is sometimes used to include UK local authority securities and Commonwealth government securities. 'Gilt-edged' derives from the original use of high quality paper with gilt-edges on the earliest certificates. Term said to have been used for first time in 1892.

Gold Standard the international monetary system in operation generally throughout the nineteenth century and up to 1931. A country was said to be on the Gold Standard when its currency was based on an agreed amount of gold, when it agreed to buy and sell gold at fixed prices and when gold could be moved in and out freely.

Government Broker a stockbroker appointed to act as the Government's agent in the gilt-edged market. Traditionally the senior partner of Mullens & Co. has held the post.

Hedging an effort to insure against price fluctuations, through the purchase of a futures contract, on the commodity markets. A 'hedge' can also be the establishment of an opposite position in the futures market to that held in the spot or physical market.

Inflation accounting a system of accounting which takes account of the changes in the value of assets and liabilities caused by inflation

Instalment credit a form of personal or industrial credit under which the ownership of the goods or equipment passes to the borrower on the repayment of an agreed number of instalments

Institutional investors the large financial institutions, such as insurance companies, pension funds, unit and investment trusts, etc., in contrast to private investors

Insurance brokers specialised brokers who secure insurance business and place it with recognised underwriters

Interbank market financial transactions between banks, often forming a base for quotation of rates for commercial borrowing from banks

Investment currency a restricted pool of money available for investment in foreign securities, property and other specified overseas assets. It usually carried a premium over the official foreign exchange rates. (See *Dollar Pool.*)

Investment houses firms, usually banks, or stockbrokers giving investment advice to clients as well as investing on their behalf

Investment trust a company which invests a fixed amount of money in a variety of stocks and shares providing a way of spreading risks. Investment trusts are companies with fixed capital, unlike unit trusts which can create or redeem units in response to demand. Investment trusts are therefore referred to as 'closed-end' funds. The price is regulated by the supply of and demand for the share and does not necessarily reflect the underlying asset value.

Invisible income foreign income from sources other than the movement of goods. It includes foreign earnings from services of all kinds, such as tourism, insurance, banking, shipping, etc., as well as from the return on investments overseas.

Issuing houses banks (and sometimes broking houses) concerned with the issue of new securities, on behalf of commercial or governmental borrowers, on the stock market

Jobbers members of the Stock Exchange who act as market makers in shares. They may only trade as principals on their own account. (See *Jobbing system*.)

Jobbing system the arrangement on the Stock Exchange whereby markets in shares are made by jobbers. The public buy and sell shares through brokers, who act only as agents for their clients and deal with the jobbers.

Joint-stock companies companies set up and owned by individual shareholders following the establishment of limited liability

Leads & lags deliberate delays in payments in some currencies, and accelerations in others, by traders or individuals attempting to protect themselves against exchange rate movements

Leasing Under equipment leasing agreements, provided by banks or their leasing subsidiaries, the assets being financed remain in the ownership of the leasing company but are effectively hired out to the customer.

Life assurance companies offices which assure the payment of agreed sums of money on a given date or on death, in return for the payment of regular premiums. Life offices can be mutual offices (owned by with-profits policyholders), proprietary companies (owned by shareholders), or friendly societies (mutual societies registered under the Friendly Societies Acts).

Life offices See *Life assurance companies*.

Liner conferences associations of shipowners which agree freight and passenger rates on scheduled shipping lines.

Liquid assets funds kept either in cash or in a form that can be easily and quickly turned into cash when necessary

Loan stock a generic term covering securities issued against loans. A distinction is made between unsecured loan stocks, which rank as creditors, and debenture stocks which are secured by a charge on assets.

Long To be 'long' implies having a surplus of a particular commodity, currency or security or having invested funds in a particular commodity, currency, security or country.

'Hot money' short-term money which moves from one financial centre to another and is quickly affected by changes in exchange rates, interest rates, economic policies or simply monetary fears

Market capitalisation the current stock market valuation of a company's outstanding capital

Mercantilism name given to a school of political economy, in the sixteenth and seventeenth century, which said that all labour should be directed towards producing goods for export in exchange for gold and silver, as the most basic form of wealth. By extension, a policy that encourages an excess of exports over imports, for the benefit of one nation above others, and not for the increased exchange and welfare of all nations.

Mercantile bills See *Commercial bills*.

Merchant banks strictly confined to members of the Accepting Houses Committee, although many other banking institutions in London, especially members of the Issuing Houses Committee, are also so described. They are specialised banking institutions, offering investment services, corporate advice, trade and project finance, exchange rate dealings, etc., to top-level clients on a world-wide basis.

Minimum Lending Rate This weekly rate replaced the old Bank Rate in October 1972, and is the minimum interest rate at which the Bank of England is prepared to lend to the money market. It is thus a basic rate in the City. For a time it simply reflected the average rate of discount established at the weekly Treasury bill tender. But the Bank of England now establishes a weekly rate in the light of current economic and financial conditions.

Multinational corporations commercial corporations with subsidiaries in several overseas territories. The definition varies from one expert to another. The United Nations prefers the term 'transnational corporation'.

'Mutual' offices insurance companies owned by the policyholders

National Giro It began operations within the Post Office in October, 1968, by offering 'an inexpensive, convenient, and speedy money transmission service'. It has since introduced the provision of overdrafts, travellers cheques, foreign currency, and personal deposit accounts.

New-issue market a primary market for the issue and placing of new shares, bonds, etc. It also includes the issue of rights shares to existing shareholders and the placing of stocks through an issuing house.

Offshore centre a financial centre free of many taxes and constraints. The term was first applied to literally offshore centres of the US, such as the Bahamas, Cayman Islands, etc. It can also be applied to certain international transactions in a City like New York or London that are specially free of normal domestic taxes and rules.

Option markets markets in entitlements to trade an underlying share or commodity at a fixed price at any time within a specified period. The buyer of the option pays a premium for the guarantee of receiving or delivering the security or commodity at the fixed price until the option expires.

Ordinary shares Holders of ordinary shares are the owners of a company, with the right to vote at company meetings, and thus collectively they control a company's overall policy. Ordinary capital is often called risk capital since, while the owners are entitled to the fruits of success, they also risk the penalties of failure. (See also *Equity stake*.)

Overnight money money lent for one day up to 3 p.m. which will be automatically repaid the following business day

Parallel money markets name given to markets in money, in both sterling and foreign currencies, which grew up alongside (i.e. parallel with) the traditional London money market throughout the 1960s

Pension funds funds created to finance the provision of pensions to employees

Physical or spot trade the buying or selling of goods for immediate delivery

Placing power the ability of an issuing bank to sell new bonds to a wide range of long-term investors so that, when trading begins, few are offered for sale on the market. The term is also used to describe the ability of stockbrokers to find institutional buyers of large lines of securities.

Portfolio investment investment in securities, in contrast with investment in fixed assets such as factories, property, etc.

Private banks banks owned by individuals and families, prior to the introduction of limited liability in the second half of the nineteenth century. Private banks continued to operate thereafter, but became fewer in number. Almost all have now become limited liability companies.

'Proprietary' companies insurance companies owned by shareholders

Quote a term occasionally used in the foreign exchange market to describe the exchange rate between any two currencies. In The Stock Exchange a quote is either the listing of a security or the price in the stock market.

Reinsurers insurance companies who help to spread risks by accepting insurance business from other insurance companies and underwriters

Reserve assets specific term to describe various categories of liquid assets of a UK bank, according to a formula laid down by the Bank of England

Reserve currency an international currency held by other countries as part of their central reserves. The main ones over the past fifty years have been the pound sterling and the American dollar, and more recently (to a limited extent) Deutschmarks and Swiss francs.

Retail banking banking business primarily related to customer affairs, in contrast with 'wholesale banking', which implies one banking institution dealing with another or with large commercial concerns

Roll-over describes a method of extending the maturity of a loan

Secondary market a place for the buying and selling of existing stocks, shares, bonds, etc. The Stock Exchange now controls the secondary market in stocks and shares in Great Britain and Ireland.

Securities the entitlement to money or other assets, which takes the form of shares, stocks, bonds, etc. They are usually traded on a stock market.

Short To be 'short' implies having oversold particular shares, currencies or commodities, or describes such assets in a particular country.

Short-dated government bonds securities issued by the government with lives of five years or less

Short- & medium-term corporate bonds bonds for varying lengths of maturity, from, say, 6 months to 10 years, issued by companies

Special deposits a proportion of a bank's assets that the Bank of England can require the bank to place on reserve with the Bank

Spot market a market in actual goods for immediate delivery

Statutory incomes policy government policy to place limits on the rise in incomes, prices and sometimes dividends, backed up by official controls approved by Parliament

Stop-go a phrase used to describe the way in which successive British Governments were forced to put on the economic brake, following a period of what was hoped to be sustained economic growth

Tariff associations associations which arrange insurance premium rates in certain trades

Term loans loans with a fixed maturity, or repayment, date

Trading currency a currency predominantly used for the settlement of trade, even by nationals of other countries, because of its ready availability and ubiquitous acceptability

Tramps ships that have no set routes but are available for hire by people who have cargo to move

Transferable sterling sterling which was transferable from one foreign holder to another outside what was once the dollar area. 'Transferable' sterling was the predecessor of 'external' sterling

Treasury bill promissory notes issued by HM Treasury usually for 91 days to finance government expenditure short-term

Treasury deposit receipt borrowing instrument introduced by the Treasury in July 1940 to raise short-term funds for war finance. Basically it had a life of six months and was confined to banks.

Trustee Savings banks savings banks managed by bodies of local trustees, which recently developed some of the features of the clearing banks

25 per cent surrender rule a levy of 25% charged on premium on currency derived from the proceeds of foreign shares when sold. The rule was abolished in 1977.

Underlying asset values the value of the assets of a company, usually expressed as a value per ordinary share in contrast to the price of a company's shares in the stock market

Underwriter the principal who signs or underwrites an insurance policy guaranteeing to pay a certain sum in the event of loss; at the time of an issue of securities, the guarantor of the funds to the issuing company or authority.

Unit Trust a fund of stocks and shares held by a trustee for the benefit of subscribing investors. They offer a cheap means of obtaining a spread of investments. Since new units can be created or redeemed, they are referred to as 'open-ended' funds.

Unmatched positions usually refers to the holding, or lending, of currencies by individual banks. A bank will sometimes deliberately hold certain currencies and have large liabilities in others, within the margins agreed with the Bank of England, as a hedge against expected movements in exchange rates. In these cases, it is described as having 'unmatched positions', since it is deliberately exposing itself to the risk of currency fluctuations.

Wall Street the financial district of New York in Lower Manhattan. The American equivalent of 'the City'.

Weekly tender the weekly auction of Treasury bills held every Friday

Wholesale money markets the markets in money in which one bank or financial institution lends to another

Index

Accepting Houses Committee 12, 21, 47–8, 222, 226
Access 28
accountancy 3
Africa, West 193, 195
Airbrokers Association 169
aircraft 62–3, 169–71
Alaska 172
Alexanders 136
Algeria 172
Allen Harvey 136
Allied Breweries 124
Amalgamated Metal 161
American Express 28, 84
Amsterdam 73, 109, 210, 240
Antwerp 240
Aramco 183n
Argentina 192, 219
Ariel 78
arranging centres 250–1
art, investment in 106, 115–16
Ashby, David 246
Asian dollar market 246, 250
Association of Investment Trust Companies 123
Astley & Pearce 136
Australia: overseas banks in 14; insurance companies 61, 69; London stockbrokers in 85; security houses in London 87; money market 137
Austria 61, 248–9

Backwardation 162
Bagehot, Walter 93, 126, 127, 194
Bahamas 85, 247, 248–9
Bahrain: Eurocurrency market 205, 242, 246–7, 251; as financial centre 240; Eurodollar market 248–9
Bain report 44
balance of payments 154, 194, 238
Baltic Exchange 156, 165–73, 242–4
Bangkok 181
Bank of America 257
Bank of England: location of 2; and monetary policy 38, 137, 145; and finance for industry 41, 49; Governor quoted 47, 124, 264n., 265; and small businesses 47, 112; and discount houses 127, 128, 136; and call money 129; establishment of 139–40; Government Broker 144; and money supply 145–7; issue of stock 150; and speculation 164; foreign exchange dealing by 176; controls on foreign exchange market 189, 226, 237; controls on sterling 201; and central bank co-operation 218; supervision of banks 224–7, 264–5; controls on Stock Exchange 228; and foreign banks 242
Bank of London and South America 208–9
bank-notes 176n.
Bank Rate Tribunal (1957) 4
Banker, The 230–1
Banker's World, A (ed. Fry) 208–9
banks: nationalisation of 1, 8, 29–30, 36; location of 2; criticisms of 4–5; number of 7; foreign 7, 15–18, 130, 208, 242, 257–8; changes in 7–8; clearing 8–10, 11, 19–21, 22–30, 40, 44, 48, 242; definition of 8–9; merchant 10–13, 21–2, 47–8, 226, 227; overseas 13–15, 19; American 16–17, 18–19, 257–8; personal services 22–30; charges 28–9; investment in industry 32–4, 92; relations with industry 34–5, 48–9; short-term lending by 39, 134; and small businesses 45–7; and discount houses 127–30, 135–7; bills 134; and foreign exchange 175–6; international 187–9, 216, 246; controls on 218–19, 264–5; fringe 225, 236, 265; foreign earnings 244
Banque pour l'Amérique du Sud 219
Banque de Bruxelles 189n., 218
Banque Commerciale pour l'Europe du Nord 205n.
Barclays Bank 9, 11, 20, 21, 124

Barclays Bank International 11, 14
Baring, the Hon. John 47–8
Barnett, Joel 151–2
Basle 184, 185, 218
Beirut 180–1, 240, 246
Belgium: support for industry 34; insurance companies 61; Eurodollar market 214, 248–9
Berlin 240
Bermuda 61, 85, 246
Billingsgate 155
Billion Dollar Killing, The (Erdman) 184
bills: of exchange 127; commercial 133–4, 137; trade 133–4; Treasury 127, 133, 145–7, 149
Birmingham 2, 72n., 90
black-market 240
Bolton, Sir George 208
Bolton Committee 47
Bombay 181
booking centres 246n., 250–1
Bowring Group, the 21
Bradford 157
Brandon, Henry 185n.
Brandts 21
Brazil 61, 84, 153
bribery 230–2
Britain: use of clearing banks in 10; economic performance 32, 34–5, 194, 198, 204; use of pension funds in 36; small firms in 46; earnings from insurance premiums 51–2, 60; insurance companies 55, 60, 61, 65; government borrowing 141–3; sterling area 192–3; sterling balances 194–5; exports 200, 203; attitude to bribery 231; Eurodollar market 248, 249; North Sea oil 263–4
Britain's Invisible Earnings 244
British Economic Policy Since the War (Shonfield) 185
British Insurance Association 58, 121, 123, 223
British Leyland 45, 65
British Rail Pension Fund 105, 106, 115–16
brokerage houses 80–1
Brown, Lord George 185
Bruges 240
Brussels 109, 266
Bucklersbury House 2
Buenos Aires 271
building societies: share of deposits 7,

26–7, 100–1; users of 102; as investors 141
bullion market 179–82
Burmah Oil 236
Burton Group 124

Call money 128–9, 146
call options 89
Callaghan, James 30, 68
Canada: insurance companies 61, 69; foreign security houses 86, 87; money market 137; dollars 206; Eurodollar market 248–9
Caracas 246, 271
Cater Ryder 136
Catherwood, Sir Frederick 231–2
Cayman Islands: taxation 4; Euro-currency market 205, 246–7; as financial centre 240, 251; Eurodollar market 248–9
certificates of deposit 130–1
Chartered Accountants, Institute of 222
Chartered Insurance Institute 60n.
Charterhouse Group 112
chartering agents 167–71
Chase Manhattan Bank 257
Chicago: competition with London 6; traded option market 86, 88–9, 255; commodity market 157, 255, 256
Churchill, Sir Winston 234
Citibank 251, 257
City, the: population 1; history 2, 138–40; functions of 2–4; criticisms of 4–6; foreign earnings 5, 243, 244; and industry 32–5, 108, 201–2; and insurance 50–2; institutional investors 107–8; government borrowing 142–4; monetary controls on 145; monetary freedom 192; and decline of sterling 198–9, 203–4; and overseas investment 202–3; and Euromarket 215; code of conduct 221–2; Bank of England controls on 224; Council for the Securities Industry 227–9; and government policy 232; government controls on 237–9, 264; advantages of 260; innovations in 260
City Capital Markets Committee 141–2, 154
City Communications Centre 44, 47, 112
City in The World Economy, The 244
Clarke, W. M. 240–1, 244, 245

clearing banks, *see* banks
Clive Discount 136
cocoa 156, 157, 160, 161
coffee 153, 156, 157, 161
commercial bills 133–4, 137
Commercial Sale Rooms 155
Commercial Union 52, 56, 69, 165
commissions, negotiated 80–1
commodity market: City's role 3; gains
    on 4; use of commercial bills 134;
    speculation on 153–4, 162–4; and
    balance of payments 154; history
    154–6; operation of 156–7; futures
    157–62; spot contracts 159–61; forward
    contracts 162; Select Committee on
    163–4; controls on 239; turnover 243;
    foreign earnings 244; New York 255;
    Chicago 256
Common Market: American investment
    in 17, 207; Britain's entry into 34;
    sources of investment in 36; and in-
    surance companies 56, 57, 67, 120;
    grain futures market 156; banking
    legislation 225, 226; European Mone-
    tary System 262
Commonwealth countries 14, 58
communications: use by City 3–4; and
    foreign exchange market 176, 178–9;
    and Eurocurrency market 212–13
Competition and Credit Control 38
computerised systems: banking 23–5, 31;
    stock market 78, 81, 82; money market
    130; Corn Exchange 156
Confederation of British Industry 34, 47,
    229
Consolidated Gold Fields 180
Consumer Credit Act (1974) 68
copper 157, 160
Corn Exchange 156
cotton 157
Council for the Securities Industry 227–9,
    239, 265, 267
Crash of '79, The (Erdman) 217
credit cards 23–4, 28
Credit Suisse 189n.
Creditanstalt Bank 219
currency: criticism of dealers 5; foreign
    exchange 174–6; rates 177–8, 183;
    forward market 177–8; dealing 182–3;
    speculation 184–5; Swiss banks 185–7;
    crises 189–90; reserve and trading
    196–7; deposits in London banks 201

Daily Mail 184
Day in the Life of a Banker, A (Higgins)
    177
de Gaulle, General Charles 179
Denmark 61, 248–9
developing countries: commodity prices
    158; shipping 172; Eurocurrency
    market 215, 219, 220; use of bribery
    232
Dickens, Charles 93, 155, 156, 273
Diners Club 28
Directors, Institute of 47
discount market 125–37, 141, 146–7,
    149, 222
Distillers Company 124
dividend control 95
dollar premium 263
Domestic Credit Expansion 145
Dubai 180, 271
Dublin 72n., 90
Dundee 157
Dunlop 161

Economist, The 115, 161, 183n., 267–8
Egypt 192, 193, 195
Einzig, Paul 207n., 241
Electra House Group 112
Electricity Supply Industry 105
endowment element 28
English language 242
Equity Capital for Industry 41
Erdman, Paul 184, 217
Eurobonds 199, 210–13, 243, 246, 255
Eurocurrency market: world 3, 246–7;
    London 6, 178, 198–9, 208–9, 242,
    243; and merchant banks 13; and
    American banks 16–17; lending in 131
Eurodollar market: development of
    16–17, 134–5, 205–7; distinguished
    from Eurobond market 213; im-
    portance for London 245; world figures
    248–9
Euro-dollar System, The (Einzig) 207
Euroloans 209–10
European Banking Corporation 17
European Monetary System 262
exchange control 175, 192, 237, 263–4
export-led growth 242, 259
exports 200, 203
Exxon 84

Far East 14, 180–1, 207

Federal Reserve Bank 143–4
Finance for Industry 41, 47
financial centres 240–1
Financial Times 257
Financial Times share index 94, 100
Finland 61
First National City Bank 21
Fleet Street 4
floating exchange rates 178
Florence 240
foreign earnings: total City 5, 244; commodities 158; shipping 171; exchange control 192
foreign exchange market: City's role 3; gains on 4; turnover 174, 242; history 174–5; operation of 176–9, 222; and Eurodollar market 213; controls on 226, 239
Fort Knox 214
forward markets 159–62, 175
France: output per head 32; support for industry 33, 34, 35; insurance companies 61, 69; security trading in 78; London stockbrokers in 85; gold hoarding 126n., 181–2; Eurodollar market 248–9; tax incentives 269
Frankfurt: foreign loans 210; Eurobonds 211; as financial centre 240, 243, 246, 253; Eurocurrency 247
Franklin National Bank 189n.
Fraser, Sir Hugh 4
freight 167–70
fur 156
futures market 158–62, 256

Galbraith, J. K. 235
gas 134
General Accident 52, 69
General Council of British Shipping 165
General National Mortgage Associates Certificates 256–7
Germany, West: output per head 32; post-war growth 32; support for industry 33, 34; banks and industry 35–6, 48; insurance companies 61; share-dealing activity 109; Government stock 142; inflation 216; currency controls 237; Eurocurrency dealing 246, 253; Eurodollar market 248–9
Gerrard & National 136
Gibraltar 85
Gillett Brothers 136

gilt-edged securities: total investments in 140, 142; marketability of 142; and monetary policy 145, 233; City investment in 150; institutional investment in 148–52, 233–4; word of mouth deals 222
Ginnie Maes 256–7
Girocentrale 218
Glasgow 2, 30
Glaxo 65
gold: world market 3, 179–82; holdings in France 126n., 182; Standard 179, 192, 219n., demand for 181; currencies convertible into 206; and dollar links 216; Baring's crisis 219n.; Zurich market 242, 254; and exchange controls 263
Government: stocks 141–52; Broker 143–4, 147; monetary policy 144–5; and institutional investors 151–2; borrowing 140, 199, 215; effect on City 237–9
grain 169
Great Crash, 1929, The (Galbraith) 235
Greece 61, 84, 165
Green, Timothy 180–1
Grindlays Bank Group 14, 21
Guardian, The 47, 153, 170
Guardian Royal Exchange 69
Guest Keen & Nettlefold 65
Guiness Book of Records 231

Hague, G. B. 24n.
Haines, Joe 181–2
Hamilton, J. Dundas 139–40
hedging 160
Herbert, Alfred, Ltd 45
Herstatt Bank 189n., 217–18
Higgins, Jack 177
hire purchase 27–8
History Today (Kirby) 138
Holland: finance for industry 35, 36; insurance companies 61; London stockbrokers in 85; Eurodollar market 248–9
Hong Kong: insurance companies 61; London stockbrokers in 85; shipping 172; as financial centre 178, 179, 240; gold market 180–1; Eurocurrency market 246, 247; Eurodollar market 248–9; as arranging centre 250–1
hot money 5, 200, 201, 216

IBM 84

Imperial Chemical Industries 45, 243

Imperial Group 110

imports 200

income tax 94, 269

India 14, 181–2, 193, 195

Industrial and Commercial Finance Corporation 112

Industrial Revolution 92–3, 127

industry: City's attitude to 5, 8, 32–5, 108, 201–2; loans for 13; investment in 32–4, 37–44, 93; and banks 47–9; insurance in 62–3; and institutional investors 110–13, 117–19, 122

inflation: in mid-seventies 94–5, 189, 236; and demand for gold 182; and Eurodollar market 216

inside knowledge 223, 229–30

Institute of Directors 47

Institute of Pensions Management 115

institutional investors: and Stock Exchange 77–8, 80, 91, 105–6; percentage of shares owned by 92; annual disposable income 92, 103, 267–70; and art investment 106, 108; power of 107, 124; criticisms of 108–10; impact on industry 110–13, 117–19, 122; and government stocks 148–52, 233–4; growth of 267–70

Institutional Shareholders Committee 123

insurance: City's role 3; underwriters 51, 54–5, 57; premium income 51–2; life 52–3, 55, 58, 68; new developments 55, 62–3; brokers 67–70, 63–5; protective legislation 68; turnover 242; foreign earnings 244; New York exchange 255–6

insurance companies: nationalisation of 1, 65, 68–70, 270; location of 2; investment by 6, 92, 102–4, 141, 152, 267–70; investment in 36, 103; payment of claims 50, 62; operating in UK 55–6; specialist 57; captive 60–1, 246; solvency margins 103; and gilt-edged stock 233–4; foreign earnings 244

interbank deposits 209

interbank market 130–1

interest: overnight 5, 133; bank rates 22–3, 38, 236; building society rates 26; monetary policy 144–5; Eurodollar market 213

International Bond Dealers, Association of 212

international business 243–51

International Chamber of Commerce 232

International Commodities Clearing House 2, 257

International Monetary Fund 199, 214, 220, 254–5

investment trusts 95–7, 244

invisible earnings 52, 243, 244, 261, *see also* foreign earnings

invoicing centres 246

Iran 172, 262

Ireland: banks in City 9; bank strike ·ion., 197; insurance companies 61; Eurodollar market 248–9

Israel 61, 218

Israel-British Bank 218

Italy: support for industry 33, 34; insurance companies 61; stock market 78; bank-note shortage 197; Eurodollar market 214, 248–9; bribery 231

Jakarta 181

Jamaica 72

Japan: output per head 32; support for industry 33, 35; insurance companies 61; London stockbrokers in 85; security houses in London 86, 87; merchant fleet 165; sterling area 192; exports 200; Eurodollar market 214, 248–9

Jeddah 180–1

Jersey 240, 246

Jessel Toynbee 136

jobbers 75–6, 78–80, 143, 222

Johannesburg 130

Johnson and Higgins 255

Johnson Matthey 179

joint-stock companies

jute 157

King & Shaxson 136

Kirby, J. L. 138

Kleinwort, Benson Ltd 12

Korea 172

Kuwait: stock market 72, 75; shipping 172; gold dealing 180; sterling held 191; as financial centre 240, 271

Labour Party: and nationalisation 1, 29, 68–9, 270; view of City 33; and

speculation 153; and foreign exchange market 174
law 3
Law Society 222
lead 157, 161
leads and lags 182, 188
Lebanon 61
Legal and General 69
Lever, Harold 153, 154, 162–3
Liberia 165
life assurance 52–3, 55, 58, 68
liners 167, 173
Liverpool 2, 72n., 90, 157
Lloyds Bank 9, 11, 20–1
Lloyds Bank International 11, 14, 20, 189n., 218
Lloyd's: overseas business 4, 52, 69, 244; operation of 50–6; foreign members 61; American bids 63–5; committee of inquiry 67; market behaviour 222; self-regulation 239
Lloyd's Register of Shipping 165, 171, 244
Lombard Street (Bagehot) 126, 194–5
London Interbank Offered Rate 209–10
London Metal Exchange 156, 157, 158, 162n.
Lonrho 4
Lowson, Sir Denis 4
Lutine Bell 53n.
Luxembourg: insurance companies 61; London stockbrokers in 86; Eurobond market 211, 246; Eurocurrency market 246–7; Eurodollar market 248–9

Macao 180
Macmillan Committee ix
Malaysia 61, 86
Manchester 2, 72n., 90
Manila 271
margin dealings 237
Marshall Plan 254
merchant banks, *see* banks
Mexico 84, 172, 271
Middle East: purchasers of gilts 142; oil funds 142, 262; gold trading 180–1; bribery 231; business in Paris 253
Midland Bank 9, 11, 17, 20, 21, 28
Milan 78, 109
Milk Marketing Board 134
Mincing Lane 155
Minimum Lending Rate 108–9, 146–7
Mocatta & Goldsmit 179

monetary policy 8, 144–5, 148, 238
money brokers 143n.
Money for Business 112
Money Markets of the World: What the Future May Bring (Clarke) 240–1, 245
Money Programme, The 176, 105–6, 231n.
money supply 144–5
Monopolies Commission 80, 89
Morgan Guaranty Bank 257
Mullens & Co 277
multinational corporations: and EEC 16–17; captive insurance companies 60–1, 246; and currency speculation 184, 185, 187–8; chemical 205; and commercial bribery 231

Nassau 205, 242, 246–7, 251, 253, 271
National Coal Board 105
National Debt 140
National Economic Development Council 202
National Giro 7, 22, 29–30, 270
National Giro (Davies) 29–30
National Savings Bank 7, 22, 26, 29–30
National Westminster Bank 9, 11, 20, 21
nationalisation: of banks 1, 8, 29–30, 36, 270; of insurance companies 1, 65, 68–70, 270; of institutional investors 108; and government debt 140; and Bank of England 241
nationalised industries 134
New Hebrides 247, 251
New York: restrictions on markets 5, 228; compared with London 6, 241–3, 254–7; and Eurocurrency market 16, 246–7; American banks in 17; insurance market 61, 63–4; Stock Exchange 73, 80, 81–2, 83, 223n., 224, 234–5; Federal Reserve Bank 143–4; commodity market 156–7; shipping exchange 166; foreign exchange 175, 179, 210–11; gold dealing 181; as arranging centre 250–1; offshore proposals 252
New Zealand 52, 61
Nigeria 172
Nightingale and Company 83
North Sea oil: finance to develop 8, 44; insurance liabilities 62–3; and tanker market 172; revenues 238, 263–4
Norway 61
Norwich 2

Office of Fair Trading 80, 89, 266
offshore centres 241, 252–3
offshore funds 246
oil: insurance liabilities 63; price in-
    creases 94, 195–6, 260; Middle East
    revenues 142; OPEC 158; shipping
    172; see also North Sea oil
option markets 86–9, 255
Orion Bank 17
overdrafts 27, 39–40
overnight money 133
overseas investment 84, 202–3

P&O 165
Panama 246, 248–9
Paris: restrictions on market 5, 254; sup-
    port for industry 32; share-dealing
    activity 109; gold market 181; as
    financial centre 195, 240, 246, 253–4;
    Eurocurrency market 247
Pearson, S. & Son Ltd 124
pension funds: investment by 6, 32,
    92, 104–5, 141, 152; investment in 36,
    95, 104; benefits paid by 105; art
    investments 106, 108; power of 107;
    funding of 113–14; percentage of in-
    stitutional investment 114; manage-
    ment of 114–16; safety of 115; National
    Association of 123; and gilts 233;
    foreign earnings 244; growth rate
    267–70
pensions, provision of 104
Pensions Management, Institute of 115
Pepper, Gordon 142, 145
Plantation House 155–6
Pocock, C. C. 122
Politics of Power, The (Haines) 191
Pool of London 154
Port of London 138–9
portfolio investment 263
Portugal 52
Post Office 4, 30, 105, 267–8
Price Commission 28, 80, 89
property investment 105–6
Prudential Insurance 56, 69, 77, 236
Public Works Loan Board 131
Pulay, George ix–x

Q, Regulation 206, 255

Radcliffe Committee ix, 125, 135–6
railways 13, 84, 93

Rank Organisation 65, 124
reinsurance 51, 56, 57
reserve currencies 196
Reuters 4
Rio 246, 271
Rolls Royce 45
Rothschild, N. M. & Sons 12, 179
Rowntree Mackintosh 153, 161
Royal Insurance 52, 56, 69
rubber 156, 160, 161
Rubber Exchange 155
Russia 172, 173, 215, 265
Radcliffe Committee ix, 125, 135–6

Salisbury 130
Salisbury, UK 2
Samuel Montagu 11, 21, 179
San Francisco 50, 178, 240
Sao Paulo 246, 271
Sarabex 226, 266–7
Sasse Syndicate 67
Saudi Arabia 172, 181, 183n., 191, 231
savings: national 2, 3; tax incentives 26,
    269; competition for 29; contractual
    36
Schroder Wragg Ltd 12
Scotland 44, 52
Scottish and Universal Investments 4
Seccombe Marshall 136
Securities Exchange Commission 223–4
shareholders 120–1
Sharps Pixley 179
Shell 122
shipbrokers 167–8
shipping: City's role 3, 173; offices 165;
    overseas 165; Baltic Exchange 166–9;
    service institutions 171; earnings 171;
    underutilisation of 172–3; oil tankers
    172
Shonfield, Andrew 185
short-term bills 145–6
short–term lending 39
silver 157
Sime Darby 4
Singapore: insurance companies in 61;
    stock market 72; London stockbrokers
    in 86; as financial centre 130, 137,
    175, 178–9, 240; rubber market 156;
    shipping 172; gold market 180; as in-
    voicing centre 205, 242; Asian dollar
    market 246; Eurocurrency market
    247; Eurodollar market 248–9

Singer and Friedlander 21
Slater-Walker 4
Sloan, R. I. 6on.
small businesses 45–7, 82–3, 110–13
Smith St Aubyn 136
Smith, W. H. & Son 77
solicitors 244
South Africa 61, 86, 137, 180
Spain 61, 170
speculation: commodity 153–4, 162–4; gold 180–1; currency 184–5, 187–8, 190
spot markets 159–62, 177
Standard Chartered Bank 14, 21
sterling: money markets 126; selling from Zurich 186; holders of 188, 191, 201; crises 192, 237; area 193; balances 194–6; oil payments 196; trading 197; City's links with 198–9, 203–4, 232–3; debts 241; and exchange rate 263
Stock Exchange: and industry 32, 33; function of 71–2; turnover 73, 243; jobbers 75–6, 78–80, 143; and institutional investors 77–8, 80, 91, 92, 108–10; bypassing 78; commissions 80–1; Talisman system 82; and small businesses 82–3; overseas stocks 84–5; option markets 86–9; regulatory functions 90–1; and individual investors 92–4; and pension funds 116; establishment of 139–40; market rules 222, 266; inside information 229–30; slump 235–7; foreign earnings 244; Council for the Securities Industry 228, 265–6
Stonier, Professor Tom 271
stop-go 191, 194, 196
Suez Canal 14
sugar 156, 157, 159, 161
Sun Alliance 69
Sweden 32, 61, 248–9
Swinfield, John 176
Swiss Bank Corporation 176n.
Switzerland: banks 10; insurance companies 61; London stockbrokers in 86; security houses in London 87; 'gnomes' 185–7; francs 206; currency controls 237; Eurodollar market 248–9

Taipei 181
Taiwan 172
take-over bids 4, 223; Panel 224, 228–9
Talisman 82

Tangiers 240
tap stocks 144, 146, 149–50
taxation: and savings 26, 269; income 94, 238; business 141; capital gains 151; effect on City 237–8; and financial centres 246, 250, 251
Tehran 180
telegraph service 14
telephones: use by City 4, 76, 242; bank accounts 24; influence on money markets 130; use by foreign exchange market 176, 222; use by Tokyo shipping exchange 166; use by Euromarkets 212, 213
telex 166, 176, 212
Tenerife 62–3
term borrowing 40
Thames, R. 2, 138–9, 154, 165
Thorneycroft, Peter 185
timber 134
time-zones 158, 166, 179, 242, 251
Times, The 84, 231
tin 156, 157
Tokyo: restrictions on market 5; as financial centre 32, 178, 180, 240, 243, 253; stock market 73, 235; shipping exchange 166; foreign exchange market 176
Too Much Money . . . ? (Pepper and Wood) 145
Toronto 130
Trade, Department of 68, 223, 224, 225
trade bills 134
trade unions 32, 70, 270; TUC 33, 117, 118, 119
trading currencies 196
tramps 167
Treasury bills 127, 145–7, 149
Trinidad 72
Trustee Savings Bank 22, 26, 29
Turnbull, M. T. 168–9
turnover: commodities 162–3; foreign exchange 174; Eurobonds 212; City totals 242–3

Uncommercial Traveller, The (Dickens) 155
unemployment 236, 261
underwriters 51, 54–5, 57, 222
Union Bank of Switzerland 189n., 218
Union Discount 136
unit trusts: proportion of shares held 92; history 97–8; number 98; operation of

98–102; growth of 99; marketing 100; Association 123; and gilts 233–4; foreign earnings 244
United Arab Emirates 87
United California Bank 184
United Nations Conference on Trade and Development 158
United States of America: 'mafia money' 5; banks 16–17, 18–19, 238; multinational companies 16–17, 186, 200; credit cards 23; computerised banking systems 23–5; output per head 32; small businesses 46; UK insurance business in 52, 57, 69; insurance companies 61; insurance exchange 64; London stockbrokers in 86; security houses in UK 88; institutional investors 107; government stocks 142–4; commodity market 156–7; shipping 173; currency exchange 183; investment in EEC 186, 207; and sterling debt 194; world use of dollar 197; exports 200; Eurodollar market 206–8, 214; commercial bribery 231, 232; taxation 238; see also New York, Wall Street
Uruguay 84

Vehicle and General Insurance Company 67–8
Vienna 240
Vietnam 261

Wages 95
Wall Street 2, 107, 144, 234–5

Wall Street Journal 187–8
Westdeutsche Landesbank 218
William Baird 161
Williams & Glyn's Bank 9, 11
Williamson, J. M. 24n.
Willis Faber 255–6
Wilson Committee ix, 1; money dealing 5; finance and industry 34, 48–9, 117–19; North Sea oil 44; small businesses 47; Stock Exchange 89; unit trusts 101; commodity market 154
Wilson, Sir Harold 91, 107, 119, 191, 267
Wood, Geoffrey 145
wool 156, 157
word of mouth dealing 4, 222
World Bank 214, 254
world trade 32, 182, 197, 261
World War, First 140, 175
World War, Second: effect on British economy 32, 241; financing of 140; exchange control during 175, 193; and sterling area 192–3; effect on Zurich 185–6, 241; effect on New York 241

Yassukovich, S. 212

Zinc 157, 161, 164
Zurich: foreign exchange market 179; gold market 180, 181, 254; 'gnomes of' 184–5; as financial centre 185–7, 240–3, 246, 254; Eurobond market 210; Eurocurrency market 247